STUDIES IN MAJOR LITERARY AUTHORS

T0352752

Edited by

William E. Cain

Professor of English
Wellesley College

A ROUTLEDGE SERIES

Studies in Major Literary Authors

William E. Cain, *General Editor*

OUR SCENE IS LONDON

Ben Jonson's City and the Space of the Author

James D. Mardock

Routledge
Taylor & Francis Group
New York   London

First published in 2008
by Routledge
270 Madison Ave, New York NY 10016

Simultaneously published in the UK
by Routledge
2 Park Square, Milton Park, Abingdon, Oxon, OX14 4RN

Routledge is an imprint of the Taylor & Francis Group, an informa business

Transferred to Digital Printing 2009

Typeset in Adobe Garamond by IBT Global

Library of Congress Cataloging-In-Publication data
Mardock, James D., 1974–
   Our scene is London : Ben Jonson's city and the space of the author / by James D. Mardock.
      p. cm. — (Studies in major literary authors)
   Includes bibliographical references and index.
   ISBN 0-415-97763-0
   1. Jonson, Ben, 1573?–1637—Homes and haunts—England—London. 2. Dramatists, English—Homes and haunts—England—London. 3. Space in literature. 4. London (England)—Social life and customs—17th century. 5. London (England)—Intellectual life—17th century. 6. London (England)—In literature. 7. Jonson, Ben, 1573?–1637. Bartholomew Fair. 8. James I, King of England, 1566–1625—In literature. I. Title.
   PR2634.M37 2008
   822'.3--dc22   2007032596

ISBN10: 0-415-97763-0 (hbk)
ISBN10: 0-415-87554-4 (pbk)
ISBN10: 0-203-92851-2 (ebk)

ISBN13: 978-0-415-97763-0 (hbk)
ISBN13: 978-0-415-87554-7 (pbk)
ISBN13: 978-0-203-92851-6 (ebk)

For Emilie

Contents

Acknowledgments

Parts of this book originated as a dissertation at the University of Wisconsin under the directorship of Heather Dubrow, whose unstinting rigor, professionalism, and energy as a director, mentor, and friend made the project possible. Various versions of the arguments herein have benefited from the critical eyes and comments of Alex Block, Justin Gifford, Marissa Greenberg, Adam Kitzes, David Loewenstein, Eric Rasmussen, Carol Rutter, Aaron Santesso, Henry Turner, Stanley Wells, Susanne Wofford, and especially Jane Rickard.

Portions of the book have been presented in abbreviated form at Shakespeare Association of America seminars organized by Jean Howard and Crystal Bartolovich, Nora Johnson, Martin Butler, and Catherine Richardson, and I am indebted to the other participants in those seminars for their insightful responses. Chapter two, in a somewhat different form, was presented to the Princeton British Studies Seminar, for which opportunity I am grateful to Peter Lake and Bill Jordan. The book has benefited from generous grants from the University of Wisconsin, the University of Warwick, and Ripon College, and I am likewise indebted for support—moral, emotional, and scholarly—to my friends and colleagues, at Wisconsin (particularly Alex Block and Jesse Wolfe), at Ripon, at Warwick, and especially at the University of Nevada, where my own friendly authorial competition with Chris Coake helped impel the production of these pages.

I would be remiss as an author if I did not acknowledge the role of place in this book's production, and so I would also like to thank the Fair Trade Coffee House in Madison, Seasons Café in Ripon, and the Bibo Coffee Company in Reno, for providing me with tables and caffeine. Finally, thanks to my family for their unflagging support over the years, and to Emilie Meyer, whose love, encouragement, and ability to maintain a long-term perspective have been indispensable. Beggar that I am, I am even poor in thanks, and yet I thank you.

Introduction

> [Jonson's] drama is deeply invested in the rhythms, meanings and struc-
> tures of the metropolis, and his works are imbued with and shaped by
> urban topographies: the urban experience was the single most determin-
> ing factor of his career.
>
> Martin Butler[1]

"Our scene is London," proclaims the prologue to Ben Jonson's *The Alchemist*, "'cause we would make known, / No country's mirth is better than our
own" (Prologue 5–6). While ironically undercut by its cheerfully amoral
attitude toward the subject matter that the early modern English metropolis
provides—"your whore, / Bawd, squire, impostor, many persons more" (7–
8)—the literary jingoism of these lines is not completely disingenuous. The
London scene is crucial to Jonson's career-spanning project of self-celebra-
tion, self-promotion, and self-fashioning. In examining Jonson's uses and representations of London, its places and its spaces, I participate in an ongoing
and vigorous response to Steven Mullaney's call, nearly two decades ago, for
a rhetoric of space in early modern London, and in the critical examination
of the drama's role in producing that rhetoric.[2] The last four years alone have
seen excellent studies—by Andrew Hiscock, Russell West, Henry Turner,
and Jean Howard, to name a few—exploring the intersections between London's urbanization, changes in the early modern spatial paradigm, cartography and other practical spatial arts, and English dramatic practices. My own
book will argue not only that Jonson's representational engagements with
the city of London potently shaped the early-modern urban experience, but
that his consciously theatrical authoring of the city aided the emergence a
new authorial subjectivity, a new idea of the author.

Most recent studies of the development of early modern dramatic
authorship have focused on textual, not theatrical matters: on authorial nego-
tiations with readership, apparatuses of state and religious censorship, systems
of patronage, and the market for books. Douglas A. Brooks, for example,
building on the work of bibliographers including Richard C. Newton and

Alexandra Halasz, focuses on the practices of the printing house, on the interventions of individual authors like Jonson in the stationers' craft, and on their participation in the marketing of their work;[3] Brooks argues that it is "the circulation and publication of dramatic texts" that "contributed to . . . the construction of proto-modern notions of authorship."[4] Joseph Loewenstein carries this focus forward in his recent dual studies of the history of intellectual property and plagiarism, arguing that the modern author, in the sense of a writer who maintains ownership over his work, arises from the competition between the stationers and the players over the rights to playtexts.[5] Other work, like Richard Helgerson's *Self-Crowned Laureates*, is less materialist in its methodology, but still focuses on texts rather than dramatic practices. Helgerson's treatment of Jonson, like that of Spenser and Milton, discusses the poet's authorial claims as inscribed on a readership, molding an authorial identity out of the differing assumptions of coterie manuscript culture and print transmission.[6]

The concerns of these valuable studies with the production of the material text have tended, understandably, to produce a narrative of Jonson's career that centers on its most lasting textual achievement, the Folio *Workes* of 1616. Jonson was, if not the first playwright to insist on seeing his plays through publication, certainly the most vociferous when it came to protecting his proprietary rights to his work, and the meticulously prepared 1616 Folio is his most overt attempt to create a lasting monument to his achievement as a poet.

But this, I will argue, is only one aspect of his authorial innovation. Covering Jonson's career from the accession of King James I to 1616, the years during which he was planning and preparing the Folio, this book will delineate a different narrative with regard to his self-construction as author. During these years, and beyond, Jonson pursued another authorial strategy, in parallel with the monumentalizing project that culminated in the 1616 *Workes*, a strategy dependent less upon written text than upon space. Despite his often-cited protestations of loathing for the public stages that provided his livelihood for much of his career, Jonson exercised as much care in establishing control over the spatial laboratory that the playhouse provided, and over the theatrically represented space of his city, as he did in shaping the textual presentation of his work. Jonson's poetry, his criticism, and especially his drama establish a range of poetic and rhetorical engagements with space that contributes to his model of the author.

Like most studies of the history of authorship, this book treats the early seventeenth century as an important transitional period.[7] My particular focus, however, is on how that transition was effected through the intersection of two factors: Jonson's role in the development of English drama, and a set of concurrent epistemological shifts—in the ways Londoners conceived of their city, in their experience of drama and its relation to their everyday lives, and in their methods for comprehending space and the lived environment. At the turn of the seventeenth century, London was changing both geographically and conceptually. The sixteenth century had seen the city's population quintuple, to around 200,000 at the accession of King James I in 1603. The civic government was faced increasingly with problems of overcrowding, plague, and crime and, after a century of responding to Tudor encroachments on its power, now had to negotiate a new relationship with an unknown Scottish king. As Raymond Williams argues, seventeenth century London saw the origin of the modern idea of the city as a "distinctive order of settlement, implying a whole different way of life,"[8] and the social and demographic changes that accompanied this paradigm shift also brought with them a disturbing epistemological uncertainty, as Jean Howard notes:

> rapid physical expansion made the city less easy to know in its entirety—"know" not just in the sense of having familiarity with the streets and buildings of various districts but also in the sense of having a conceptual image of the activities imagined to characterize these new areas and the kinds of people who inhabited them.[9]

In this context, the writers of Jacobean London were largely concerned with defining what it meant to live in (and rule over) the newly "British" capital. Significantly, Jacobean London also brought an effective end to the tradition of touring theater in England, already declining late in Elizabeth's reign, as playing companies became a primarily and almost exclusively urban phenomenon. London's dramatic poets advanced the development of the theater business under the city's occasionally hostile regulatory authority, but they also wrote plays for citizen audiences and devised entertainments for the civic government. The establishment of permanent urban playhouses and the accompanying explosion of dramatic production helped form a response to the new English urban experience, providing a mode of representation based on the individual's experience of the spatial environment as a form of interpretation.[10]

In other modes of literature, the author's processes can arguably be divorced from the personal or sociopolitical processes of place-making, but place and space are integral to the production of drama, since for the dramatist meaning is achieved in part through bodies in space. The practices of place and space, that is, form for dramatic authors a syntax and vocabulary as important as those of language. Moreover, the conventions of stages both public and private in early modern London—bare of all but the most portable scenery, with setting entirely established by dialogue—foreground the role of the individual in producing and interpreting space.[11] The environmental poetics that emerged from Jonson's employment of and reflection on the dramatist's potential to shape space—not only the space of the stage, but the space of the city—deserves consideration alongside textual and material factors in the development of authorship.

With this in mind, I trace Jonson's career from 1604 to 1616, demonstrating the ways in which Jonson consistently asserted his authorial identity by foregrounding drama's power to represent space, a project that ran alongside, if sometimes seemingly at odds with, the concern with textual self-monumentalization that culminated in the Folio. My first chapter demonstrates how intricately these two strategies could be related, and also illustrates Jonson's lifelong interest in spatial poetics, even in non-dramatic poetry like the scatological mock epic "On the Famous Voyage." Chapter two turns to a very different Jonsonian portrait of London, and examines what I argue was a transitional moment in Jonson's career, his employment (along with Thomas Dekker) to produce the pageants celebrating the newly crowned King James's royal entry into London in 1604. I argue that from his competition with Dekker, played out in the matrix of London's temporary transformation into stage space, Jonson gained an awareness of the potential for dramatic control over urban space as a tool for the assertion of authorial agency.

The remainder of the book turns to the representation of London onstage in Jonson's London comedies, where, as I argue in chapter three, individual virtue is shown to be analogous to the character's mode of inhabiting and moving through the space of the city. In the revised *Every Man in His Humor* (1605?-1616?) and the collaborative *Eastward Ho* (1605), Jonson established a model of urban cultural competency that depends on one's ability to apply a playwright's representational practices to the city's places. When he returned to London comedy after a four-year hiatus following *Eastward Ho,* Jonson was able to refine this model further, staging his characters' own dramaturgical manipulations of urban space in order implicitly to foreground his own authorial practices. The subjects of my fourth chapter, *Epicoene* (1609) and *The Alchemist* (1610), two plays written during the closure of the playhouses during seventeenth-century London's longest-lasting plague visitation, present an implicit competition for dramatic authority between the characters in his plays and Jonson himself. Finally,

I turn to *Bartholomew Fair* (1614), a play omitted from the Folio but crucial to Jonson's alternate, spatial, authorial strategy. Chapter five reads that
play—in which Jonson implicitly inserts himself into the dramatic fiction
and explicitly into the playhouse itself—as Jonson's fullest articulation of
spatial authorship and of the potential for considerations of urban and theatrical space to express his poetic ideals.

In recognizing the part that space plays in what David Riggs calls
Jonson's "extraordinary campaign to secure his authorial prerogatives," I am
not necessarily arguing that that campaign was "successful" in some essential sense.[12] After Wimsatt and Beardsley questioned the relevance of authorial intention, after Barthes wrote the author's obituary, and after Foucault
replaced him with a function, we may be forever beyond the naïve assumption that claims of authorial agency are ever successful.[13] But neither can we
ignore the existence of those claims if we wish to historicize authorship as an
idea. Barthes's famous declaration of the author's death was wishful thinking
as much as a statement of what has happened; he acknowledges that "[t]he
author still reigns in histories of literature."[14] And for Foucault, if the historical author is always in the act of disappearing into the "author function," he
remains a "necessary or constraining figure."[15] At any rate, my arguments
do not depend on a reactionary reassertion of or submission to the tyranny
of the author, but rather on the view that Jonson's claims—"successful" or
not—to a privileged role as maker and interpreter of the meanings of London expand and color our sense of what counts as text, of what counts as
authorial practice, and of what constitutes an assertion of authorial agency.

Chapter One
Space as Authorial Strategy

> I'll never
> Be such a gosling to obey instinct, but stand
> As if a man were author of himself,
> And knew no other kin.
>
> William Shakespeare, *Coriolanus* 5.3.34–37[1]

The banished Coriolanus's declaration of independence, his attempt to "stand / As if a man were author of himself," has already failed. He will not resist the pleas of his kin to spare his native Rome, and in these words of defiance, Shakespeare, as the real author of Coriolanus, marks his failure—with that bathetic "As if"—as a tragically ironic joke. For the world of the play, and perhaps for Shakespeare himself, attempts at self-authorship are dangerously hubristic and even absurd. As a fictional character, Coriolanus is authored not by himself, but by Shakespeare, and as a man, he is defined by his community, given one name by his mother and a second by his city, the two dominant agents in his life that do prevail upon his instinct and convert his doomed attempt to stand as a self-author into a tragic death.

The irony of the passage from *Coriolanus* suggests the inseparability of the individual from his society, which seems appropriate for a dramatist like Shakespeare who left posterity comparatively little trace of his own personality, and no explicit authorial self-portrait, in his writing. The Shakespearean canon and the scant biographical details available to us do not allow critics much insight into Shakespeare's own self-fashioning. For as immediate as his characters seem, their author is distant and demonstrably unknowable; even in the sonnets, with all their temptations toward biographical interpretation, the speaker and the author are never unproblematically equivalent.

The case with Shakespeare's contemporary and colleague Ben Jonson could not be more different. He strove throughout his career to construct and present himself as a poet, which partly explains why generations of critics—influenced by Romantic authorial ideals like Keatsian "nega-tive capability"—have maligned him as a lesser poet than Shakespeare.[2] Instead of disappearing behind his works as Shakespeare does, he con-stantly points to himself as their creator and origin, and C. H. Herford found his constant presence in his texts to be a transparent expression of his personality, seeing in "every sentence he wrote . . . an unmistakable relish of the man . . . a document of the Jonsonian temperament."[3] Twen-tieth-century criticism, showing the influence of Freudian psychoanaly-sis and deconstruction, has seen the "Jonsonian temperament" as much more opaque and conflicted and has judged his project of self-authorship by the same standards by which *Coriolanus* judges its central character's failure. The comparison, if perhaps unfair, is apt in some ways. If Rich-ard Helgerson's suggestion that Jonson's poetic career is characterized by a disillusionment and alienation almost as tragic as Coriolanus's is perhaps exaggerated, it is nevertheless true that Jonson's career was complicated by the same factors that bring Coriolanus to his death.[4] Jonson, despite his repeated insistence on his status as the individual creator of his poetry and of his career, led a life defined by his relationships.[5] Moreover, as with Coriolanus, the one relationship that defines Jonson most fully, and from which, this book will argue, his model of authorship emerges, is his rela-tionship to the city in which he lived and on whose stages—in playhouses, streets, and bookstalls—he performed. This performative relationship with London, and a corollary conception of London and its spaces as fun-damentally theatrical, helped give Jonson the scope and the method for his self-construction as author.

It is an axiom among many critics and literary historians that Jon-son was involved in the development of a form of authorship new to his period and recognizably modern in sensibility, but claims about the nature of Jonson's innovation are often treated as unspoken assumptions or are very generally stated. We know that Jonson was doing something new, but exactly what it was is a question as difficult to delineate as a portrait of Jonson himself. Broadly speaking, we can group the innovations of the Jon-sonian "author function" into two related claims: that Jonson was engaged in technical practices that helped define ideas of copyright and intellectual property; and that he was promulgating a new role and function for the poet, a new configuration of the relationship between author and audience or author and society. These two observations combine to form, in the views of Jonson himself and of his critics, a distinct and new form of authorship, one that is inseparable from his meticulously crafted authorial persona. For Jonson, being a poet *required* a man to stand as author of himself.

THE FOLIO OF 1616

Given the emphasis by historians of authorship on the developments in the material literary culture of the seventeenth century and on the evolving interaction between systems of patronage and the literary marketplace, it is understandable that the dominant narrative about Jonson and his authorial self-construction centers on the publication of his *Workes* in 1616.[6] It is true that this book stands as a textual monument of his literary life, a well-wrought picture of Jonson's poetic career. He constructs himself as an author by emphasizing in his *Workes* the four principles of unity proposed by St. Jerome and cited by Foucault in "What is an Author?": a constant level of value, a conceptual coherence, a stylistic unity, and most importantly for Jonson, a historical presence.[7] The artifice with which he makes these claims for authority is quite apparent, however. The Folio does not contain the *complete* works of Ben Jonson, in Herford and Simpson's sense; he avoids any works that landed him in legal trouble and includes only those works that are entirely his, omitting his collaborative plays and reducing Inigo Jones's considerable contribution to the masques to anonymous "scenes" channeled through Jonson's textual descriptions of them.[8] Additionally, by revising the plays while stressing on the title pages that the play-texts in the Folio are those performed by a specific troupe at a particular moment in history, he creates the illusion of a constant level of artistic excellence. The Folio version of *Every Man in His Humor*, the most heavily revised of all the plays, is quite decidedly *not* the play "Acted in the yeere 1598. By the then Lord Chamberlaine his Seruants" (A1).

As textual critics such as Jerome McGann have stressed, authorship—insofar as it is defined as the production of a text—does not lie solely in the human being who first conceptualized that text, but in all the people, institutions, and other factors involved in the production of the document in which the text is contained and the reception of the text in any medium.[9] Thus, in the case of Jonson's texts, we should recognize that authority lies to some extent in the palace, the playhouse, and the printing house; with the acting company and the prompter no less than with the bookseller; with the masques' scenic designers and the compositor who set the type for the Folio, and with the audiences—courtly and popular, oral and textual—that received the texts.

Jonson, however, seems almost to have anticipated the poststructuralist insistence on the cultural production of texts and attempted to challenge it. As we will see again and again, his authorial strategies place himself in competition with all these competing claimants for authorial production, and he sets about to suppress or overcome each of them.[10] The Folio of 1616 is only the most obvious example of this, an attempt to establish himself as sole author and controller of his texts, and to determine how and by whom they are received. His most powerful tool for achieving this scheme in his book is the use of the folio format. The large format, as G. E. Bentley reminds us, was "generally reserved for sermons, geographies, the classics, royal books like *The Works of King James*—also printed in 1616—and other such literature thought to be of permanent significance."[11] For Jonson to produce a folio volume that included a genre as trivial as plays written for the public theaters can be seen as an almost unprecedented act of authorial hubris. The Folio's printer, William Stansby, was known for meticulously prepared, expensive presentation volumes, several in folio—Florio's *Dictionary*, the histories of Ralegh and Camden, and Seneca's *Workes*, for example—as well as high-quality books in smaller format. Stansby had worked with several of the playwright's friends and Jonson contributed commendatory verses to many of Stansby's volumes.[12] He had also worked with Jonson himself earlier, having printed the neoclassical playhouse flop *Catiline* in 1611 and *Certayne Masques* in 1615.[13] Jonson carefully chose a printer who would not compromise quality in favor of large sales, a printer who was, as the Folio title page declares Jonson to be, *Contentus paucis lectoribus*. This is appropriate to Jonson's stance in Epigram 3, where he begs the bookseller not to advertise and force his book on the masses. Jonson would rather his book "lye vpon the stall, till it be sought" than be "ofer'd, as it made sute to be bought" (5–6).

Jonson was not content, however, to give Stansby complete control of his texts. He personally selected and edited the play-texts and poems—although he did not reedit the masques—and corrected proof in the printing house. While it was not unusual for an author to usher his texts through publication like this, the courtly tradition of authorial *sprezzatura* dictated—for a poet as scornful of the market as Jonson tried to seem—a calculated appearance of ease and carelessness about a work's printing.[14] Perhaps, as Sara van den Berg suggests, James I's publication of his works in 1616 legitimized print as a means of self-representation and began to remove the stigma of professionalism associated with publication.[15] At any rate, Jonson ignores the self-effacing courtly tradition of manuscript circulation, and indeed his epigrams—particularly 81 ("To Prowl the Plagiary") and 56 ("On Poet-Ape")—express a real anxiety that his texts be kept in their integrity and associated with his name. This abandonment of the *sprezzatura* associated with earlier aristocratic authors is Jonson's main effect on the developing significance of print, according to Richard Newton: "Jonson's own insistence on his place in [the] professionalization of the book business marks an important step. He completely abandons the pretense of the gentleman amateur and emphasizes his professionalism in his metaphors for writing."[16]

Newton, with the benefit of historical hindsight, reads Jonson's insistence on his role in the production of his book as "integration into the corporate enterprise of book production,"[17] but I would argue that at the moment of the Folio's production, such insistence was one of many ways in which Jonson effaced or diminished the contributions of the other producers. His participation in the printing process allows him to exert editorial authority over the printer, who becomes merely the employee of the author. Indeed, this insistence on seeing his works through the printing process is one of the primary ways in which critics have defined the novelty of Jonsonian authorship; James A. Riddell, for example, discusses Jonson's obsessive editorial eye for small corrections in printed texts because "they are necessary to illustrate how the modern idea of an 'author'—one who takes particular care with the exact appearance of his words—began with Jonson."[18]

Jonson's choice of Stansby—a printer not known for printing plays or other ephemera of the sort usually associated with inexpensive chapbooks—gives Jonson's Folio a monumentality; it claims for the *Workes* a permanent status, and allows Jonson to place himself and his works historically. The folio format gives his book the status of a history, not of England or of the world or of the church, but of Jonson himself. The plays, which take up well over half the volume, are arranged chronologically, with the original performance date stated on each play's individual title page and again in a sort of program note following each play that also lists the principal players and the location of the first production. As Timothy Murray points out, by presenting the plays this way, in an author-based chronological order, Jonson suppresses the playhouse as an operating force in textual production, "fabricat[ing] a textual temporality transcending the sporadic moments of theatrical performance."[19] In the pages of the *Workes* the players and the public audiences become secondary, mere markers of and witnesses to the historical provenance of Jonson's texts. Even as the title pages and actor lists remind us of the works' theatrical origins, they distance the plays from those origins and allow Jonson to assert his authorial power over that of the players, as W. H. Herendeen argues:

> In specifying at the end of each play which companies originally performed it, and even in identifying the original actors, Jonson proclaims his independence from any single company and presents himself as an employer of actors rather than as an employee.[20]

This process of distancing himself from his background among the players and playhouses of London is reflected emblematically on the Folio's title page. While the triumphal arch that frames the book's title acknowledges the dramatic nature of Jonson's works, it specifically excludes the stages of contemporary London. The arch is founded on two blocks, the left one—labeled *PLAVSTRVM*—carved with an image of Thespis driving a pageant wagon, and the right one—labeled *VISORIVM*—depicting a Greek chorus in a round auditorium. Directly above the title is a Roman theater, marked *THEATRVM*, appropriately elevated by Jonson the Romanophile to a pride of place as the totemic locus of Senecan and Terentian drama. Nowhere is a Blackfriars, Globe, or Fortune to be seen on the title page, which indeed has no hints of Englishness about it other than the author's and printer's names.

JONSON'S SPATIAL AWARENESS

This effect of distancing the textual monument to Jonson's career from its origins in the drama would seem to lend credence to another piece of received wisdom about Jonson, the idea that he was a paradoxically antitheatrical playwright.[21] The method of authorial construction that the Folio advances by abstracting the poet from the ephemeral vagaries of theater, however, is only one of the strategies Jonson employed in the years leading up to 1616. The textual monumentalization that has been the focus of Jonson's critics is certainly part of his assertion of authorial agency, but we must supplement our understanding of Jonsonian authorship with the awareness of another strategy working parallel to it, if not always in concert with it: over the course of those same years, Jonson became more and more interested in the role of space—the space of the playhouse and the urban space it could represent—in his authorial claims.

In this concern, Jonson was very much of his time; early modern Europe was a transitional, revolutionary period with regard to the conceptualization and representation of space. As Edward S. Casey has argued forcefully in his work on the ideas of place and space in western philosophy, the sixteenth and seventeenth centuries saw a fundamental "early modern paradigm shift" in the priority of the terms in the popular and intellectual imagination. Scientific revolutions like Cartesian geometry and Galilean astronomy required a conception of undefined, limitless space as epistemologically prior to place, the bounded, local, topographical knowledge of our everyday lives.[22]

This early modern shift in spatial awareness corresponds to what Bernhard Klein, in his study of mapping in Renaissance England and Ireland, calls "the 'cartographic transaction': the mental and material renegotiation of the lived space of experience."[23] The mapping of England became a widespread science in the latter half of the sixteenth century, and at the same time the genre of chorographic descriptions of local British natural and social landscapes—like the *Britannia* of Jonson's beloved tutor William Camden (1586) and William Lambarde's *Perambulation of Kent* (1576)— carried out the cartographic process in descriptive prose. And in 1598, the historian John Stow's *Survey of London* turned the chorographic gaze to the capital city, with a ward-by-ward description of London, its structure, its streets, its history, and its monuments.[24]

In this wider cultural and intellectual context, playwrights are uniquely placed to serve both as objects of inquiry and as experimenters themselves. After all, playhouses, especially the playhouses of early modern London, which can serve as "metaphors of the city and the urban experience generally,"[25] provide a wonderful petri dish for the observation of interactions with—and production of meaning through—space and place. It is no coincidence that Stow's *Survey*, the first systematic description of London's spaces in print, appeared in the same year as the first play—William Haughton's *Englishmen for my Money*—to be set in the contemporary London of its audience. Jonson's London was a city "in a state of flux and in the continuous process of reinventing itself,"[26] and the drama of the period was crucial to this process of reinvention. If the city, as Jean Howard has recently argued, was disturbingly unknowable to its inhabitants, "[w]riting about London, as many dramatists did, was one way . . . discursively to manage change and to provide interpretations and conceptualizations of both new and old aspects of the city."[27]

I hope to show that Jonson, more than his contemporaries, recognized this implicit foregrounding of the epistemological role of space and place in the intellectual imagination of early modern England. His participation in the processes and relations of space and place, and their implications for politics and poetics, is crucial to his awareness of himself as author. Moreover, his exploration of these processes anticipates some central theoretical debates of modern materialist theorists, geographers, and social anthropologists.

An effective starting point for our consideration of space's role in Jonson's production of authorial subjectivity is Yi-Fu Tuan's study of psychological geography and the "perspective of experience," which focuses on the individual's internal cartographic processes.[28] Tuan articulates a useful binary of space and place that reflects Casey's description of the Renaissance relationship between the terms: *space* is the undistinguished "out there" that we conceive only vaguely until we apply experience to it, allowing us to distinguish and define *places*, points in space that derive meaning from our experience and naming of them. Tuan articulates a view of space as the amorphous precursor to place, and emphasizes that space exists only until the experience of the mind names it, a blank page—or an empty stage—upon which the individual inscribes meaning.

Tuan may seem to offer the most intuitive way of thinking about stage space, especially given the spatial conventions of early modern English drama, which, as Alan Dessen's seminal work on the subject has demonstrated, used characters' behavior, appearance, and speech rather than stage properties to determine locale. To put this in Tuan's terms, the individual character's subjective experience, and the audience's experience of her, makes place out of the space of the unmarked stage.[29] Dessen does not mention Jonson in his chapter on "The logic of 'place' and locale" except to suggest that Jonson characteristically scoffs at the conventional fluidity of the Renaissance stage, and that Jonson, as a self-consciously literary rather than theatrical playwright, hampered by the self-imposed strictures of the classical unities, is the exception that proves the rule of Elizabethan drama's representation of space.[30] I would contend that, far from being less attuned than his contemporary dramatists to the potentialities of dramatic space, Jonson is merely interested in a more competitive subjectivity, one that conceives of space not as an amorphous and undefined thing, but as an already existing definitional matrix that always precedes the individual's experience of it.[31]

After all, authors who work, as Jonson did, in a specific urban milieu do not write in an ahistoric void, any more than the inhabitants of any city create its fabric out of their own minds. Cities are not blank books, but palimpsests, and Michel de Certeau offers a model of space and place more applicable to the everyday, "real" urban experience, and to Jonson's authorial project, than Tuan's. De Certeau does posit a binary relationship similar to Tuan's—defined, located place (*lieu*) and dynamic, mobile, shifting space (*espace*).[32] He reverses the direction of the relationship, however, presenting place as the preexisting term. Place (*lieu*) is defined and located by semiotic markers, but it is meaningless by itself. It is something to be worked on, an "instantaneous configuration of positions" that "implies an indication of stability," but that requires space to give it meaning.[33] Space (*espace*), for de Certeau,

> exists when one takes into consideration vectors of direction, velocities, and time variables. Thus space is composed of intersections of mobile elements. It is in a sense actuated by the ensemble of movements deployed within it. Space occurs as the effect produced by the operations that orient it, situate it, temporalize it, and make it function.[34]

Espace, that is, is human action that makes sense of preexisting, pre-ordered, but as yet meaningless place. "In short," as de Certeau says, "*space is a practiced place.*"[35] This model is much more amenable to a playwright who saw dramatic authorship primarily as a way to represent and rewrite the city he inhabited, making London—a city of pre-existing places to be practiced— into a stage, as well as representing it in the playhouse.

Another of de Certeau's analogies (with an inescapable echo of Saussure's *langue* and *parole*) demonstrates his model's applicability to dramatic authorship: "in relation to place [*lieu*]," de Certeau writes, "space [*espace*] is like the word when it is spoken." *Espace*, that is, is performative; it can be seen as analogous to the theatrical utterance of a playwright's script. In repeatedly returning to this analogy of place as text, and space as the performance (practice) of it, I hope to show that de Certeau's model provides a way to conceptualize the various roles that Jonson, as a dramatic author, could take: as a producer of texts on the one hand, as a producer and performer of plays on the other.

Jonson's authorial strategies are intrinsically competitive. If the production of the Folio is an attempt to efface the other producers of his book and his text, his authorial wrangling in the realm of urban space is no less agonistic, bound up in contests to produce place and to practice space, to write, read, and rewrite the city. Thus the fact that de Certeau's model places *lieu* and *espace* in competition with each other would seem to be especially appropriate to our understanding of Jonson. We must, of course, be careful with this as with all binaries not to reduce it to overly simplistic oppositions of class, or of subversion and containment. When mapped onto structures of power, de Certeau's model of cultural practice is, at a first glance, unapologetically binary and inescapably antagonistic in its terminology. Dominant classes and institutions use "strategies" in an attempt to define their power, to establish fixed and delimited knowledge, untainted by the uncertainties of historical change. Dominated classes, "the weak," or "the other," use "tactics" to turn place, the product of these strategies, to its own ends, and to seize opportunities for subverting them from within.[36] In the terms of his space binary, strategies are associated with *lieu*; they include mapping, building monuments, inscribing the names of leaders into the physical fabric of the environment. Those in power rely on the primacy of place, the idea that it is static and unchanging and can monumentalize their control, offering a resistance to time, a sort of fantasy of ahistoricity. "The 'proper,'" as de Certeau says, "is *a triumph of place over time.*"[37] Tactics, on the other hand, "gain validity in relation to the pertinence they lend to time;" they depend on ephemerality, change, and unknowability.[38]

Tactics are the work of *espace*, the way the individual can plot his or her own trajectory through the planned architecture of a cityscape to change its meaning. Merely by the way he or she moves through the city, the individual complicates and subverts the strategic attempts of power to create permanent, unchanging place.

Despite the number of related binary oppositions that de Certeau's model describes—strategy/tactics, space/place, dominant/dominated—his emphasis on the infinite vectors of space, and by extension the infinite multiplicity of the subject, give his theory a potential that exceeds the potential limitations of dualism. The opposition of *lieu* and *espace* is useful as a preliminary model of the social and ideological relations of space, and it also delimits a position for the emergent individual author. Jonson, I will argue, recognized the potential friction between the institutional strategies of the powerful and the individual tactics of the dominated. His authorial claims, however, come not from association with either term of the opposition—or with "subversion" or "containment" to put it in terms of another well-worn binary. His claim comes instead from the recognition that, as geographers like David Harvey and Doreen Massey have argued, there are no *a priori*, unpracticed places but rather that both *lieu* and *espace* are continual processes in constant interaction.[39] The sense of Jonson's potency as author emerges from his conscious participation in both of those processes, of forging a third way that avoids the limitations of *lieu* and *espace* while exploiting the potential of each. Jonson's construction of himself as a dramatist, as an author of space, produces a third term between the oppositional binary of space and place that contributes to both practices, that seeks in fact to make the author's privileged *espace* into a substitute for institutional *lieu*.[40]

For Jonson, spatial practice—in the sense of de Certeau's *espace*, the way the individual inhabits, experiences, and makes sense of his or her environment—is a figure for and expression of moral and mental capability. Throughout his writing, not only power, but also virtue, intelligence, and the capacity for critical judgment are all characteristically associated with space. Also characteristically for Jonson—perhaps reflecting his status as a bricklayer *cum* poet—the analogy between the construction of physical place and the construction of poetry is particularly appealing.[41] In the *Discoveries*, the miscellany of observations "made upon men and matter" that Jonson compiled from his extensive reading, both classical and contemporary, he makes this analogy in an argument concerning the ordering of poetry:

> if a man would build a house, he would first appoint a place to
> build it in, which he would define within certaine bounds: So in the

Constitution of a *Poeme*, the Action is aym'd at by the *Poet*, which
answers Place in a building; and that Action hath his largenesse,
compasse, and proportion. (2686–2691)

This is only one of many metaphors for poetry and poetic style in the *Discoveries*, but inasmuch as Jonson was a dramatic poet, whose tools necessarily included physical space as well as words, it is perhaps the most apt
formulation in Jonson's criticism to his own poetry. As a playwright—on his
own home ground, as it were, of the playhouse—Jonson was accustomed, in
de Certeau's terms, not only to produce *lieu*, to define the "certaine bounds"
and plot the thoroughfares of his drama, but also to populate them with
competing practitioners of place, creating varied vectors of theatrical space,
practices over which he could both pass judgment and have control. His
poetry, both dramatic and non-dramatic, celebrates the author's control in
spatial terms derived from and enabled by these theatrical practices.

Moreover, Jonson demonstrates this simultaneous involvement in the
processes of both *lieu* and *espace* in the spaces of both the page and the stage.
The 1616 Folio does employ a strategy of distancing Jonson from the immediacy of the theater, constructing Jonson primarily as a poet rather than a
playwright, but even there he exhibits a playful awareness of the role of space
in his authorial assertions. In his book he can manage and delimit the competing authorities of printer and publisher more successfully than he could
the questionably reliable players and the exigencies of performance. When,
for example, his epigrams engage with rival playwrights, Jonson imagines
the engagement of wits on the page, not the stage: "PLAY-WRIGHT," he writes
in Epigram 49, "I loath to haue thy manners knowne / In my chast book:
professe them in thine own" (5–6). In praising the great player of his time,
Edward Alleyn (Epigram 89), Jonson does not allow the player's skill and
fame to speak for itself in the playhouse. The player, after all, merely speaks
the poet's words, and Jonson claims both the right and the responsibility to
validate Alleyn's virtuosity; as Roscius required Cicero, Alleyn needs Jonson
to "publish" him, to remove him from the playhouse and give him eternal
life in the book: "'Tis iust, that who did giue / So many *Poets* life, by one
should liue" (13–14). Players may animate poets' work onstage, but the final
triumph is the dramatist's, in the space of the text.

Even as he abstracts playhouse space into the more controllable textual
fixity of the book, however, he is imagining competitive spatial practices.
Epigram 112, "To a Weak Gamester in Poetry," is a translation of Martial's
"To Tucca," an expression of exasperation to a poetic rival who insists on
imitating the poet's efforts in every genre. Significantly, Jonson's major

innovation on his original is to imagine the "game" of poetic rivalry in spatial terms, as indicated by the use of deictics of place (*where, there*):

> I cannot for the stage a *Drama* lay,
> *Tragick* or *Comick*; but thou writ'st the play.
> I leaue thee there, and giuing way, entend
> An *Epick* poeme; thou hast the same end.
> I modestly quit that, and thinke to write,
> Next morne, an *Ode*: thou mak'st a song ere night.
> I pass to *Elegies*; thou meet'st me there:
> To *Satyres*; and thou dost pursue me. Where,
> Where shall I scape thee? (7–15)

Jonson's irritating competitor does not merely imitate him, he *pursues* him through different genres, which Jonson, unlike Martial, presents as though they are physical places, as if trying to find the most advantageous ground on which to stage a duel.[42] On the one hand, the Folio allows Jonson to withdraw from the physical, urban environment in which he, his colleagues and his rivals lived and competed to the higher ground of his book, but he imagines the book itself as an alternate space, one that remains subject to his authority.

Moreover, in Jonson's non-dramatic poetry, as well as in the plays, he stages the association of space and place with the virtues of the mind. A favorite metaphor for virtue in Jonson's epigrams and lyrics is the transformation of the object's body into an urban place, inhabited by virtue or vice. Thus the gluttonous lecher "Gut" of Epigram 118 "makes himselfe a thorough-fare of vice," while Jonson's patron Sir Kenelm Digby

> is built like some imperiall roome
> For [virtue] to dwell in, and be still at home.
> His brest is a brave Palace, a broad Street,
> Where all heroique ample thoughts doe meet:
> Where Nature such a large survey hath ta'en,
> As other soules, to his, dwell in a Lane (*Underwood* 78, 7–12)

It is worth noting in this comparison that virtue is seen as static, dwelling and still at home, while vice traverses a "thorough-fare."[43] Digby's breast may be a street as well as a palace—suggesting the importance of both the public and private self—but it is the sort of street that is less a passage to somewhere else than a place of congregation for "heroique ample thoughts." Like

London's central avenue of Cheapside—which was at once a street, a sort of mercantile plaza, and a staging ground for civic ceremony—Digby's breast is a street but also a *lieu*, a well-mapped spot, surveyed by Nature herself; vice, by contrast, defines Gut the glutton's body by movement, by practicing its own *espace*. Moreover, and unsurprisingly, Jonson allies himself as author with Nature; after all it is the poet himself who builds Digby as a place for virtue to dwell. Conversely, Jonson dissociates himself from the "thoroughfare of vice," which is of Gut's own making.

The morally definitive movement of vice through "Gut's" guts is a particularly transgressive portrait of *espace*, but not all mobility is vicious in Jonson's spatial figures. Mere stasis is not virtue, and knowledge of the world is not to be found except by moving through it, as Epigram 92, "The New Crie," makes clear. The pretenders to statecraft that Jonson satirizes "know the states of *Christendome*, not the places" (8). Their knowledge, that is, comes from hearsay, not from traveling or inhabiting the places themselves: "Yet haue they seene the maps, and bought 'hem too, / And understand 'hem, as most chapmen doe" (9–10). The experience of place merely through the textual medium of cartography leads to a ridiculous parody of topographic knowledge. Just as the foolish reader of poetry, for Jonson, is more prone to acts of plagiarism than true understanding (see, for example, Matthew in *Every Man in His Humor*), the reader of cartography lacks any agency with regard to place. By contrast, Epigram 128, "To William Roe" presents the ideal of travel through the world, an ideal that informs all of Jonson's practices of place, and also his conception of the author's self-construction, and his relationship to antiquity and his readers. Roe is encouraged "to goe / Countries, and climes, manners, and men to know, / T'extract, and choose the best of all these knowne, / And those to turne to bloud, and make thine owne" (1–4). Jonson's ideal practice of place, that is, must be tempered by judgment; the virtuous man maintains his subjectivity as he performs *espace*, refusing to be fundamentally altered by the places that he visits. It can be said that he, like Aeneas, "past through fire, / Through seas, stormes, tempests: and imbarqu'd for hell, / Came backe vntouch'd" (12–14). The epigram to William Roe describes his ideal journey as an ideal shape: "may all thy ends," Jonson writes to Roe, "As the beginnings here, / proue purely sweet, / And perfect in a circle alwayes meet" (6–8).

Late in his life, Jonson presented the path of his own career with an image similar to that of the Roe epigram. In the Induction to *The Magnetic Lady*, a "Boy of the house" presents the picture of Jonson's dramatic career coming to a close with a comedy of humors, the sort of play with which it began; *The Magnetic Lady* constitutes therefore "the close, or shutting up of his Circle" (104–105).[44] This image of spatial practice, orderly and almost mathematically traced like a compass, is part of a larger pattern in Jonson's canon, as Thomas Greene has argued,[45] an ideal version of *espace* that stands in contrast to the endlessly mobile, hectically intersecting vectors of the characters in Jonson's London comedies. Whereas Greene sees in the compass image one side of a binary of selfhood in a confrontation that Jonson staged throughout his career, I would suggest that Jonson's own emblem, a broken compass with the motto *Deest quod duceret orbem* ("that which would draw the circle is missing"),[46] is a winking acknowledgement that the perfection of the circle is artificial, achievable only through dramatic invention. This book will argue that Jonson saw both the compass metaphor's geometric ideal and the unbalanced, uncontrolled fluidity of the humors characters, rogues and gulls of his London comedies as poetic constructs. What his career really demonstrates is not the failure to achieve an ideal, but the extent of his control over competing representations of spatial practice.

AUTHORING LONDON: "ON THE FAMOUS VOYAGE"

Jonson's interest in space and place is not confined to theoretical constructs or abstract metaphors, however. His authorial project is intimately dependent on the medium of London's physical places and spaces, on demonstrating epistemological control over a city that was already in the process of becoming the vast, urban unknown that Samuel Johnson and Charles Dickens would inherit. Nowhere in his non-dramatic poetry is this demonstration more apparent than in the long poem that crowns and concludes the Folio collection of epigrams, "On the Famous Voyage." This mock-epic and gleefully scatological narrative documents the 1610 rowing excursion taken on a dare by two of Jonson's acquaintances, a journey that extends from Bridewell dock on the Thames to the village of Holborn, north of London. Their adventure is notable because it carried the men, Shelton and Heyden,[47] along with the two watermen hired to row their wherry boat, up Fleet Ditch, the open sewer that formed the westernmost border between the city and Jonson's native Westminster. In effect the colon of the city, the ditch ran past two prisons, through London's most notorious neighborhoods, and past the butchers' district; it was filled with excrement, offal, and dead animals, made worse in the plague year of 1610 by "the cryes of *Ghosts*, women and men, / Laden with plague-sores, and their sinnes" (16–17).[48]

Shelton and Heyden's journey was an example of a phenomenon popular in late Tudor and Stuart England, a form of highly publicized travel that, through the descriptive writing it produced, became part of early modern

England's cultural imagination. "Putting out" voyages, as they were called, involved a sort of mercantile adventure, and the term combines two meanings of the phrase *to put out*: to embark on a journey, and to invest money. A prospective voyager publicly proposed a trip to be undertaken within a certain space of time—typically with outlandish restrictions on his behavior—and invited people to bet on his failure. Bonds were drawn up and the voyager traveled with a supervisor to ensure that he stuck to the conditions of the bet. Jonson himself parodies the phenomenon with Puntavarlo in *Every Man Out of His Humor*, who ventures to travel to Turkey and back while managing to keep his pet dog and cat alive. While Puntavarlo is the object of satire—and his pets do not even survive to the outskirts of the city—his plan seems not to have been comparatively dafter than others. The "Famous Voyage" up the Fleet has terms more outlandish than most putting out voyages: Shelton and Heyden must make it to the Three Sergeants' Heads pub in Holborn without holding their noses or turning back. They see themselves, Jonson tells us, in direct competition with several of the most well-known of such stunts, proposing their wherry voyage

> in worthy scorne
> Of those, that put out moneyes, on returne
> From *Venice*, *Paris*, or some in-land passage
> Of sixe times to, and fro, without embassage,
> Or him that backward went to *Berwicke*, or which
> Did dance the famous Morrise unto *Norwich* (31–36)[49]

Putting out voyages like those Jonson lists were most often documented in first-person accounts like *Kemps Nine Daies Wonder*, which highlighted the voyager's experience of the journey and of the places he or she encountered. Unlike cartography and even first-person chorography, which ostensibly create place (*lieu*), the genre of putting out literature was usually a means of privileging, indeed *marketing*, the individual's *espace*.[50] Jonson's "On the Famous Voyage," however, is the only surviving account of Shelton and Heyden's "most liquid deed" (193), and in spatial terms it has another function entirely, to celebrate the control that Jonson has over the meanings of London's space. Jonson turns Shelton and Heyden—the originators of the Famous Voyage—into mere dramatic characters in *his* poem, and he hardly allows them a voice at all. He appropriates their spatial practice and classicizes it, abstracting a historically immediate experience of London space into the arena of the page, where he can attempt to assert sole control (to the extent that printing practices allowed), where his third-person, cartographic eye can define the *lieu* of the poem and the event, and where his authorial *espace* can replace that of the voyagers.

The classicizing of the jaunt up Fleet Ditch into a mock-epic journey to the underworld is for comic effect, of course, but it also illustrates Jonson's exertion of authorial control over urban space. In addition to the ironically heightened rhetoric, the archaic vocabulary, and the epic similes, Jonson enacts a transformation of London's familiar places into classical analogs. Thus the three sergeants on the pub sign at Holborn become a version of Cerberus, the three-headed guard dog of hell; a garbage barge is mistaken for Scylla or Hydra, and the watermen employed to row the wherry are a "brace of CHARONS" (87). The wherry embarks at a spot that becomes in Jonson's hands a conflation of Aeneas's entryway to the underworld and a more mundane urban place: "A docke there is, that called is AVERNVS," he declares, then adds parenthetically, "Of some *Bride-well*" (41–42). Fleet Ditch combines all the horrors of Hades's rivers, "of STYX, of ACHERON, / COCYTVS, PHLEGETHON . . . in one; / The filth, stench, noyse" (7–9), and to structure his poem, Jonson uses the rivers as stages of their journey: "COCYTVS" (89) is the first stage, where they encounter the garbage barge; "the *Stygian* poole" is next (121), the stretch of the Ditch before Fleet Street bridge, where they are tormented by floating turds and "ghosts . . . of farts"(124–25); Acheron is the dumping sink of the butchers, or "*Fleet*-lane *Furies*" (143), and it is also the site of Fleet Prison, where the noises of inmates become in Jonson's poem the "out-cryes of the damned" (172).

Jonson's mock-epic, reveling so grossly in filth that William Gifford refused to annotate it, hardly glorifies the city, as do Jonson's other examples of classicizing London. In the next chapter we will see him help to transform London into a neo-Roman triumph for King James, and he often Londonizes Roman models of poetry with specific reference to place, as with the song to Celia that appears as the sixth poem in *The Forest*, wherein he compares his beloved's kisses—Catullus's *basia mille*—to

> All the grasse that *Rumney* yields,
> Or the sands in *Chelsey* fields,
> Or the drops in siluer *Thames*,
> Or the starres that guild his streames (13–16)

It is one thing to transform Cheapside into Rome, and quite another to make Fleet Ditch into a classical, if overly scatological, Hades, but the function of both is the same, to glorify Jonson himself, to celebrate the poet's interpretive and transformative power over London's places. Jonson suggests as much when he implies that the monumental function of his poem for Shelton and Heyden has a counterpart in monumental civic architecture; "The citie," he claims, "since hath rais'd a Pyramide" in their memory (194). This purported monument to the voyagers' exploits is a fiction, as would have been obvious to Jonson's readers, either in 1610 or in 1616. The line functions ironically to remind us that the only monument that remains of Shelton and Heyden's "Famous Voyage" is Jonson's poem, which claims its author as the primary agent in the memorializing of urban space.

As the next chapter will show, Jonson had some experience with the more usual, unironic sort of civic monumentalism, as he had been employed in 1604 to help the city celebrate the accession of King James I, a project that involved him in portraying an idealized, antiseptic version of London as far removed as possible from the filth of Fleet Ditch. In undertaking to bring this most vulgarly intimate thoroughfare into his poetic control, though, Jonson illustrates the scope of his spatial authority over the places of London. He can paint vivid portraits not only of the city's face, but also its fundament. As we will see, in the official civic pageantry for King James, Jonson is just as concerned with using his privileged, authorial view of London and his capacity to define its places as he is in "On the Famous Voyage." He demonstrates that his authorial *espace* can replace that of the king on his progress through London, just as he had effaced the voices and spatial practices of Shelton and Heyden. Moreover, 1604 was a defining moment in Jonson's career. If there is a moment to which we can trace the beginnings of his exploration of dramatic space as an alternate strategy for the assertion of authorial identity, it is in his experience working with his rival playwright Thomas Dekker on the royal entry pageant. From his competition with Dekker emerges a new awareness of the potential of urban space, not only as a writable, controllable text, but as a stage for contests of performative, dramatic authority.

Chapter Two
Londinium
The 1604 Royal Entry of James I

The entertainment celebrating King James I's ceremonial entry into London on 15 March 1604 provides a remarkable example of the complex competition—among institutions and individuals alike—for the authority to define and control the uses and meanings of London's place. It was a climax and a turning point in the dramatic development of London's civic pageantry because it includes mature character development and replaces static tableaux with dramatic action and dialogue, and also because the city employed the best dramatists then available to design the shows and write the scripts.[1] But the royal entry pageant was also a turning point in Jonson's career; through his employment on its production alongside his rival Thomas Dekker, he realized the potential to be gained by the application of theatrical methods of spatial representation to the overdetermined, ritualized places of London.

James's *Magnificent Entertainment* (as Dekker's published text would call it) was more than a show; it evinced not only shared cultural attitudes, but also complex conflicts.[2] The texts that Dekker and Jonson sent to the press illustrate a struggle between the two playwrights to describe the triumphs, pageantry, and symbolism of the entry. Theirs is an authorial competition to interpret the events of 15 March 1604 correctly, to preserve an ephemeral phenomenon in such a way as to replace the spatial practices of the king and his audience with practices that remain in the authors' control. This struggle with Dekker gave Jonson a model for the competitions of cultural competence in the arena of urban space that his middle and late comedies repeatedly stage.[3] From the playwrights' competition, from their reconstruction of the king's performance, and from their subordination of that performance to their own authority, emerges a sense of the dramatic author as a privileged interpreter of London space that would inform Jonson's dramaturgy for the rest of his career. Jonson, like Dekker, embraced the opportunity to treat London as a stage, and learned from it that using dramatic practices to assert his authority over the city's space, as over any other stage, could be a viable authorial strategy.

CITY AND CROWN: POLITICAL CONTEXTS

Jonson's competition with Dekker is underscored by its historical concurrence with a pre-existing competition between the city and the crown. Such competition was not new, but because of the unprecedented situation of 1603–4—the peaceful succession of a foreign monarch with no previous relationship with the government and people of London—James's pageant occurred in a particularly charged political climate that both imposed certain strictures on the two playwrights and encouraged them to turn their contributions into claims of authorial agency.

Traditionally, the interdependence of the civic and monarchial governments, and the authority of both city and crown, were ceremonially reasserted on the streets of London through the ritual of the royal entry, which brought the crown itself and its wearer onto the stage of London's streets, but the relationship thus illustrated was rarely free from tension. The steady escalation in the complexity of discourse in civic pageantry during the sixteenth and early seventeenth centuries, as Lawrence Manley points out, is closely associated with the recognition of the pageants' potential for expressing political agendas.[4] Thus, the maturity of dramatic structure so notable in the 1604 entry may be traceable to the fact that relations between London and King James in 1603 were particularly unsure and complex, with neither side altogether certain of its place in the pageant's ritual of exchange and mutual affirmation of authority.

Britain was unique in Europe in that the triumphal entry associated with a new monarch's coronation traditionally occurred *before* the actual coronation. At the death of a king or queen, the Lord Mayor of London was held to be the highest-ranking official in the land, and one of the chief functions of the succeeding monarch's entry into the capital was a ritual demonstration of the citizens' approval of their new leader, the residue of Saxon London's tradition of electing kings.[5] The approval of God would be ritually demonstrated in the coronation at Westminster Abbey, and the city served as a parallel stage for secular approbation. The welcome for the new king was the city's to plan (and to pay for), and the climactic ritual at St. Paul's established London's authority and its place in national government. The recorder, a civic official who served as the voice of London's government, delivered a speech in Paul's churchyard to demonstrate the allegiance of the city, the mayor presented the new monarch with gifts, and the symbols of royalty were transferred to the mayor, who led the procession the rest of the way to the Abbey.[6] The city was both host and stage, and the ceremony of the royal entry made the city's representatives crucial players in the day's drama.

For a variety of reasons in 1603–4, however, the city's role in the new king's triumph and coronation was constantly questioned and undermined. To begin with, the appropriate processional syntax for James's entry was already in question. Traditional coronation entries had the new monarch housed in the Tower of London for days before the event, under the protection of London's largest and most visible fortress. Issuing from the Tower, the procession would wind its way toward the central avenue of Cheapside through Tower Street, Mark Lane, Fenchurch Street, and Gracechurch Street. At Cheapside it would proceed to St. Paul's for the recorder's speech, and after joining the Lord Mayor it would go finally out of the city past Temple Bar and to Westminster for the coronation proper. London would thus have visible ritual control over the entire ceremony, sending forth the fledgling king from its protective bosom.

On the other hand, royal entries by monarchs already crowned—visiting foreign royalty or English kings returning triumphant from battle—had a significantly different symbolic structure. A previously crowned king would approach London from outside its bounds, usually from south of the Thames, and be met at the southern end of the bridge by a pageant of ritual warding off, often featuring giants or allegorical figures on horseback offering battle to the approaching force.[7] This ritual threat would be dispelled at the revelation of the king's identity, and he would enter the city over the bridge, joining the traditional coronation route at Gracechurch Street. The apotropaic figures of protection might reappear at the monarch's exit, as a sort of allegorical bouncers vigilantly policing London's borders. This type of entry evoked a city besieged, if only temporarily and ceremonially. It could allow the city to exhibit the role of protector of the realm—warden in the English king's absence, or vigilant guardian against foreign incursion, however peaceful—but the siege structure could also make explicit in ritual the shifting and uneasy negotiation between crown and city over London's spaces and prerogatives.

Given these two traditional options for royal entries into London, the succession of James I offered a conundrum unique in English history. Never before had an heirless monarch died having named an already-reigning king as her successor. The coronation ceremony demanded one processional syntax, demonstrating the city's ceremonial protection and election of the new king, but James, at thirty-six, was no fledgling Prince of Wales. He had been crowned at the age of thirteen months and had reigned successfully in Scotland for years. On the other hand, he had only just acceded to the English throne and the traditional royal entry for a visiting foreign king or a returning English one, with its rhetoric of siege and symbolic surrender, was likewise inappropriate. With a king who was neither native nor foreign, the city's ceremonial role in James's first royal entry was uncertain, and in the context of this uncertainty the arrangement of the route planned for James's royal entry took on added political significance.

In addition, the relationship between the new king and his new capital city was strained from the beginning for a variety of other reasons. Most prominently among these was the fact that Queen Elizabeth had died £60,000 in debt to the Corporation of London. Immediately upon her death, and perhaps more urgently because they were conscious of the expenses that the coronation ceremonies would incur, the aldermen began to petition the new king for repayment of the debt, a petition they would repeat with increasing frequency over the following months.[8] Before the city could take on their expensive ritual role, moreover, the king had to appear, and James was in no particular hurry that spring, forestalling their royal welcome by taking his own time in making his way to London. James was not ignorant of the necessity for royal display and ostentation to mark the beginning of his reign; quite the contrary. He did insist, however, that he, not the traditions of England's or London's government, would dictate the manner of such display, and he made his trip southward a series of royal entries—into Berwick, Newcastle, York, etc.—that would culminate, not begin and end, with the London entertainment.[9]

The growing anticipation of James's arrival in London was tinged with anxiety, partly because his visit occasioned a temporary population increase of more than a third of the city's inhabitants, which brought with it a plague epidemic: in all, over 30,000 in London and the vicinity would die of the infection over the course of 1603, making it the worst visitation for a decade.[10] On 6 July, after the city had already spent thousands of pounds in preparation for the king's entry, a royal proclamation effectively removed London from her traditional role in the ceremony; the king ordered the city to "deferre all shewe of State and Pompe accustomed by our Progenitors."[11] The coronation ceremony itself would go forward at Westminster Abbey, but the thirty-nine aldermen allowed to attend the coronation were a far cry from the thousands of liveried merchants that were planned to have flanked the king in his progress through the capital, and the concession to the dignity of the civic elites hardly repaid the city's monetary outlay for the event.

The triumphal arches, costumes, and other salvageable material from the pageant were put into storage at further expense, for eventually, James determined that he would make his long-delayed entry into London the following spring on 15 March, to celebrate the opening of his first parliament.

The city had time to complete, improve, and perhaps reconsider its preparations for the event, and it was at some point during the winter of 1603–4 that Jonson was brought in to help Dekker script the shows at the triumphal arches. Little occurred in the intervening months, however, to dismantle the tension implicit in the competition for authority between the city and the crown. The king, constantly on progress to avoid the plague and retiring from the public eye, remained to his English subjects the nearly unknown factor that he had been since his accession.[12] His elaborate progress southward had devalued the centrality of the London royal entry to the coronation ceremonies, and his cancellation of the entry had ultimately denied the city its traditional right to approve the monarch's accession. The unique situation of a coronation for a foreign monarch made the city unsure about its place in the ritual, and the civic government's anxiety was compounded by the chaos of the plague and the attendant monetary tensions between city and crown. It was in this atmosphere of conflict that the royal entry pageant of 1604 was conceived and created.

This aura of conflict can be overemphasized, of course, and the simple reduction of the ostensibly laudatory, ludic, and communal function of events like royal entries to encrypted political conflict is not my concern here.[13] Surely, however, some critics too unproblematically accept these functions at face value. Graham Parry's treatment of Jacobean iconography, for example, contends that the royal entry "demonstrates compactly how the arts served the monarchy by projecting a state mythology," but largely ignores the disjointed nature of the pageant's composition.[14] In the royal entry the city becomes a text to be written, rewritten, and interpreted by a number of potential authors, institutional or individual, each with his own agenda.

That text, moreover, could never be written on a clean page, as it were; history had already given meaning to London's spaces, making the city's processional route a palimpsest, with ceremonial baggage dating to Roman and medieval rituals of boundary-marking, each with the potential for topical political discourse.[15] The 1559 coronation entry of Elizabeth in particular had embedded itself on the cultural imagination and established the most memorable precedent for the ideological and political potential attached to the places on the processional route. Elizabeth had been presented with a protestant English bible at the Cross in Cheap and in kissing it with a speech of acceptance had both established herself as the defender of her father's faith and acknowledged the demands of her subjects.[16]

The political climate in which the designers of the pageant were working, then, had already made the event into a competition for authority, a rivalry between crown and city over the question of whose pageant it was, and that atmosphere informed a second competition for authority, since Dekker did not long remain the sole poet-playwright responsible for planning the entertainment. Jonson—having recently established himself as a maker of royal entertainments with his *Entertainment at Althorp*—was assigned to provide scripts for three pageants: the entertainment's first triumphal arch in Fenchurch Street, another arch at Temple Bar, and a final entertainment in the Strand.

In light of this institutional rivalry over meaning-making in the royal entry, it is tempting to align Jonson and Dekker—both in the design of their parts of the pageant and in their subsequent representation of the royal entry in their printed texts—with either the city or the crown, and indeed critics have done so, but it is difficult to pin either playwright down to one political agenda.[17] Their interpersonal competition, however, is clear. Jonson apparently did not collaborate with Dekker in any way. The two playwrights had established themselves as rivals in the recent "war of the theaters," satirizing each other in *Poetaster* (Jonson, 1601) and *Satiromastix* (Dekker, 1601), and the two separate printed texts presenting their work in the pageants are significantly different in tone and function; there is even some indication that Jonson's text was rushed to press in order to beat Dekker's into print.[18] As these texts will illustrate, the playwrights were more interested in establishing their individual poetic roles—in relation to the spaces of London, and to each other—than they were in associating themselves with either of the competing governments. Their appropriation of the institutional struggle for control of city space to the individual would underpin Jonson's authorial claims for the rest of his career.

Jonson and Dekker's texts illustrate their claims for authorial agency by suggesting that the individual author has the potential to change significantly the interpretation of London space. With such a multiplicity of potential meaning makers—crown, city, multiple designers and reporters, and the historical palimpsest of the city's space itself—the royal entry could never be a simple or unambiguously interpretable event. Each playwright wrote a text onto the city and made a text out of it, but the way James, the members of the city government, and the onlookers read this text can only be imagined through the printed texts that remain. The authors not only made a text out of the city; their writing makes a "city" out of their texts, reproducing and practicing the city's place imaginatively on their pages. In Michel de Certeau's terms, Dekker's and Jonson's texts, conceived ostensibly to enforce the "strategies" of either the city government or of James, are themselves "tactics," individual acts and utterances that put their own meaning on the space of London, and work to efface the spatial practice of the king.

King James's own *espace*, his practice of London's ceremonial place as it was produced out of the already meaning-laden fabric of the city, was an opportunity for him to perform kingship, to inscribe his authority upon the city. Ostensibly, it should have been an example of what Clifford Geertz identifies as "the ceremonial forms by which kings take possession of their realm":

> [R]oyal progresses . . . locate the society's center and affirm its connec-
> tion with transcendent things by stamping a territory with ritual signs
> of dominance. When kings journey around the countryside . . . they
> mark it, like some wolf or tiger spreading his scent through his terri-
> tory, as almost physically part of them.[19]

Despite having taken some pains to "mark his territory" in this way during his journey from Scotland, in his royal entry James apparently neglected to assert his ceremonial authority to a conspicuous degree, and the absence of such an assertion left a vacuum in authority, leaving open the question of who has interpretative power over the space of London.[20] Into this vacuum Jonson and Dekker seem to have been only too happy to step. Ostensibly, the guiding desire (or mandate) of a royal entry pageant is to praise the king by reifying his practice of the place of London as the ideal reading of the city's spatial text, but the project of praise is complicated by the agendas, the subjective quirks, the frustrations, and the individual urges of the authors as they foreground their own spatial practice.

Not content simply to record the king's journey through London on that Ides of March, the playwrights seem more concerned with infusing themselves into their texts. That desire surely stemmed in part from their ongoing rivalry: not only did the authors become litigious about copyright for their contributions to the entertainment, but Dekker's work is full of jibes at the ostentatious pretension of Jonson's learning; and Jonson, for his part, simply omits all mention of any contributor to the entertainment other than himself in his precisely titled quarto, *B[en] Jon[son] His Part of King James his Royall and Magnificent Entertainement*. More importantly, how-ever, the pageant texts presented them with the opportunity to assert the importance of their own authorial *espace*. Writing the devices for the royal entry entertainments was for Jonson and Dekker another form of practice of the ideal place of London, and they make no attempt in their texts to hide the fact that they consider the authority this granted them to be as important as the king's.

As a comparison between the methods employed by both playwrights will show, however, their strategies for inserting themselves into the day's entertainments and asserting their authorial agency seem very different. Jonson, rigorously jealous of his proprietary rights to his own work, writes himself into and onto the pageant, and makes certain that his contributions are his property by making text—as printed in his book and as inscribed on the fabric of the city—more important than performance. Dekker's text, on the other hand, essentially re-performs the royal entry, usurping the perspective of the king, sharing it with the reader, and ultimately eclipsing it.[21] Jonson's text would seem to be of a piece with his often-discussed authorial strategy of textual self-monumentalization, and he pursues some of the same methods of self-presentation that he would later use in the production of the Folio. Unlike Dekker, who describes the entire event, including his contributions and those of his colleagues, Jonson's printed text, as his title indicates, is concerned only with his contribution; as with the Folio, he is not interested in presenting collaborative work.

The royal entry texts, however, present a picture more complicated than a performative Dekker and a textual Jonson. The process of designing and scripting these pageants required each playwright to employ a blend of strategies, working with both text and physical space as media for authorial assertion. And ultimately, although their methods may seem incommensurable, and despite the competition between them, Jonson was influenced by Dekker, gaining from him a broader sense of the employment of theatrical control over urban space as a potential authorial strategy.

CITY SPACE AS PAGE: *B. JON HIS PART*

Jonson's contributions to the royal entry would seem to reinforce the picture of his authorial innovations—exclusively scholarly and textual—that the Folio would construct twelve years later and that generations of critics have tended to accept. Indeed, the title page of Jonson's 1616 Folio would bear a striking resemblance to his 1604 triumphal arches, one of which he actually refers to in his royal entry text as a "frontispice."[22] His first pageant, the "Londinium" arch in Fenchurch Street, demonstrates the most singular characteristic of his work on the royal entertainments: the arches themselves are *written* texts. Jonson covers the surface of his pageant structures with writing, to the extent that Stephen Harrison's illustrations can only abbreviate the most complex bits.[23] The arches are meant to be read, and their intended audience is clear. The Fenchurch Street arch's "whole frame, was coured with a curtaine of silke, painted like a thicke cloude, and at the approach of the K. was instantly to bee drawne" (B2).[24] Until the approach of James, that is, the texts of the arch are closed to all other potential readers.

Alongside the overt textuality of the Fenchurch Street arch, however, Jonson was also concerned to control the significance of physical space, not just in the shape of the pageant structures, but in the architecture of their meaning. He uses the layout of the temporary stage, the position of his actors, and the position of his mobile audience, to ensure that he emerges as the principal controller of spatial meaning throughout his contribution to the royal entry. Jonson, that is, effectively blends the text-based authority of the poet-critic with the space-based authority of the theater.

On the Fenchurch Street arch, he disposes both written word and image in such a way as to address his several audiences appropriately. At the apex of the arch was a model of the city, with particular monuments, spires, and buildings—St. Paul's, the Tower, Bow Church, the Royal Exchange— clearly discernible. This model, like all miniature representations of this kind, reduces the city in the most literal way possible to a manageable space; even as the image of London is given pride of place atop the foremost triumphal pageant, it is made into a figure of itself, whose meaning can be determined by Jonson's arrangement. Important with this regard is the perspective used in the model, as far as it can be determined from Stephen Harrison's illustration. From the position of the king as he approached the Fenchurch Street arch, at London's eastern end moving westward, one might expect the model to present a view of the city from the west, as if it were that of a bird following the route above the king's head. Just as appropriate, perhaps, might have been a view from the east, imagining the king's prospect from Whitehall. Harrison's engraving of the model, however, depicts the city viewed directly from the south, over the river. This was the traditional pictorial perspective on the city, since the spires of Southwark Cathedral (then St. Mary Overy) afforded the best view of intra-mural London, but it also approximated the perspective from the Bankside theaters, including the Lord Chamberlain's Men's Globe, for which Jonson had written *Every Man Out of His Humor* in 1599. The layout of the model London thus indicates Jonson claiming a theatrical, and personal, perspective on the city and on the king's triumph.

Beneath this proud but controlled image of London sat a female figure called *Monarchia Britannica*, holding in her lap a globe inscribed *Orbis*

Britannicus, the British World (A2-A2ᵛ). This figure was "the highest person aduanc'd therein," portrayed by an elaborately costumed player, but she did not speak in Jonson's device, and neither did the figure of Divine Wisdom at her feet, nor the six figures flanking her, representing the six daughters of the Genius of London, the proper offerings of London to a monarch (named Gladness, Veneration, Promptitude, Vigilance, Affection, and Unanimity). These actors' purpose was to serve as living images, firmly under the author's spatial control; they had no lines, songs, or dumb shows, but stood in their niches, their names painted above them and their significance explained by the inscribed Latin mottoes Jonson assigned to their spots on the arch. Closer to street level were the only speaking figures in Jonson's device, the *Genius Urbis*, played by the renowned actor Edward Alleyn (and flanked by mute figures representing the Counsel and Warlike Force of London), and the Thames, played by one of the Children of the Queen's Revels.[25] Their position made it possible for Alleyn to deliver the speeches, in Dekker's words, "with excellent Action, and a well tun'de audible voice," and the placement also allows for two significantly different interpretations of these figures' importance.[26] On the one hand, the Genius of the city stands well below the figure of British monarchy, perhaps indicating London's submission to the crown; on the other, he is at the eye-level of the approaching dignitaries, and placed in the most prominent position thrust out from the arch, a position from which he can direct their gaze wherever Jonson wants.

The various inscriptions on the arch are placed in a similar relation to the images and figures, likewise arranged to guide interpretation. The word "LONDINIVM"—a cognate understandable even by those literates in the crowd who had no Latin—dominates the upper frieze underneath the model of the city, in such a position as to be read by all. Standing alone as a label for the magnificent model of the city, it could be read as a triumphant proclamation of London's architectural glory. Underneath, and as Jonson writes, "in a lesse and different Character," the words *Camera Regia* ("the King's chamber") appeared, a metaphorical inscription that serves to glorify both the king and the city: if the king can be glad that London is *his*, the citizens can rejoice that the epithet ennobles their city. The third most prominent inscription on the arch was less accessible to the crowds; written just above the king's passageway was a quote from Martial: *par domus haec coelo, sed minor est domino*, "This house is on a par with the heavens, but less than its master" (A2ᵛ). The praise of both city and king are still evident, but the hierarchy—with the royal *domino* greater than the civic *domus*—is made clearer in the inscription closest to the royal reader's eye. Jonson can thus please all parties, and arranges the text spatially to accommodate this interpretive variety.

The fact that he makes his audience read an unchanging text apparently gives Jonson more explicit personal control over the interpretation of his device than Dekker's, which, as we will see, relied on long orations by actors to explain the allegorical imagery. Jonson uses his own written word instead, and one of the most extensive welcomes given James at the Londinium arch is Jonson's own Latin elegy, not spoken, but painted into the central space, at the feet of Divine Wisdom. Even those speeches that *are* spoken in Jonson's device participate in the privileged place of the written over the oral word. The speeches of Jonson's dramatic characters are performed from the stage of the arch, with no spillage of action into the streets, no interaction with the royal audience or invitation to the king to participate. Genius and Tamesis stay obligingly in their places near their inscribed "words" like the silent characters, and the speech itself, paradoxically, expresses a preference for silence. Jonson's Genius bids London's people rouse themselves for the glory of the day, and wonders why his six allegorical daughters forbear to voice their praise: "Why keep you silence Daughters? What dull peace / Is this inhabites you?" He then likewise chides his companion, the Thames—"Vp thou tame RIVER, wake"—who defends the daughters' silence, explaining that excess loquacity is needless, even unnatural:

> Not my fishes here,
> Though they be dumbe, but doe expresse the cheere
> Of these bright streames. No lesse may These, and I,
> Boast our delights, albe't we silent lie.[27] (B3ᵛ)

Genius stands corrected, conceding, "Indeede, true Gladnesse doth not alwayes speake: / Ioy bred, and borne but in the tongue, is weake" (B4). Genius does go on to welcome the king orally in the name of the civic government, his "sons" (specifically indicating another speechless actor at the king's side, the Lord Mayor), but this exchange between Genius and Tamesis subordinates theatrical speechifying to Jonson's silent symbols and written words.

As well as this first, the last arch the king passed through before leaving the city—at Temple Bar in Fleet street, the easternmost extent of London proper—was also Jonson's, and although the device there included the most dramatically sophisticated playlet in the day's entertainments—a small dialogue and scene played out on a miniature stage over the archway—the same subordination of action to text is apparent. The Temple Bar pageant,

like that at Fenchurch Street, held several living but mute figures in separate, silent tableaux. In a neat reversal of the six daughters of Genius that
began the royal entry, representing London's intangible gifts to the king,
the figures at Temple bar present the benefits the king bestows on London.
James's mascot virtue of Peace is given the topmost position; attended by
the boy Plutus, or wealth, she is shown trampling on a groveling Mars. Her
handmaidens, each in their own niche, accomplish similar static victories:
Quiet treads on Tumult, Liberty on Servitude, Safety on Danger, and Felic-
ity on Unhappiness. Each has her classically derived motto inscribed on her
spot, and each is steadfastly silent.

The playlet that Jonson stages in the small space makes no attempt to
expound on these figures, but it does illustrate Jonson's interest in acquiring
definitional authority over London's spaces, and the blend of textual and
theatrical strategies that characterizes his work on the royal entry. Just as
he draws upon Roman poetic models and emulates Horatian *sententiae*, he
uses classical authority to produce a sort of archeological reconstruction of a
Temple of Mars. Jonson employs his classical scholarship, that is, to establish
a new meaning for this London place, but then he uses the spatial practices
of theater to effect a further transformation of the place's significance. The
pageant presents a confrontation between London's Genius and a resurrected
Flamen, or pagan priest of Mars, who, aroused by the pomp and finding it
to be the feast day of Anna Perenna (a goddess associated with Mars), has
kindled a sacrifice at the altar. The Genius's rebuke of the Flamen's "eth-
nicke rite" appropriates all the symbolism and glory of the classical religions
for King James and his celebration: Queen Anne eclipses the goddess Anna,
the arch becomes a "translated Temple," and, Genius says, no pagan sacrifice but "My Citties heart" shall be offered at the altar (D2-D2ᵛ).[28] All the
while it highlights Jonson's dramatic virtuosity, however, this effective scene
points the audience's attention ultimately to the centrally placed altar, which
serves here, as did the central spot in the Londinium arch, as a page for Jonson to write his final message on. An inscription on the altar—apparently
too lengthy for Harrison's book to reproduce fully in its engraving—declares
that the altar has been erected and dedicated to the virtues of the king and
those of his family by the *S.P.Q.L.*, the Senate and People of London.

The ostentatious learning apparent in the Temple of Mars pageant is
also a hallmark of Jonson's printed text. His contributions to the entry fore-
grounded textual representations of his learning by writing on the very fabric
of the place, and his text is a practice of that written place in a correspond-
ingly literate manner. The writing on Jonson's pageants, the inscriptions and
labels and mottoes, serve a double purpose: they give some explanation of

the visual allegory, but they also lead Jonson's ideally intelligent and curious reader on to require more explanation, more words. Graham Parry sees Jonson's use of the "burdensome book-learning of the English Renaissance" as a form of flattery to his elite audience, "a towering mass of classical scholarship to honour the scholar-king."[29] The complex challenge of Jonson's inventions was pleasing to the well-educated Elizabethan aristocracy fed on emblem books and heraldic *imprese*, Parry argues, and "the act of perceiving these truths, with Jonson's tactful help, flatters the beholder into a satisfying estimation of his own powers."[30]

This may be true, but the "tactful help" Jonson offered the audiences of the actual pageant, including the royal audience, was very nearly nil. He scorned Dekker's technique of giving his characters explanatory speeches, commenting that it did not "stand with the dignity of these shewes (after the most miserable & desperate shift of the Puppits) to require a Truch-man, or (with the ignorant Painter) one to write. *This is a Dog*; or, *This is a Hare*" (B2ᵛ). By contrast, Jonson's own devices left the viewers of the pageant on their own, without even the aid of his marginal notes, to take in as much as they can. The devices were so presented

> as vpon the view they might without cloude, or obscurity declare themselves to the sharpe and learned. And for the multitude, no doubt but their grounded iudgments gazed, said it was fine, and were satisfied. (B2ᵛ)

Much of the writing on the arches must have been almost invisible; how could the king or anyone else make out the inscription *orbis britannicus* on a "little globe" in the lap of a figure nearly forty feet above the street? The commentary and sidenotes in Jonson's printed text point out the references to Claudian and Virgil that give context to Monarchia Britannica's motto *divisus ab orbe*. Surely, though, even the most well-educated observer, and many a reader of the printed book, could not find his way from the pageant inscriptions to Claudian on his own. One main function of Jonson's first text, the pageant, is to point up the necessity of his second, the book; its complexity demands the use of Jonson himself as a "truch-man," or interpreter. The fact that the arches *require* commentary and sidenotes—and that the only interpretation offered is Jonson's—makes them flatter their author as much or more than those who passed beneath them.[31]

The text of Jonson's *Part of King James his Entertainment* makes the claim that the reader has a more complete and perfect experience of Jonson's part of the royal entry than any experience available on the actual day. His text is loaded with supplementary material, quotes from Tacitus, Martial, and Ovid that appear nowhere on the arches themselves but help set the inscriptions in context. Dekker's jibe at Jonson for "Anatomizing *Genius*, from head to foote, (only to shew how nimbly we can carve vp the whole messe of the Poets)" is well deserved (A4ᵛ).[32] Jonson's text does indeed anatomize the character of the Genius of London, whose description and speech is nearly overwhelmed by Jonson's learning and crowded off the page with sidenotes. The learning is given a dominant position in the text, just as writing was given the central physical position in the arch structure. In each section Jonson first describes the arch and its iconography, contextualizing and expanding upon the mottoes and dutifully citing his sources. The actual words that the audience heard are added in the text almost as an afterthought, and nestled within a glossatorial frame.

The text does not simply engage in this glossatorial process; it self-consciously defends it and reflects upon it. Jonson claims to know the proper function of a triumph, and proudly distinguishes his composition from Dekker's mere "pageantry." The ideal receiver of Jonson's text, as the text itself points out, is an educated reader, not Dekker's "multitude . . . whose heads would miserably runne a wooll-gathering, if we doo but offer to breake them with hard words" (Dekker, A4ᵛ).[33] Jonson theorizes the design of the royal entry and explains his compositional strategy:

> the *Symboles* vsed, are not, neither ought to be simply *Hierogliphickes*, *Emblemes*, or *Imprese*, but a mixed Character, pertaking somewhat of all, and peculiarly apted to these more magnificent Inuentions: wherein the Garments, and Engines deliuer the nature of the person, and the Word the present office. (B2ᵛ)

The well-wrought triumph, in other words, is the "complementall parte" (in Jonson's phrase), both in the sense of "complimentary" and "complementing"—each aspect complements the others (B2).

For Jonson, images may have a part, but words—specifically *his* words—always have the final say; the images require naming, and an inscribed motto (or as Jonson simply calls it, the "Word") to guide their interpretation. Figures and symbols point to the words inscribed on the arch, but the arches themselves are not enough, requiring the supplement of Jonson's printed text to show whence the costumes and props were derived. Moreover, the "Word" points to more words, and the line between the writing on the pageant and the writing on the page begins to blur. The name "Londinium," Jonson's printed text implies, must be explained by Tacitus's history, quoted in the book as if it, too, is inscribed on the arch. Likewise the image of Janus on the Temple Bar arch was explained by the inscription *Jano Quadrifronti Sacro*, but this itself, Jonson suggests, requires justification, and his text quotes from Martial, Ovid, and Cicero to justify the name *Janus Quadrifrons* ("four-faced Janus") for the device's patron god. Jonson's text leads the reader on a journey: image points to inscribed "Word," which points to more words—classical tags and citations—which in turn point to still more words—commentary and side notes on the classical sources—which point to the royal entry's ultimate authority, Ben Jonson.

Jonson's own name is the only contemporary name other than King James's that appears anywhere in his printed text. It is also the first name a reader encounters in the book, in large type, if in abbreviated form ("B. JON"), advanced at the top of the title page above that of King James just as *Londinium* was advanced over *Monarchia Britannica*.[34] The quarto in which his contribution to the royal entry appears also contains a "brief *Panegyre*" on James's opening of parliament on 19 March, and the text of his entertainment for Queen Anne and Prince Henry at Althorp the previous June. The volume is thus bound together not by the particulars of 15 March, but by Jonson's authorship and his growing role as poet to the royal family. Jonson hardly acknowledges that his text bears any relation to the ephemeral performance, the actual execution of the royal entry entertainments; the only real hint we get of performance comes in the passages that snipe at Dekker, and the king's reactions to the entertainment are not mentioned at all.

Notwithstanding all this emphasis on written text, Jonson's quarto description of the events played out upon the stages of London's streets does imagine an authorial spatial practice, even if, this early in his career, he figures it in terms of the book and not the stage. Graham Parry's description of the triumphal arches as "frontispieces to the Jacobean era" is particularly apt for Jonson, whose textual practices make walking in the city and reading essentially the same act.[35] He conflates the geographical space of London with that of the printed page, attempting to recreate the king's experience of the arch by reconstructing it typographically. "LONDINIVM," for example, appears at the top of the first page in a larger typeface, with the other two prominent inscriptions on the Fenchurch arch, "CAMERA REGIA" and "PAR DOMVS HAEC COELO, SED MINOR EST DOMINO" appearing on the same page, in their respective positions and in smaller capital letters, just as they appeared on the arch. Likewise, when he comes to the inscription on the Flamen's altar at Temple Bar, Jonson gives not so much a transcript as a typographical illustration of the altar; the words appear surrounded by a rectangle, in their proper blocks and type sizes, the Latin abbreviations intact.

Jonson's most remarkable equation of urban space with page space—an explicit association of the act of reading with that of walking—comes in his address to the reader between the description of the Temple Bar pageant and the final device he designed to be performed in the Strand. The reader is assured that his or her textual version of "our portion of the deuice for the Cittie" is superior to the pageantry, or "the *Mechanick* part yet standing." Any distaste that this mechanic part gives to "the wrye mouthes of the time"—presumably those who only saw the pageants but have not read the book—is pardoned, "for their owne ambitious ignorance doth punish them inough." But despite this apparent privileging of readerly practices, it is here, at a spot in the text that looks back at the devices for the city and forward toward Westminster, that Jonson's imagined conflation of geographical and textual space becomes most apparent: "From hence we will turne ouer a new leafe with you, and lead you to the *Pegme* in the Strand" (D3ᵛ). Turning the page and walking become one; Jonson has written his text onto the city, and now he writes the rewritten city into his text.

The 1604 royal entry entertainment, and Jonson's printed textual commentary on it, show us a Jonson already thinking about urban space as a medium through which to present his authority. With its burden of classical scholarship, its emphasis on the role of textuality and readership alongside dramatic performance, its jibes at the ignorance of Dekker and Dekker's audiences, it also seemingly delineates a categorical difference between his own authorial identity and the practices of his rival. For all their differences, however, Dekker's example would broaden Jonson's awareness of dramatic space's potential, and give Jonson a model for the representational engagements with London and its spaces that he would undertake throughout his dramatic career.

DEKKER'S *MAGNIFICENT ENTERTAINMENT* AND THE PRIVILEGED SPACE OF THE PLAYWRIGHT

When we compare Jonson's devices to those that Dekker designed, we are struck by the apparent methodological differences between their assertions of authorial agency. While Jonson's tight control of urban space is always bound up with his sense of the city as a page on which to write and publish his text, Dekker, even in his printed quarto, emphasizes the performative nature of his incursion into the royal entry, and the extent of his authority not just over the places of the city, but over the ways in which those places, in de Certeau's sense, are practiced.

Dekker's contribution to the royal entry as it was performed consisted mainly of the design of the three arches forming the central axis of the processional route, as well as the scripts for the entertainments performed there and several songs to accompany the passage between the arches.[36] His contributions account for less than half of the day's shows as they were actually seen, and in the event not everything he wrote was performed, but his three devices had pride of place along the central segment of the procession, from the western end of Cheapside past St. Paul's to the end of Fleet Street. After the two fairly static shows by the Italian and Dutch merchants that preceded them—two highly decorated arches and two short speeches, which Dekker calls "pageants" to distinguish them from his own more complexly dramatic "devices"—the sophistication and vigor of Dekker's three central devices must have been remarkable. Moreover, these three devices illustrate most fully the exertion of dramatic authority over the space of London that was to influence Jonson so strongly. Jonson rewrote Temple Bar into an ancient Roman temple, but each of Dekker's arches, and the playlet that accompanies it, imagines a much more emphatic physical transformation of London into someplace else: a British Arabia, a Garden of Plenty, and a mystical *Cosmoz Neoz*, or New World.

More strikingly, unlike Jonson's controlled, silent actors, confined to their niches or small stages, the dramatic elements of Dekker's entertainments spill into the larger space of London, as demonstrated most fully by the second of the three arches (and the fifth of eight total). Standing at the center of the day's events, Dekker's second arch was the site of his most daring authorial reshaping of space. After the king heard the city recorder's speech at the Cross in Cheap, his progress was halted in the street by the wild-looking figure of Sylvanus, god of the woods, whose long prose address to James transformed London's busiest street into an idyllic pastoral setting: "Most happie Prince, pardon me, that . . . I presume to intercept your royall passage. These are my walkes: yet stand I heere, not to cut off your way, but to giue it a full and bounteous welcome" (F4). This imagined transformation not only sets the stage for the upcoming device at the little conduit in Cheapside, the *Hortus Euporiae* or Garden of Plenty, it makes a proprietorial claim on the places of London. Cheapside and its environs are Sylvanus's "walks," and even if he gives the king permission to pass through, Dekker's character's claim not just to reinterpret but in some sense to own the place is a particularly bold one.

In Dekker's part of the entertainments, the interpretation of allegorical tropes—carried out in Jonson's devices by the text inscribed on the arches themselves—is instead scripted and performed. Sylvanus, while leading James to the garden arch, tells him that he has been sent as a messenger from Irene, or Peace, the principal figure in the Garden of Plenty. She, along with her daughter Euporia (or Plenty) sit "vnder yonder Arbour" having languished for months at the delayed arrival of James, the sun that brings nourishment to all growing things. Peace, says Sylvanus, is the one who has given the foreign merchants leave to share in the day's happiness; she is the agent that welcomes James at this most topographically significant spot of London.[37]

Here, at James's approach to the central spot of the procession, came the most dramatically significant moment of the day's entertainment, the only time when the king himself was specifically invited to participate, as his predecessor had done, as an actor in his show. Sylvanus ended his first speech with an invitation to the king (or perhaps a challenge) to dismount and enter the stage set, to bless the entertainment with the physical magnificence of his own royal person. Peace herself—symbolically the most persuasive figure for a king whose motto was "blessed are the peacemakers" (Matthew 5:5)—entreats the king in Sylvanus's voice "that ere [he] passe further, [he] would deigne to walke into yonder Garden" (F4ᵛ). The stage could not have been more perfectly set for James, who prided himself on being a scholar, philosopher, and poet, as well as a peacemaking king and statesman: in addition to Peace and Plenty, the arch featured two galleries wherein sat figures representing the seven liberal arts and the nine muses. Moreover, the pageant was expressly built for James to become physically part of it, as the engraving in Stephen Harrison's text makes clear. In the building's center, between the two arched passages, a stairway led up to an empty throne marked with small flags reading "I" and "R" for *Iacobus Rex*. A song of joy had been prepared for the muses, and a speech written for another character, Vertumnus the gardener, to deliver to the king. This speech seems to have been written with the prospect of impromptu interaction with James in mind: Dekker only records the "tenor" of it, indicating that it may have been loosely composed to accommodate the possibility of a dramatic dialogue with the king. The speech praised the civic government as faithful gardeners themselves, and—in a move that echoes the recorder's traditional gift to the royal entrant—Vertumnus submitted these gardeners, the arbor, bowers, and walks, and all the fruits of peace to the king "to be disposde after his royal pleasure" (G3ᵛ). Everything points to this moment being intended for a climactic bit of stagecraft—with the king as an actor—that would vie in the cultural imagination with Elizabeth's participation in her own civic pageantry. Instead of receiving and claiming a protestant Bible, though, James would have taken symbolic possession of London's space by physically inhabiting it. Given the historical context of rivalry between crown and city, this was an unparalleled opportunity for the king to assert his authority.

As far as can be gathered, however, James did not take the opportunity, and indeed things seem not to have gone as planned at the *Hortus Euporiae*. Neither Dekker's commentary text nor Gilbert Dugdale's eyewitness account mention any interaction or suggest that the king dismounted or entered the arbor. It is even possible that Sylvanus's speech of invitation to explore the arbor went entirely unheard: Dekker's commentary tells us that "his Grace was (at least it was appointed he should haue beene) met on his way neere to the Crosse, by Sylvanus," perhaps an admission that the speech went unspoken (F4). It seems certain that the king, for whatever reason, did not respond to the chance to interact, and forfeited the opportunity symbolically to receive the space of London when it was proffered to him.

Despite—or perhaps because of—the king's refusal to participate, Dekker emerges as the primary, privileged interpreter of space: he claims possession, through his characters, of Cheapside, and demonstrates not only the dramatic author's ability to construct the nature and meaning of the *lieu*, but his claim to control the *espace* of others. Even James's noteworthy refusal to sit in his chair illustrates the king's power less than it reverses the usual hierarchy of authority over place and space; the king becomes a recalcitrant actor, resistant but still subject to the playwright's spatial script.

Moreover, Dekker's printed text, inasmuch as it is more in his control than the king's whim, furthers his authorial assertion, substituting for the king's experience of space a more perfect authorial one, and offering that experience to his readership. What is most remarkable about Dekker's text is not its much-praised thematic unity, but the extent to which he does not so much memorialize 15 March 1604—let alone provide scholarly commentary on it as Jonson had done—as he recreates the experience. In *The Magnificent Entertainment*, Dekker imagines himself walking down the processional route, and gives himself and the ordinary reader—for "[t]he multitude," not the king, "is now to be our audience"—a privileged and more proper peripatetic view of the show than the king's (A4ᵛ). It is a view, moreover, that allows him to ignore the laws of physics; the imagined spatial practice of the reader traces the path of the king, but it also exceeds the capability of any physical person. Not satisfied simply to give an idea of the pageants' grandeur, Dekker (D4-E1) leads us on a physically impossible three-dimensional tour of the arches. At the Dutchmen's arch he guides the reader's gaze ("Lift vp your eyes a little"), then guides us inside ("you may with little labour walke into the *Mart* [a representation of a Dutch market-place on the arch]), and then to the nearly eighty-foot height ("Let vs now clime vp to the vpper battlements").

Dekker makes no attempt to disguise the fact that his text presents an idealization of the event. That idealization coexists, in fact, with a tone very like disappointment when Dekker recalls the actual performance. Repeatedly he regrets the hurried pace with which the king made his way through the route that had been months in preparation. His Majesty dwelt at the Fenchurch pageant, for example, for "[t]oo short a time (in their opinions that were glewed there together so many houres, to behold him)" (C1ᵛ). At times, indeed, the text exhibits a scarcely concealed tension between the king's progress and the pace of the entertainment. The Dutchmen's speech was apparently not heard in its entirety, and Dekker, in a tone that sounds quite like amusement, uses racing terms to express this tension: "Whilst the tongues of the *Strangers* were imployed in extolling the gracious Aspect of the King," he writes, James had "won more ground, and was gotten so far as to *S. Mildreds* Church" (E2). Where His Majesty's pace on the day conflicted with his own devices, Dekker is more circumspect. He omits any mention of James's failure to take his seat in the *Hortus Euporiae* arch, and where the king was apparently wearied with the length of the *Nova Faelix Arabia* device, Dekker mentions it only in the politest of terms: after the last speech, "His Maiestie (being readie to go on,) did most graciouslie feede the eyes of his beholders with his presence, till a Song was spent" (F2).

Dekker seems quite willing to take such royal weariness in stride, perhaps understandably so, since he could be confident that his lines, if lost to the king, would not be lost to posterity. A final note to the reader explains that

> a regard, being had that his Maiestie should not be wearied with teadious speeches: A great part of those which are in this Booke set downe, were left vnspoken: So that thou doest here receiue them as they should have been deliuered, not as they were. (I4)

Whether or not that "should" contains an air of authorial frustration at the cutting of his text in performance, or at the imperfect hearing given his speeches by the royal audience, the note makes clear that the reader has, in *The Magnificent Entertainment*, a more perfect version of Dekker's show. Unlike the king, a reader can spend as much time as he or she likes at each station of the progress, and indeed Dekker shapes the reader's experience of the royal entry in such a way as to encourage just the sort of contemplation and interaction that the king apparently neglected. Dekker presents the reader an opportunity to relive the procession whenever the book is opened. Unlike Jonson's book, which calls upon readers to witness his *authoring* of the city, Dekker's invites them to participate in a *performance* of it. Moreover, skillful manipulation of verb tense gives the illusion of perpetual present-ness; the past tense is generally used for remembrances of the king's reception of the events on the day (e.g. "His Maiestie dwelt here a reasonable long time" [H1]), and present tense for passages wherein Dekker gives agency to the reader's imagination (e.g. "Having hoysted vp our Sailes . . . let our next place of casting anker, be vpon the Land of the 17. Prouinces [i.e., the Dutch pageant]" [D1]).[38]

At times, this juxtaposition of the king's practice of space with the reader's—in two different time signatures, as it were—seems to create a further tension. The pace of James's progress is imagined not only to be conflicting with the intended pace of the entertainments, but also with the pace of Dekker as he guides the reader. If James pressed on in his progress, ignoring speeches that took too long, neglecting to note the extent of the arches' iconography, or failing to interact with the pageant even when the stage was set for him as it was at the *Hortus Euporiae* arch, we readers are able to engage with every section at leisure while Dekker's present tense manufactures a feeling of immediacy. The experience of the text becomes in effect a speed-reading competition between the reader and the king, and one remarkable passage makes this competition explicit: "Wee haue held his Maiestie too long from entering this third Gate of his *Court Royall*; It is now hie time, that those eyes, which on the other side ake with rolling vp and downe for his gladsome presence, should inioy that happinesse. Beholde, hee is in an instance passed through" (D4). In Dekker's text the king can be imagined as just another piece of the scenery to be moved along his processional route at the convenience of the author and his readers (the "Wee" who have held the king too long). Moreover, this rhetorical fantasy—holding the king still while Dekker guides the readers' eyes over the front of the Dutch pageant—is imagined as ending not to suit the king, but for the benefit of the spectators who ache to see him. Much was dependent, during the actual entertainment, on the king's whim; in *The Magnificent Entertainment*, the king himself is moved at Dekker's.

Like Jonson, Dekker makes an authorial claim on the pageant, and like Jonson he does so in terms of spatial practice, but whereas both of Jonson's texts—the planned devices and the printed memorialization—treat the city as a text to be written and read, Dekker treats it as a stage, performing his authority by recreating the experience, putting his own performance on that stage in competition with that of the king. Jonson's sense of his role as an author was always intrinsically competitive, but his competition with Dekker taught him that if part of the dramatic author's stock in trade is the manipulation and control of the spatial practices of others, and if even kings can be made into actors on a stage, then the dramatist's use of stage space, and its extension into the space of the city, is itself potent enough to serve as an assertion of the privileged societal position of the author. Dekker's exertion of control over both the *lieux* of London and the *espace* of the king was to lead Jonson to broaden the range of authorial strategies at work in his later drama. From 1604 onward, as the following chapters will show, his London comedies hinge on contests of cultural competency illustrated by competing practitioners of urban space.

Chapter Three
London on Stage, London as Stage

The simplest definition of the popular subgenre of early seventeenth-century drama that critics have variously identified as "city comedy," "citizen comedy," or "London comedy"—or at least the one aspect that most critics can agree on—is that they are plays set in the contemporary London of their audiences. Beyond that, the definition of the genre becomes more vexed; are city comedies characteristically satirical or celebratory? Do they champion one social class or another?[1] More important for my purposes is the question of the genre's role in Jonson's self-construction as author. I argue that Jonson found in city comedy, in the processes of transforming stage space into urban space and vice versa, the means to explore the potential of dramatic authorship. In *A Midsummer Night's Dream*, Shakespeare's Theseus famously claims that the poet "gives to aery nothing / A local habitation and a name" (5.1.16–17), but city comedy begins not with aery nothing, but with local habitations that already have names, with London places that are already laden with meaning. Jonson's city comedies are often centrally about London as a stage, and as a corollary, about the playwright's ability to shape the meanings of familiar space and the audience's perception thereof. They expose London, the London inhabited by Jonson and his audience alike, as inherently dramatic. Theater is shown to be how their city *works*, and the playwright thereby takes on an immediate presence, whether through representation as an author figure within the dramatic fiction, or as an implied physical presence in the playhouse or its surroundings at the moment of performance. Throughout Jonson's career, he used London city comedy as a demonstration and a celebration of the playwright's power to shape communal urban consciousness.

With *Every Man in His Humor* (1598) and its sequel, *Every Man Out of His Humor* (1599), Jonson had made excursions into urban comedies, but if they suggested the concerns of London life, they distanced it behind an

Italianate façade, and significantly, it was not until after 1604 that Jonson began to write comedies set explicitly in London. In part, I have argued, this is because the experience of his competition with Dekker in that year gave him a keener interest in the meanings of London place and the potential contribution that asserting control over those meanings could make to the construction of his authorial identity.

Perhaps another reason for his initial hesitation to set a comedy in London also has something to do with Dekker. In 1599, when the first version of *Every Man In* was printed, and in the years immediately following, the London setting had been confined to plays celebrating a particular set of values and ideologies. The late Elizabethan London comedy was limited to moralistic, romance-inflected genres that appealed to the citizen classes, but apparently did not inspire Jonson. Plays like Thomas Heywood's *Four Prentices of London* (c. 1594) and Dekker's *Shoemaker's Holiday* (1599) portrayed idealized, heroic apprentices, and applied the nostalgia and the popular conventions of prose romances like *Mucedorus* and *Palmerin of England*, popular with the urban mercantile middle class. And moralistic plays like *Liberality and Prodigality* (published 1602) and *The London Prodigal* (c. 1604) showed thriftless prodigals whose vices whip them into the path of bourgeois virtue.

These were plays whose ideological work, as Susan Wells has demonstrated, was of a piece with the city government's annual Lord Mayors Shows.[2] In these "elaborate and costly exercise[s] in legitimation and back-slapping,"[3] the merchant guild from whose ranks a new Lord Mayor had been elected commissioned a parade with dramatic and allegorical devices praising the magnificence of the guild, the virtue and benevolence of the new mayor, and the glorious history of his fellow Drapers, Goldsmiths, or Grocers throughout the city's history. Like *The Shoemaker's Holiday* and Thomas Heywood's *If You Know Not Me, You Know Nobody* (c. 1604), the Lord Mayor's shows celebrated the accomplishments of great citizens and mayors of the past like Simon Eyre and Thomas Gresham, the building of civic monuments like Leadenhall and the Royal Exchange, and the traditional values of hard work, generosity, loyalty, and mercantile prosperity.[4]

In the last years of the sixteenth century and the first of the seventeenth, London comedy must have seemed a genre quite limited in its potential tones, arguments, and ideological stances, and it should come as no surprise that Jonson, writing satire and classically-inflected comedy and tragedy, writing also primarily for the so-called "private theaters," with audiences that demanded other fare than didactic moralizing, eschewed a setting that must have seemed to carry such limitations. At the turn of the century, however, partly in response to the banning of prose satire by the ecclesiastical courts' Order of Conflagration in 1599,[5] satirists had begun to move their critiques of English culture and society to the stage; in the years following James's accession, other playwrights—mainly Thomas Middleton and John Marston—expanded the potential of city comedy to include a variety of voices. Jonson may well have turned to London comedy—changing the location of his revised *Every Man in His Humor* and collaborating in 1605 on *Eastward Ho*—in response to a new, growing awareness of the potent and varied effects made possible by making the stage represent London and making London itself into a stage.[6]

SPACE AS "HUMOR": *EVERY MAN IN HIS HUMOR*

Every Man in His Humor is a valuable case study by which we can begin to understand the potential that Jonson found in putting London on stage, partly because of the considerable differences between the quarto text of 1601 (Q) and the version of the play with which Jonson chose to open his 1616 Folio (F). The play's Folio title page gives the mistaken impression that the later text of the play was that "Acted in the yeere 1598. By the then Lord Chamberlaine his Seruants," but in fact Jonson had revised the text substantially by 1616, possibly, but not certainly, for the Folio publication itself.[7] The revisions have some effect on the tone and arguments of the play, but the most striking and significant changes in the Folio version are in setting. The quarto version had been set in Florence, albeit a Florence undistinguishable as such by specific reference to place. The Italian city was, as J. W. Lever, points out, already a thinly disguised version of the English metropolis, "a purely conventional backcloth for English characters and manners. Cob and his wife were undisguised Cockneys; even references to the Exchange, the Mermaid Tavern, pence and shillings, intruded."[8] In revising, however, Jonson transferred the action explicitly to an English setting, anglicizing the characters' names. Thus Matheo becomes Matthew, Stephano becomes Stephen, and Bobadilla becomes Captain Bobadill. Other characters acquire names that indicate character or behavior: thus the Lorenzos, Senior and Junior, become Kno'well and Edward Kno'well, and the quarto's amiable gallant Prospero becomes Wellbred in the Folio. The tricky servant, familiar from Plautine comedy, is Musco in 1601, and the more precise-sounding Brainworm in 1616. The shift from Florence to London, however, is more than another of these name changes. Jonson goes beyond merely removing the Italianate disguise to create a London in the second version thoroughly recognizable to the playhouse audience.

On the one hand, the addition of local color in the Folio version may seem no more than a case of a more mature playwright clarifying bits of his play that seemed vague in the earlier draft. Placing the play in a recognizable London has the advantage of employing the audience's local knowledge as stage dressing, whereas Florence—especially the indistinct Florence of the quarto—must have been as conceptually blank to the average playgoer as the Jacobean stage was bare of scenery. "[I]n this sense," notes Richard Dutton, the thoroughgoing and strategic Londonization of the play is

> no more significant that [*sic*] Jonson's obvious efforts to clarify the sister/sister-in-law/brother/half-brother relationships complex, which is needlessly confusing in the quarto, or the tightening-up of the denouement in the last act. We expect this kind of care from an experienced professional.[9]

This is certainly true; with the obsessive attention to details of place, often specific addresses, we can at many points trace the characters' movements on a map. Edward and Stephen go from Hoxton to Moorgate, then down Justice Clement's Coleman Street and into the Old Jewry, site of Kitely's house and the Windmill tavern. But Jonson's reimagining of the play in London is much more than draft revision, or clarification of abstruse action for the audience's benefit. The substantial differences between the two texts of the play highlight and distill Jonson's own awareness of the potential for specificity of place in his comedy. He found such topographical specificity to be a useful corollary to the psychological experiment of his humors play, and in the revised *Every Man In*, space and place become analogs for, and reflections of, individual character.

Places have specific meanings for the London audience, particular significances derived from institutional or experiential designation—"representational spaces" and "representations of space" respectively, to use Henri Lefebvre's terminology—and Jonson continuously emphasizes the local associations the places of London hold for his characters as well. He rarely refers to a spot merely to create an empty signifier, or to generate easy audience sympathy like a modern touring rock band ("Hello, Cleveland!"); he evokes locales for specific dramatic purposes. Most of the characters seemingly know these local significances, and they quickly become part of their vocabulary and idioms.

When Old Kno'well, for example, intercepts a bawdy-filled letter beckoning his son to a day's entertainment in London, he can sum up its offensive tone with reference to place: "From the Bordello it might come as well; / The Spital or Pict-hatch" (F 1.1.172–73). Presumably the virtuous suburbanite Kno'well has no intimate knowledge of "the Bordello"—the Bankside stews—the "Spital" (a hospital for venereal diseases near Hoxton), or "Pict-hatch," the prostitution district in Clerkenwell,[10] but the associations serve him as metaphors in his inaccurate judgment of the letter writer Wellbred's profanity and dissolution. Similarly, when Brainworm fetches one of his disguises from a second-hand clothing broker, the Folio has him specify that the seller is "a Houndsditch man" (3.2.235). Houndsditch was not only, as John Stow tells us, "for the most part possessed by Brokers, sellers of olde apparel, and such like,"[11] but it is particularly appropriate to supply costumes for Brainworm's impromptu theatricals, as it borders the extramural liberty of Shoreditch, site of the Curtain playhouse where *Every Man In* had its first performance. Likewise, when Brainworm—triumphing over having deceived his master Kno'well in a soldier's disguise—needs a shorthand for the military that will forever be distasteful to his master, he makes another reference to place: Kno'well will "hate the musters at Mile End for it, to his dying day" (F 2.3.140–41). This is particularly apt, since the Mile End muster, where the amateur city militia trained, was a running joke for its pretension and ineptitude; Brainworm's successful attempt to play at being a soldier makes the prentices' failure to do the same at Mile End all the more ridiculous.

The play's places thus have metaphorical meanings in themselves, but they also transfer those meanings to the characters associated with them. *Every Man In* consists of various conflicts and wit battles between characters, but while there are conventional comic plot strands like an over-jealous husband learning his lesson and a pair of young lovers eloping, the play is mostly what the title indicates, a parade of humors, that is, foolish obsessions and affectations, and the chief action of the play is observation and mockery of these; it begins with a Londoner inviting his suburban friend to join him as the audience for London's idiocies. It has been noted that in the absence of a unifying plot, London becomes the central character in *Every Man In*,[12] and Jonson's use of spatial specificity is intricately linked with his characterization. Nowhere is this more apparent than in the first scene, which, in addition to being one of what Dutton calls "strategic bursts" of local coloring, establishes the play's pattern of spatial representation.[13] The first person in the scene to call on specific place is the country gull Stephen, who affects "the hawking and hunting languages" of the gentry as more valuable than the classical tongues. Jonson heightens his idiocy and his affectation in the Folio by having him pour scorn not only on the social groups from which he would escape, but also on the places associated with them:

> Because I dwell at Hogsden, I shall keep company with none but the
> archers of Finsbury? Or the citizens, that come a-ducking at Islington
> Ponds? A fine jest i'faith! (F 1.1.47–49)

This spatially-inflected scorn for the suburban sports of city-dwellers
expresses the pretension to gentility that is Stephen's defining characteristic. Ironically, when Edward Kno'well brings him along to the city, his
affectation of gentle behavior promises to make Stephen himself a sport
for citizens, "a suburb-humour" (1.2.115), or out of town novelty, like the
Islington ponds.

The first scene also transforms the quarto's jealous merchant, Thorello,
into the Folio's Kitely, and again the change is most notable in the specifi-
cation of locale. Where Thorello was merely a "rich Florentine merchant"
(Q 1.1.125–26), Kitely becomes "the rich merchant in the Old Jewry"
(F 1.1.138–39), the street in which Jonson sets much of the play's action.
Named for its function as a London ghetto before the official expulsion of
the Jews in 1290, in the play this street retains associations with familiar
early modern anti-Semitic stereotypes. For Wellbred, who also dwells there,
the Old Jewry serves mainly as a source for puns that characterize the city/
suburb dichotomy: "Do not conceive that antipathy with us and Hogsden as
was between Jews and hogs' flesh" (F 1.1.155–57), but when Jonson associates Kitely, his humorously jealous and close-fisted merchant, with the Old
Jewry, he can quietly evoke comparisons with Shakespeare's Shylock and
Marlowe's Barabas.

Jonson's use of specific localities helps him to define his characters,
but his treatment of London in the play goes beyond fixing static meaning
to places or to characters, and here we must return to Michel de Certeau's
distinction between space and place. If *Every Man In* acknowledges the *lieux*
of London and uses the audience's and character's assumptions about them,
it depends no less upon the *espace* of London, that is, the individual's rewriting of the city's meaning by moving through and becoming a part of it. The
meaning of London emerges in the play as an amalgam of spatial practices
analogous to the characters' "humors."

In the introduction to her edition of the play, Gabrielle Bernhard Jackson hints at this analogy between physical space and moral/psychological
space in the play. Seeing *Every Man In* as the epitome of what she calls Jonson's "comedy of non-interaction," Jackson identifies a dramatic structure
of competing vectors: "[e]ach character . . . moves along the line of force
directed by his nature, and comes into collision, when time or a manipula-
tor decrees, with another character moving on an intersecting line." Each of

the characters "think[s] himself central, while his author knows him to be tangential."[14] "Tangential" is a key word, for the play's characters define the moral space of London just as tangents can describe a circle in geometry; the absent moral center of the play—the mainly unillustrated virtues that oppose the foolish errors of the humorous characters—emerges from the combined understanding of the characters' practices of moral space.

The main accomplishment of Jonson's use of specific localities is to map this practice of *moral* space onto the characters' practice of *civic* space, to map the humors onto the topography of London. Jonson, it has long been noted, uses the concept of the humors in a broader and vaguer sense than the medieval medical sense of an imbalance in the four fluids of the human body; the butts of his satire are never identifiable in a simplistic way as phlegmatic, sanguine, choleric, or melancholy.[15] One aspect of the humors theory did directly influence his use of it in both *Every Man* plays, however: the property of fluidity, or "fluxure." As Asper explains in *Every Man Out of His Humor*, the broadest definition of the word is simply anything fluid: "in every human body, / The choler, melancholy, phlegm, and blood, / By reason that they flow continually / In some one part and are not continent, / Receive the name of humours" (Induction 96–100).[16] In *Every Man In*, Jonson needs no more than this broad definition to ground his satire. His particular brand of humoral psychology suggests that inhibitions of flow lead to fixed, unhealthy characteristics. It is precisely his characters' fluidity and mobility, or lack thereof, that defines their particular "humors," as each of the characters has his own particular way of flowing through the body of London.

Every Man In consistently applies this fluid aspect of the humor theory to the arena of spatial practice, and the contrast between healthy fluidity of thought and unhealthy or affected—that is, humorous—mental rigidity is mirrored in the characters' practices of physical space. London provides Jonson with a physical template, recognizable from the audience's own experience, on which to portray this psychological satire; the city becomes a metaphor for the mind and its relative rigidity or fluidity. The imaginative London topography employed metaphorically by playwright and characters alike ranges geographically from Mile End in the east to Bridewell prison in the west, but with the exception of the first scene in suburban Hoxton, the onstage action is restricted mainly to a very small area of the city, between Kitely's house and the Windmill Tavern in the Old Jewry, the Royal Exchange, some two hundred yards to the east, and Justice Clement's house in Coleman Street, a block north of the Windmill. This topographical constriction is not accidental; once Jonson gets his characters into the same space, the moral and physical vectors on which they travel are strictly contained in such a way as to reflect the humors.

Jonson subtly foreshadows this constriction even before the action moves to London. When the country gull Stephen protests that he "speak[s] to serve his turn," his cousin Edward teasingly quibbles upon the word in order to provoke Stephen into an even more ridiculous register of gentlemanly affectation: "Your turn, coz? Do you know what you say? A gentleman of your sort, parts, carriage, and estimation, to talk o' your turn . . . like a tankard-bearer at a conduit: fie! (F 1.2.90–93). "Turn" being a term used by water carriers to describe a circuit from the conduit to a customer's house and back, the word carries a potential association of baseness, and Edward's mockery is ironically appropriate, for Stephen's mind is just as limited in scope and flexibility as a water carrier's urban, physical practice of place.

This association of mental and physical space is emphasized all the more by the appearance of a literal water carrier in the scene immediately following. Cob, the play's clown, has a wit limited to punning on his name and claiming a lineage from a long line of herring, and his mental practices are as restricted as his professional circuit to and from the Great Conduit in Cheapside. Shortly after his first entrance, Cob worries that "It's six o'clock: I should ha' carried two turns by this" (F 1.3.53). He thus establishes both the temporal setting and the locality, bringing us swiftly into Jonson's London with its collection of intersecting individual vectors, but in addition to setting the scene, these lines emphasize that Cob's profession is circumscribed by his practice of place, and as the play progresses we see that his very nature is also so circumscribed. Thus, when Cob swears to the suspicious Kitely that Dame Kitely is innocent of adulterous intent, the terms of his oath are ironic: "I am a vagabond, and fitter for Bridewell than for your worship's company, if I saw anybody to be kissed" (F 3.3.36–37). Cob is, in fact, the *opposite* of a vagabond—far from being a transgressive wanderer in need of imprisonment in Bridewell prison, his movements are already completely constrained by his profession.

The image of the water carrier's turn permeates the play as a metonym for the humorous spatial practices of its characters, but Cob is by no means the only character whose limited mental range is reflected in the way he inhabits London's spaces. The two most prominent "humors" characters of the play—the jealous Kitely and the swaggering Bobadill—are likewise confined in ways that parallel their psychological constriction, and Jonson's satirical treatment of them is consistently, if implicitly, spatially inflected.

Kitely is bound by his unfounded jealousy to the confines of his own house. So obsessed is he that he cannot even carry out his professional duties, instead delegating his servant Cash as a proxy for him at the Royal Exchange so that he can stay home and guard his wife. His agony at the internal conflict between commercial interest and jealousy is expressed in the dueling proverbs that he mouths in the same scene: the misogyny of "He that lends / His wife, if she be fair, or time or place, / Compels her to be false" (F 3.2.30–32) is set against his recognition that there is "No greater hell, than to be slave to fear" (138). Nevertheless, he is a slave to fear, and his spatial practice is limited to pacing back and forth in his home, trying to work up the courage to step out his front door.

Captain Bobadill's humor is similarly linked to the London setting. Despite repeatedly having his pretensions stripped away, he is utterly indefatigable in clinging to his braggadocio. Even when his bluff is called and Downright beats and disarms him, he attempts to scrounge some dignity by claiming weakly that the law prevents him from retaliating. Again, Bobadill's stubbornness in his ostentatious bravado, like Kitely's insistent jealousy, is mirrored by his spatial practices. His claims to have been in the Indies and to have done service at two foreign sieges, his professed expertise at the Spanish dueling forms, even his swearing by "Pharaoh's foot" are exotic pretensions to a vast international experience, and when Jonson deflates these pretensions, he does so through a constriction of space and scope. For all his claims, Bobadill is, as the *dramatis personae* list him, a "Paul's Man," that is, one of the gallants who pace the middle aisle of St. Paul's Cathedral, a ridiculous microcosmic version of his claimed worldwide wanderings.[17] Richard Dutton succinctly describes how Jonson uses London and its places to mark the disparity between Bobadill's illusion and his reality:

> When Bobadill lets the ease of his braggart façade get the better of him, he inadvertently mentions "Turnbull, Whitechapel, Shoreditch, which were then my quarters, and since upon the Exchange" [F 4.5.42–43]. The sordid reality of brothels and doss-houses suddenly invades his fanciful bravado and the result is a laughable incongruity which "explodes" his pretensions.[18]

London, in short, becomes inescapably a part of the humors characters. Just as Kitely is bound by jealousy to his house in the Old Jewry and becomes, as he fears, a laughingstock, "talk for the Exchange" (F 3.2.62), precisely by avoiding the Exchange, so Bobadill cannot escape the taint of his former lodgings, his actual experience of London "invading" his imagined world.

If Jonson marks the butts of satire in *Every Man In* by highlighting the self-imposed constriction of their spatial practices, his equation of the freedom to think with the freedom to move is made even more explicit in the way the play's protagonists use, represent, and imagine urban space. The merchant Kitely has the "freedom of the city" in the economic sense—that is, he has a citizen's right to buy and sell—but he is paradoxically the least free character in the play. The "heroes" of *Every Man In* (admittedly a troublesome word in a comedy of this sort) are those who claim and exercise their freedom in a different sense, the freedom to move at their leisure, and the freedom that Jonson has as playwright, to reinterpret London's places and their experience of them for their own ends. They have, in short, the sort of authorial agency over the space and place of London that Jonson claims for himself.

Wellbred and Edward Kno'well, the two witty and affable young men who serve as the audience for the play's parade of humors, are the clear exponents of the play's values. This is most apparent in that young Kno'well (and to a greater degree his original in the quarto, Lorenzo Junior) is Jonson's mouthpiece in a debate about the merits of poetry. This debate is framed as a battle between the generations of Kno'wells, with the elder—ironically in the verse that is characteristic of Old Kno'well's speech—condemning his son for "Dreaming on nought but idle poetry, / That fruitless and unprofitable art, / Good unto none, but least to the professors" (F 1.1.18–20). With this opinion we are obviously not meant to sympathize. In the quarto, his son mounts a thirty-line defense of poetry (Q 5.3.294–325), but in the Londonized version, Old Kno'well's objections are answered by no less a personage than Justice Clement, the play's magistrate *ex machina*, who leaps in to "sav[e Edward] the labor of a defense" (5.1.239). Poets, Clement declares, are more valuable even than the governors of the city: "They are not born every year, as an alderman. There goes more to the making of a good poet than a sheriff . . . I will do more reverence to [a poet], when I meet him, than I will to the Mayor" (F 5.1.232–36). This transfer of the defense of poetry from the mouth of a young poet into that of a presumably less biased authority figure enhances the argument's validity, and what is more, it makes explicit an analogy between poetic abilities and the urban experience that Jonson explores throughout the play.

In opposition to the young protagonist-poet Kno'well and his companion Wellbred—praised as "the choicest brain the times hath sent us forth" (F 1.1.175)—are the "paper-peddlers" and "ink dabblers" represented by the plagiarist Matthew. In passing off Christopher Marlowe's verses as his own, Matthew incurs the harshest condemnation of any of the humors characters. In the same way that Cob the tankard bearer is confined to pacing over the same "turns" throughout the day, Matthew treads and retreads the same route through the "commonwealth of paper" that he carries in his hose. Bobadill is likewise confined in his poetic experience to quoting Thomas Kyd's *Spanish Tragedy*—an exceedingly old-fashioned play by the time of *Every Man In*—which Bobadill declares is the greatest play written, ensuring his condemnation by Jonson and his fashionable audience: "I would fain see all the poets of these times pen such another play as that was!" (F 1.3.133–34). Even Kitely, who is allowed to repent of his jealous humor, undercuts his repentance in the Folio version by showing himself to be a plagiarist; the verse with which he dismisses his cuckold's horns comes, as he confesses, "out of a jealous man's part in a play" (F 5.1.275–76). Jonson's comedy of humors draws a correspondence within the humorous characters between their textual acts of reading and writing and their *espace*; a mind incapable of escaping the texts and meanings of other men's poetry is likewise incapable of experiencing an adequately free, that is, individually determined, practice of place.

Jonson's heroes, on the other hand, are not only poets, but characters who enjoy the flexible spatial practice that the playwright claims, who do not merely accept the institutionally or socially determined meanings of London places, but rewrite them, appropriating and transforming their meanings, as Jonson himself does, for their own purposes. Kitely condemns Wellbred's behavior in terms of his spatial habits, complaining that Wellbred's "course is so irregular . . . as scarce no note remains / To tell men's judgments where he lately stood" (F 2.1.49–53). If we compare Kitely's own "course," however—cooped up bodily and mentally by his jealous humor—Wellbred's irregularity (which we might read as a comparatively healthy fluidity) is an obvious improvement. Nor is the audience likely to object as vehemently as Kitely does to Wellbred's ability to transform place, specifically Kitely's own house: "He makes my house here common as a mart, / A theater, a public receptacle / For giddy humour and diseased riot" (57–59). Jonson, after all, has invited us into the theater's infinitely transformable space for exactly this purpose, the display of "giddy humour."

It is in this potential to transform the meaning and purpose of place that the distinction between the humors characters and the play's protagonists lies. Wellbred and Edward, for all their plans to spend the day as detached observers of city humors, soon develop their own romantic scheme to wed Edward to Kitely's sister Bridget. In planning the elopement, Wellbred arranges for the couple to remove from Kitely's house to the Tower of London,

> for here . . . the house is so stored with jealousy there is no room for love to stand upright in. We must get our fortunes committed to some larger prison . . . and than the Tower, I know no better air; nor where the liberty of the house may do us more present service. (F 4.6.57–63)

The quarto originally had the meeting place as a "Friary," a conventional dramatic site for illicit elopement familiar from *Romeo and Juliet* and impossible to translate from Florence to Protestant London.[19] But in transforming the assignation spot in the Folio to the Tower of London, Jonson adds more than practical specificity or local color. The Tower was paradoxically both a prison and a "liberty," an area outside city jurisdiction and thus potentially a place where immediate marriage could be effected, a more convenient version of Gretna Green. This juridical and terminological paradox is the source of Wellbred's wit in the passage just quoted, but it also provides him with an opportunity to exercise an interpretive, even transformative practice of place. Just as the presence of a monarch, as in James's residence there in 1604, could transform the Tower from a political prison into a royal privy chamber, Wellbred and Edward Kno'well can define it by their flight not as a place of confinement but as a symbol of individual freedom.

It is clear that Wellbred and Edward Kno'well have some sense of this transformative potential, and they also seem to be aware of the connection that Jonson draws between self-determined spatial practice and unfettered wit. When they learn from Brainworm of Edward's steps having been dogged from Hoxton by his father, Wellbred makes this connection explicit. In Wellbred's formulation, Kno'well senior's physical chase becomes a metaphorical footrace between minds, and the two gallants' wits, he assures his friend, are not "so wretchedly dull that one old plodding brain can outstrip us all" (F 3.2.229–30). Their imagined punishment for losing this generational battle of wits is also appropriate to Jonson's motif of the equation of mental and physical space. If Kno'well's brain does indeed outstrip them, declares Wellbred, "would we were e'en [im]pressed, to make porters of; and serve out the remnant of our days in Thames street or at Custom house quay" (F 3.2.230–32). In a play where walking in the city is parallel to thinking, where free movement equals wit, and "humor" is reflected in confinement of spatial practice, the worst punishment that Wellbred can conceive for faulty wits is to be forced into a porter's job, a profession, like Cob's, wherein movement is restricted to mechanical "turns" in a circuit to and from the river.

Wellbred and Edward Kno'well are almost the only characters in the play that have no discernible humor, no restriction on the movements of their minds and their bodies. Poetically-minded characters whose critical faculties and opinions on poetry clearly link them with their creator, their awareness of their power to reinterpret London's places reminds us of Jonson's own practices in writing the play. The association between the playwright's art and that of his characters is epitomized mostly, however, by the third "humorless" character, the protean Brainworm, who hides his effortless fluidity of mental and physical movement in a series of disguises, playing roles as apparently constricted in movement as Cob, Kitely, and Bobadill are.

After his introduction as a witty household servant in Hoxton, he reappears in act two in the disguise of "Fitzsword," a veteran of foreign wars reduced to beggary. This disguise, which he adopts through act four in order to trace Kno'well Senior's movements and relay them to Kno'well Junior, has a specific association with place. The disguise involves adopting a perceived spatial practice as limited as Cob's: he appears to be one of the "worm-eaten gentlemen of the round"—that is, a patrol, the poorest class of soldier whose job it is to make "turns" about the camp, and whose civilian spatial practice after discharge is just as determined, as they have "vowed to sit on the skirts of the city" in defiance of beggary laws (F 3.2.217–19).[20]

It is on the skirts of the city that "Fitzsword" worms his way into Old Kno'well's service, and once he enters the city proper he adopts two more disguises. In both of these—first the habit of Justice Clement's clerk in which he forges an arrest warrant at Bobadill's behest, and second as the sergeant who can put the arrest into effect—Brainworm is apparently bound to follow the directions of others; sergeants, after all, are civic versions of patrols. In each case, however, as with "Fitzsword," his apparently restricted function masks the fact that he is the character in the play most free of movement, and that he engineers the movements of others as well.

In effect, Brainworm functions as the direct agent of the playwright. Wellbred and Edward Kno'well are analogs of the perceptive audience member: they have come to the city, just as the audience has come to the playhouse, to observe every man on the stage play out his several humor. Their distance from the spectacle of the humors characters going through their paces on the stage and in the city is the same as the audience's; their witty asides commenting on Bobadill, Kitely, Cob, Matthew, and Stephen are a link to the epigrammatic quality of judgment and wit that Jonson tries to evoke in his audiences; and their cleverness as protagonists and onstage audience is a compliment to the clever playhouse observers.[21] Their power to construct their own romantic elopement plot, however, is enabled by and pales in comparison to Brainworm's consistent function in the play as an avatar for Jonson himself. The sort of simple observation that the two wits have planned makes for good entertainment, both for them and for us, but it does nothing to purge the individuals of their humors or the city of its "corporate insanity" (to use Richard Dutton's phrase).[22] Although the aim of Brainworm's "day of metamorphosis," he claims, has been merely wit for its own sake, the play's conclusion and the purgation (or at least exposure) of the humors are only achieved through his agency, and he does it by prodding the humorous characters out of their constricted spatial practices, returning them to a more normal "fluxure." Kitely, trapped by his silently seething jealousy within his own house, is only drawn out by Brainworm—disguised as Justice Clement's clerk—to face the insanity of his jealousy in the open street before Cob's house. Similarly, Brainworm channels Downright's choler and Bobadill's pacing braggadocio into open conflict, exposing both to the scrutiny of the public and of Justice Clement. In this "comedy of non-interaction," in which humors are maintained by the limited spatial and mental practices of the afflicted and the affected, Brainworm brings about the resolution of the play by channeling all the humors into one spot, Clement's house, where resolution can take place.

Brainworm is both a player, as Jonson had been, and a playwright as Jonson was, with London as his stage and Houndsditch, where the costume brokers live, as his tiring house. The play's structure, especially in the Folio version, thus contains a reflection of the playwright's art, with Brainworm as the surrogate and champion of Jonson. In later plays, Jonson would become increasingly ambivalent in his attitude toward characters like Brainworm whose theatricality is dramatically delightful but morally questionable. *Volpone*'s titular rogue and his servant Mosca—even Subtle and Dol in *The Alchemist*—are subject to harsher judgments than Brainworm, who Clement immediately pardons: "Thou hast done or assisted to nothing, in my judgment, but deserves to be pardon'd for wit of the offense" (F 5.1.173–75). Brainworm, of course, is more harmless than a pseudo-alchemist or legacy hunter; he even returns the jewels and stockings that he cons from Matthew and Bobadill. But his comparative lack of censure is as much attributable to his function as an analog for the playwright as it is to his lack of pecuniary interests. Brainworm illustrates the potential that theater has to create a London in which poetry and wit can trump even civic authority in the contest to determine the meaning of urban space. Just as Clement values a poet above the Lord Mayor, Jonson valorizes the characters—regardless of social rank—whose spatial practices allow them the sort of authorial agency that Jonson himself has over his play, whose urban experience involves reading and rewriting the places of London as Jonson himself does.

PLAYWRIGHT'S PLAY: *EASTWARD HO*

Depending on the date of the Londonizing revisions to *Every Man in His Humor*, *Eastward Ho*, Jonson's 1605 collaboration with George Chapman and John Marston, may have been his first real excursion into London city

comedy. As a collaboration, of course, the play was unsuited to Jonson's textual monument to his unified poetics, and it consequently does not appear
in the Folio of 1616, but it nevertheless demonstrates Jonson's growing concern with the alternate authorial medium of dramatic space. As the revised
Every Man In depicts the power of dramatic authorship to purge the symp-
toms of London's spatial pathology, *Eastward Ho* illustrates Jonson's awareness of theater's potential to shape place, and the dramatic author's ability to
transcend the interpretive limitations of class.

Eastward Ho places city comedy's characteristic concern with the
morality of class interaction within a framework that highlights the role of
the spatial practice of dramatic art; it implicitly claims that drama is the
medium through which early modern London is to be most effectively interpreted and created. In presenting a parodic challenge to the earlier citizen
genres of drama exemplified by Dekker and Heywood, and to the assumptions of those plays about the urban experience they portrayed, *Eastward Ho*
illustrates Jonson's growing consciousness of the genre's potential for ideological variety.

The class ideology and biases of *Eastward Ho* are notoriously ambiguous. The play certainly appears on the surface to be wholeheartedly and
unproblematically pro-citizen, with the thrifty and virtuous goldsmith
Touchstone—whose name reflects not only a tool of his trade but also, seemingly, his function as the play's moral benchmark—achieving an easy victory
for citizen virtues over the spendthrift gallantry and mounting class ambi-
tions of his prodigal apprentice Quicksilver, his foolish daughter Gertrude,
and her affianced "carpet knight" Sir Petronel Flash.[23] The play's debt to the
English morality tradition is apparent, with its sets of opposed pairs of moral
exemplars, delineated in the first act: the virtuous apprentice Golding and
the malcontented apprentice Quicksilver, a would-be gallant; the humble and
obedient daughter Mildred versus the gold-digging Gertrude; and the con-
tention between Touchstone and his socially climbing wife. Those characters
who violate the bourgeois code of thrift, honesty, and satisfaction with their
lot are punished by near-drowning and imprisonment, while the adherents
to the code are rewarded by marriage and advancement. There could be, it
seems, no more obvious example of the moralistic prodigal play, championing
citizen values in the most precise way possible, and most critics for three centuries read *Eastward Ho* in exactly that way, seeing it as an exemplary citizen
comedy, remarkable only for the exactitude with which it fits its genre.[24]

As most more recent critics and editors have realized, however, *Eastward Ho*'s class ideology is difficult to pin down. The levels of irony are
quite complex, if at times deeply embedded, and the parody extends to the

characters whose virtues the playwrights apparently champion. Although Touchstone and Golding's point of view seems to vanquish the other characters'—and critics such as C. G. Petter see Golding as the unambiguous moral center of the play[25]—the victory is undercut by the shallow, formal propriety of their characters and the unpleasant smugness of their victory. The main function of Golding's virtue is to set off Quicksilver's prodigality; when taken alone he is a much less vital character, and his frugality and loyalty to his master and father-in-law Touchstone are portrayed too cartoonishly to take seriously. Indeed, loyalty and frugality are the only values that Golding seems to possess. When Touchstone perfunctorily offers his good daughter Mildred to him in order to spite his bad daughter Gertrude, who has run off with the foolish Sir Petronel, the unison response of the couple is as joyless as it is automatic: "*Touch.* . . . Y'are both agreed, are ye not? / *Both.* With all submission, both of thanks and duty" (2.1.164–65).[26] And their marriage is celebrated with the same caricature of "thrift, thrift" that provides Hamlet a sardonic joke: when Touchstone offers them a marriage feast, Golding protests, in all seriousness, "Let me beseech you, no, sir; the superfluity and cold meat left at their nuptials will with bounty furnish ours" (172–74). The extent to which the apprentice goldsmith gilds the lily of his bourgeois virtues strongly suggests satirical caricature. The playwrights "see to it that we find Golding a precise, unpleasant little conformist."[27]

Critics have proven unable to come to a consensus on how to read the ambivalence of the play's class ideology. In light of the fact that city comedy, by and large, has a clear bias either toward abused gentry plagued by grasping citizens, or toward virtuous citizens cuckolded and beggared by spendthrift gentry, the apparent ideological neutrality of *Eastward Ho* is something of an anomaly. Louis B. Wright views the balanced satire as one of the play's strengths, assuming that the play could be subtly attuned to different audiences, the citizens being burlesqued at the Blackfriars for a private audience, but played unironically for the citizen audiences at the Fortune.[28] Wright is an exception, however, and the majority of the play's critics have assumed that it must have been pitched toward one class group or the other. Until the 1930s the play was seen as presenting a neat if unremarkable bourgeois moral paradigm, but Una Ellis-Fermor recognizes in it a "sub-sardonic comment . . . on the citizen virtues of thrift and patience," and H. W. Wells reads it as a straightforward satire on citizens' simple tastes and morals. Similarly, M. C. Bradbrook, Marchette Chute, and Jill Phillips Ingram see it as a burlesque response to the tradition of prodigal plays.[29]

Given that city comedies do, in the main, project a bias that would appeal to the intended audience, this desire of critics to attribute a clear-cut class bias to *Eastward Ho* is understandable. The immediate occasion of the play is as a response to Dekker and Webster's 1604 *Westward Ho*, which does depend on a bias toward citizens threatened by lascivious gentlemen. In light of this, and of the fact that *Eastward Ho*'s satire on court practices brought imprisonment for two of its authors (a voluntary punishment, Jonson claimed to William Drummond) and exile from London for the third, we might be forgiven the assumption that the play's main conflict, whether one reads its irony correctly or not, is between civic and courtly ideologies and values.[30] After all, the binaries of the play—Quicksilver/Golding, Gertrude/Mildred, etc.—are boldly drawn, and the generic assumptions of economic and sexual conflict between citizens and gentry do make appearances.

As Petter points out, however, *Eastward Ho*'s refusal finally to take sides ultimately removes this conflict from a central position, "presenting all classes in a mood of critical enjoyment which depends neither on sympathy for, nor antagonism against, any particular class."[31] The playwrights hold up this generically traditional conflict to our scrutiny, but the play marginalizes the conflict, if it does not dismiss it, and the implications of this marginalization, I would argue, are important for our understanding of Jonson's awareness of the power of dramatic authorship over London and the urban experience. Since everyone is satirized equally, in this "playwright's play"[32] the true heroes emerge as the playwrights themselves, the most effective values those of theater itself. Moreover, the celebration of the playwright's art, as in *Every Man In*, plays out in terms of a contest of interpretive control, through the characters' exercises in theatricality, over London place.

Ralph Alan Cohen calls *Eastward Ho* the period's purest specimen of "topographical comedy." The play, he points out,

> abounds with allusions to places with infamous associations and men-
> tions, among others, the disreputable precincts of Whitefriars and St.
> Katherine's; prisons such as Bridewell, the Fleet, King's Bench, and the
> two city prisons, the Counters; and even Tyburn and Wapping, notori-
> ous as places of execution.[33]

Not only is the play heavy, as city comedies tend to be, with allusions to specific London places, but "[t]he meaning of *Eastward Ho* is inseparable from its setting: place functions both as protagonist and theme."[34] Cohen neatly articulates the social aspirations of Petronel, Gertrude and Quicksilver in terms of place: all three long to go eastward, Petronel to begin his journey to Virginia, Quicksilver to court in Greenwich, Gertrude to escape the "chitty" and its "chittizens," the class to which she was born. The play forms a structural "magnetic field," according to Cohen, that draws all these potential escapees who would disrupt the status quo back to Cheapside at the end.[35] Cohen stresses what he perceives as *Eastward Ho*'s frankly middle class morality a bit too heavily, suggesting that the city and the Thames as its agent punish those who aspire to higher social status. He is certainly correct, however, to point to 4.1, in which the characters' eastward journeys are brought to ignominious ends by a storm on the Thames, as the play's most effective demonstration of theater's power over place.

In this lengthy scene, the only one written in concert by all three playwrights, who divided the rest of the play between them by scenes,[36] the authors demonstrate the infinitely malleable qualities of the stage's spatial function to a degree unique in Jacobean drama. The scene introduces us to Slitgut, a butcher's apprentice who appears nowhere else in the play. He climbs the tall pole at Cuckold's Haven, a point on the south bank downriver from London, in order to adorn it with the horns that make it a symbol of cuckoldry and a well-known landmark. Slitgut's only function is to serve as the audience's eyes and to determine the setting of the lower stage, which must become several different locations on the banks of the Thames—where the various eastward voyagers are washed up—in quick succession. Through the device of Slitgut poised upon this prospect and describing what he sees, we are transported miles at a time—from Cuckold's Haven itself, to Wapping, to the Isle of Dogs—in what is among the most brazen abandonments of classical unities to be seen in Renaissance English theater. Like Virginia Woolf's airplane in the stream-of-consciousness spatial shifting of *Mrs. Dalloway*, the cuckold's pole acts both as a fulcrum for these shifts and as a shifting point of view. As the text of Dekker's *Magnificent Entertainment* had lifted readers imaginatively to the heights of the triumphal arches, Slitgut serves as the audience's surrogate and lifts them to a prospect where they can see two miles about. The lower stage becomes like a map that they can read, zooming in and out and gaining the aspect of a controlling, superior reader, omniscient, omnipresent, and capable of comprehending multiple simultaneous scenes at once, like the split-screen effect in cinema.

Henry Turner has argued that this scene, although it was "demanded by the logic of the action they had themselves begun" threatens to sweep the playwrights away like their shipwrecked characters by virtue of its "scope and movement that far exceeded the stage's capacity." The scene's spatial displacement, "unthinkable" on Jonson's stage, required Slitgut, who is "at once character and Chorus, actor and author, playwright and surveyor, a figure brought onstage to contain a plot threatening to overspill its bounds by re-creating a unity of place through the power of his word and view."[37]

But this double function of Slitgut need not be seen, as Turner's reading suggests, as an expedience of authorial desperation, nor must we read the scene's vast scope as a loss of control. The scene's dramatic efficacy derives from its demonstration of the cartographic power of the stage and the power of the playwright to control the audience's perception of London places and their meanings. Each of the spots we are taken to is symbolically appropriate as punishment for the character who washes up there. The usurer Security, who has gone to great lengths to commit adultery but risked cuckoldry in the process, washes up at Cuckold's Haven, as Slitgut says with metatheatrical equivocation from both the upper stage and the cuckold's pole, "even just under me" (4.1.28). His would-be adulterous wife Winifred comes to shore nearly three miles upriver at St. Katharine's, formerly a reformatory for fallen women. The prodigal apprentice Quicksilver alights at Wapping, a place of execution. And when Sir Petronel appears at the Isle of Dogs believing he is in France, his aspirations as an adventurer are burlesqued, and the spot is appropriate for his discomfiture since it was a haven for debtors.

This scene constitutes the playwrights' deft demonstration of their power over London space, and in *Eastward Ho*'s denouement—written by Jonson alone—it becomes clear that this, the potential of theater and the privileged spatial practice of the playwright, is the point of the play, rather than any expression of class-based morality. In the resolution, Jonson turns the focus of the characters to theater itself. Touchstone, for example, comes to present a strange amalgam of citizen attitudes toward plays and theater. He has a clear contempt for the falsity of drama, dismissing Quicksilver's offer of repentance because the latter has "learned to whine at the play yonder" (4.2.350–51). On the other hand, Touchstone also seems to recognize the value of theater to promote just the sort of citizen values that *Eastward Ho* both burlesques and ironically celebrates. When congratulating his former apprentice Golding on his meteoric promotion through the ranks of city government, he partakes in John Stow's discourse of glory as permanent monumentalization, imagining Golding's glory inscribed on the fabric of the city: "I hope to see thee one o' the monuments of our city," he tells Golding, "and thou and thy acts become the posies [inscriptions] for hospitals, when thy name shall be written upon conduits" (4.2.80–86). Touchstone, however, lives in the London of the Lord Mayor's Show, and shows an awareness of theater's role in this sort of monument making. In an addition that Stow never would have countenanced, he claims the public stage as a monument-making site, hoping to see Golding's "deeds played i' thy lifetime, by the best company of actors, and be called their get-penny" (87–89). Theatrical *space*, according to Touchstone, can be put to the ideological uses of monumental *place*.

This assertion is implicitly complicated, however, by its placement just after the *coup de théâtre* of 4.1. That scene's ample demonstration of the ephemeral, protean nature of stage space undermines Touchstone's claim that theater can make a monument of a man's name. Stage space is the opposite of monumental inscription; a more appropriate metaphor would be the blackboard, infinitely, constantly, and ephemerally reinscribed. Golding's deeds may be played by a company of actors, and his monument built in the stage space that currently represents London, but that same stage space will be Verona tomorrow, and as *Eastward Ho* 4.1 demonstrates, it can be multiple places almost simultaneously. Attempts to use theater as an agent of establishing permanence and power serve only to establish the near infinite power of theater over place.

Moreover, just as Wellbred, Kno'well, and Brainworm demonstrate their superior ability to navigate London by assuming a power over the city's spaces analogous to that of the dramatist over the space of the stage, so the characters in *Eastward Ho* bring the comedy to a satisfactory resolution not through exhibitions of traditional virtue, but through their own practices of theater. In the end, Golding and Quicksilver are competing again, but it has become a competition of poetics and playcraft. Golding's promotion to magistrate enables him to become, in essence, a playwright. He "venture[s] on a device" (5.3.118) to trick the adamantly unforgiving Touchstone into coming to the Counter, where Quicksilver is imprisoned, "to be a spectator of [his] miseries" (5.3.117–18) and to hear the prodigal's ballad of repentance.[38] And if Golding is a stage manager, Quicksilver is all too delighted to become a player. As Jean Howard puts it, "[i]f the Counter typically represents social death, in this play it is rewritten as a stage upon which the would-be gentleman is reborn as star cultural performer."[39] Quicksilver's ballad is so overwrought, so opposite to what we have seen of his character, and so tinged with excess, that its sincerity is questionable; indeed Brian Gibbons takes it as self-evidently hypocritical because of its Puritan jargon.[40] The song is, however, a successful performance for the play's onstage audience. In Leggatt's words, "[o]ne feels that [Touchstone] pardons Quicksilver not so much for moral reasons as because he finds him satisfying artistically."[41]

The apprentices' dramaturgical efforts, while they complement each other in bringing about the play's resolution, can be seen as competing dramatic forms. Golding is analogous to an unironic dramatist establishing the good citizen moral of the prodigal play, while Quicksilver is analogous to the playwrights of *Eastward Ho* itself, writing and playing a part in which he does not believe and letting different audiences, onstage and off, determine the sincerity of his repentance and thus the moral ideology of both his performance and of the larger play. This competition is apparent in the moral doubleness of the play's conclusion, its dueling epilogues. At the characters' emergence from the Counter, Quicksilver caps his repentance by offering to make an inglorious journey in his prison garb from there back to Goldsmiths' Row, significantly along the traditional route of the Lord Mayor's Show: "I . . . here make it my suit that I may go home through the streets in these [clothes] as a spectacle, or rather an example, to the children of Cheapside" (5.5.214–17).[42] Touchstone, apparently well pleased with this moralizing inversion of the Lord Mayor's Show, delivers directly to the audience lines that sound like the play's ending, a summation of lessons learned:

> Now London, look about,
> And in this moral see thy glass run out:
> Behold the careful father, thrifty son,
> The solemn deeds, which each of us have done;
> The usurer punished, and from fall so steep
> The prodigal child reclaimed, and the lost sheep. (218–23)

Touchstone's epilogue-like lines accord with the mini-drama that Golding has produced in the prison, and all-too-neatly affirm his citizen values. They are not, however, the larger play's ending. Quicksilver gets the last word, the true epilogue, and though his lines do nothing directly to subvert Touchstone's bourgeois moral, they divert the attention away from class ideology and toward theater. Presumably stopping Touchstone's intended final exit with "Stay, sir," he works one last act of transformative magic on playhouse space, extending it to include not only the stage, but also the galleries. Surveying the audience, Quicksilver declares,

> I perceive the multitude are gathered together to view our coming out
> at the Counter. See, if the streets and the fronts of the houses be not
> stuck with people, and the windows filled with ladies, as on the solemn
> day of the Pageant! [*To the audience*]
>   O may you find in this our pageant, here,
>   The same contentment which you came to seek;
>   And as that show but draws you once a year,
>   May this attract you hither once a week. (*Epilogue* 1–10)

Quicksilver the character, poised as he is on the verge of a version of a pageant procession of his own, seems to evoke here an equation of pageantry with the citizen morality of Touchstone's sententious ending. Quicksilver's last final verse lines, however, undercut Touchstone, in that, as R. W. Van Fossen argues, it is not any moral at all, but "merely contentment that Quicksilver hopes London will find in their play."[43] Indeed, these lines put the Lord Mayor's Show directly in *competition* with the performance of *Eastward Ho* at the Blackfriars. "The play's real epilogue," writes Leggatt, "is not a moral tag but an appeal for a long run."[44] The comparison of the audience of the Blackfriars with the crowds at the Lord Mayor's Show, however, is more than just a commercial issue. Indeed, it is not a comparison at all, so much as a transformation, a final assertion of the playwrights' ability to manipulate the signification of urban and playhouse space. Just as the actor playing Quicksilver is both himself and his role, or perhaps steps out of character during the course of the speech, the "here" of his epilogue is both the street in front of the Counter and the Blackfriars stage, or perhaps it transforms as Quicksilver moves from prose to verse. Most remarkable is the prose section, wherein the playwright's power over stage space—and over the London that it represents—extends to the entire playhouse. Jonson makes the galleries into shop windows and the audience into a pageant audience. Neatly and chiasmically, the stage becomes the city in the context of civic pageantry, a phenomenon wherein the city is transformed into a stage.

In the portraits of London life in the revised *Every Man in His Humor* and in *Eastward Ho*, Jonson incorporates a demonstration of theatrical virtuosity on the stage of London. The characters who emerge victorious in these plays are those who can shape the interpretation of London space as successfully as the playwright himself, a fact that emphasizes Jonson's own artistic skills and authorial identity just as effectively as does Justice Clement's speech in praise of true poetry. Jonson was just as invested as Shakespeare in the *theatrum mundi* trope, the idea that all life is a drama, and for Jonson, that drama was inherently a competition of authority: "our whole life is like a *Play*," he writes in the *Discoveries*, "wherein every man, forgetful of himselfe, is in travaile with expression of another" (1093–95). If, for his more celebrated contemporary, the corollary of all the world being a stage is that the men and women are merely *players*, the upshot of Jonson's city becoming a stage in his London comedies is that the ideal Londoner is a *playwright*, and specifically the sort of playwright that Jonson himself was, always in travail with others. For Jonson, the profession of playwright produced agonistic relationships with his fellow dramatists, with the players, with his audiences, with his readers. And as the following chapter will discuss, his next comedies would begin to put Jonson in competition with his characters, as well.

Chapter Four
Jonson's Plague Year Plays

His collaborative experience on *Eastward Ho* aside, Jonson did not write a play pointedly set in London until *Epicoene, or, The Silent Woman* in 1609.[1] As we have seen, his earliest city comedy, *Every Man in His Humor*, was originally set in Florence. The setting of its sequel, *Every Man Out of His Humor*—notwithstanding references to Pict-Hatch and almost an entire act set in the middle aisle of St. Paul's—alternates between a generalized, vaguely Italianate urban space and the rarefied metatheatrical mindscape inhabited by Asper and the Grex. *Eastward Ho* seems to have whetted his appetite for the London setting, however. In the Folio texts of both *Epicoene* and Jonson's next comedy, *The Alchemist* (1610), the setting is specified on the *dramatis personae* page ("THE SCENE LONDON"), and the dramatic action depends on a consistent, intricate play of references to specific London topography. These plays mark an important further transition in Jonson's career with regard both to the playwright's representation of London and to his exploration of the potential of theatrical space.

This transition comes, at least in part, as a response to two practical contexts for the writing of these plays. The first of these is the acquisition of the Blackfriars playhouse by the King's Men in 1608, and the subsequent change in the legal status of the Blackfriars itself. Once a Dominican monastery in the southwest corner of intramural London, the Blackfriars district, upon Henry VIII's dissolution of the monastic houses, had fallen into the possession of the crown, and as such was outside the jurisdiction of the City of London, geographically part of the city, but legally a liberty. Since 1576, theatrical performances had taken place in the Blackfriars, and Jonson had written plays—*Cynthia's Revels* and *Poetaster*—to be performed by the Children of the Chapel Royal in the private space there.[2] Not until the King's Men's lease of the permanent indoor playhouse there, however, had professional adult companies been allowed to play in the Blackfriars, and not until that time had Jonson written a play for an adult company to be performed in an interior playing space.[3] Moreover, the Blackfriars district, where Jonson himself had taken up residence by February 1607,[4] passed for the first time under the city's jurisdiction shortly after the King's Men signed the lease to the theater there, a legal change that highlights the potentially uneasy contest between theater practitioners and civic government over the theatrical deployment of space in an urban setting.[5] This watershed event, placing the preeminent adult playing company inside the city and in Jonson's own neighborhood, seems to have contributed to the new concern in his next two city comedies with the control of interior, private space and the implications of theatricality on that control. *Epicoene* and *The Alchemist* constitute Jonson's playful and complex exploration of the intersection between two types of household, the domestic and the dramatic. As Ann C. Christensen points out, from *Every Man in His Humor* onward, Jonson had had a concern with doors, thresholds, and the private spaces that they demarcate: "In Jonson's plays, it is at the domestic threshold where the artistically, socially, and thematically most important scenes occur."[6] This concern of Jonson's is in part, of course, inherited from Roman New Comedy, with its traditional setting of an urban street with two or three doors opening onto it. After 1608, however, Jonson began to move beyond the legacy of classical theater, and to investigate the mastery of his own private, theatrical house in order to delineate the authorial role with regard to space.

It was not only the King's Men's lease of the Blackfriars theater that encouraged this investigation, however, for although the company had the house, they were largely unable to perform Jonson's plays there, or anyone else's, until late in 1610, because of the plague. The closure of the playhouses during periodic visitations of plague, of course, was part of the theater business throughout the Elizabethan and Jacobean periods, and the necessity of stripping down a cast and adapting scripts for tours of East Anglia and Oxfordshire was a common inconvenience for playing companies. Even dismissing the arguments of theater's detractors based in theology, marking the plague as divine punishment for playgoing, those based in biology were practical and harder to counter—infectious diseases, when their causes are poorly understood, can only be fought by the spatial confinement and quarantine of infected bodies, and popular gathering places like playhouses were hotbeds of contagion.[7]

London's plague-time quarantine practices, however, were far more extensive than playhouse closure. When the meticulously recorded numbers of plague deaths reached epidemic levels (defined in various periods as thirty, forty, or fifty deaths per week), as they did during the great visitations of

1603 and 1625, the city enforced the policy, introduced in the early sixteenth century, of shutting up infected houses and confining within them their inhabitants, both sick and well, for a period of forty days. This practice of segregation, in use during every epidemic up to the last great plague of 1665, was enforced by specially appointed officials called warders or watchers, and the doors of infected houses were marked with bills declaring their status and reading "Lord have mercy upon us," or with large red crosses—less easily defaced than paper bills—painted on the doors.[8]

The period of plague during which *Epicoene* and *The Alchemist* were written and performed was not as intensely deadly as the visitations of either 1603 or 1625. It did, however, last longer. From 1605 to 1606, yearly plague deaths in London nearly quintupled, from 444 to 2,124. Annual mortality rates remained above 1,800 for the next four years, peaking in 1609, the year in which Jonson wrote *Epicoene*, at 4,240.[9] Playhouses were regularly closed during this period, a nuisance tiresome enough to theater practitioners to give force to Surly's assertion in *The Alchemist* that anyone who could drive the plague out of the kingdom would earn the sung praises of the players (2.1.71).[10]

The frequent plague closings led to the fallow period that produced Jonson's two comedies most concerned with household prophylaxis and the control of interior space. Not coincidentally, both *Epicoene* and *The Alchemist* are set (and performed) in the plague-ridden London that produced them, a city whose spatial practices were in a state of heightened control. *Epicoene* was written not for the King's Men and the Blackfriars, but for another professional company, the so-called "Children of Her Majesty's Revels;" by 1609 this was, as Richard Dutton argues, only nominally a boys' company, its mainly young adult members functioning more as a professional adult troupe than anything resembling the boys companies of the 1570s or the turn of the century.[11] The play was performed at the Whitefriars playhouse—an indoor theater near the Inns of Court, outside the walls but within the Temple Bar, with dimensions much smaller than those of the Blackfriars[12]—sometime after 7 December 1609, when the playhouses were reopened after an eighteen month closure, most likely in January 1610.[13] *Epicoene's* performance, in a window between plague closures (the playhouses would be darkened again from July to November) would surely be heightened by the temporal setting of the play: Truewit refers in the opening scene to the perpetual ringing of funeral bells "now, by reason of the sickness" (1.1.176–77). More pointedly, *The Alchemist*, despite its likely first performance on tour in Oxford (also by reason of the sickness) was written for the grand opening of the Blackfriars playhouse with its new company, the

King's Men, and its plot turns on the setting during a time when, "The sickness [being] hot" (Argument 1), the city and its houses are empty enough to be used as sites of con artistry.

Ian Donaldson is certainly correct in his assertion that

> [n]o dramatist before [Jonson] ... so fully explores the psychology of urban indoor living, so instinctively perceives the correspondence between the fixed space of a house and the fixed space of the stage on which the actors must work.[14]

This concern with interior space, though, does not arise *ex nihilo*, and it is attributable, more than anything else, to the confluence of these two circumstances in the plague years. The plague, and its attendant quarantine procedures, inevitably brought with it an awareness of a certain prophylactic form of spatial control. And this awareness, for Jonson, must have been compounded by the transition of the companies for which he was writing to indoor theaters, for the two plague year comedies heighten the playwright's growing sense of his own uses of space and their authorial potential. As we have seen, since 1604 he had already begun to think of dramatic authorship as the ideal means of achieving epistemological control over urban space, and during this time of heightened anxiety about household permeability, Jonson uses *Epicoene* and *The Alchemist*—plays whose action depends on the theatrical management of entrances and exits to houses, the fictionalized equivalents of the indoor private theaters—to demonstrate the control he has over the space of the playhouse. More importantly for the development of his authorial strategy, in these two plays, more than in *Every Man in His Humor* or *Eastward Ho*, Jonson begins to situate his characters' often explicitly theatrical spatial practice in direct competition with his own.

"BY REASON OF THE SICKNESS": *EPICOENE*

The character of Morose, the neurotic monstrosity at the center of *Epicoene*, can be seen to represent a step in the evolution of the Jonsonian "humors" character. The causes of his mental affliction are more nuanced, more rooted in something like realism than the baseless jealousy of a Kitely or the cartoonish swaggering of a Bobadill. Morose's father, he tells us,

> in my education, was wont to advise me that I should always collect and contain my mind, not suff'ring it to flow loosely; that I should look to what things were necessary to the carriage of my life, and

what not, embracing the one and eschewing the other. In short, that I should endear myself to rest and avoid turmoil, which now is grown to be another nature to me. So that I come not to your public pleadings or your places of noise; not that I neglect those things that make for the dignity of the commonwealth, but for the mere avoiding of clamours and impertinencies of orators, that know not how to be silent. (5.3.46–54)[15]

The passage, with its quite reasonable explanation for Morose's aversion to noise, can be read as proto-Freudian psychological sophistication, but such readings lead all too easily to the insupportable assumption of the character's basis on a real acquaintance of Jonson's, as Dryden suspected, or on Jonson himself, as Edmund Wilson argued.[16] The passage also belies Morose's grotesquery elsewhere in the play, which surely makes him more a descendant of those earlier Jonsonian humors characters—also unable to "flow loosely"—than of anything in his experience, and the uses Jonson makes of Morose's humor are similar to those he finds in Cob's, Kitely's, and Bobadill's. Like theirs, the humor of the "gentleman that loves no noise" is reflected in his practice of urban space. Morose lives near—although importantly, not *in*—the fashionable Strand, in the area between London and Westminster now referred to as the West End but in the early seventeenth century coming to be known as "the Town."[17] He attempts to create a microcosm of silence in this busy urban environment, obsessively attempting not only to block off his house from noise, but also to block or divert the normal currents of urban space outside his walls.

The play's concern with the control of space is not confined to Morose, however. As Adam Zucker argues, *Epicoene* presents a hierarchy of "cultural competence," whereby power is gained and articulated primarily by "managing one's relationship to urban spaces."[18] I would add that by explicitly demonstrating the most effectual management of these spaces to be theatrical, Jonson uses the play to assert his own ascendance in a world made up of competing pretenders to that most privileged relationship to urban space produced by dramatic authorship. Inspired, perhaps, by the plague-time practices of household quarantine, and encouraged by the tiny playing space of the Whitefriars stage for which it was written, *Epicoene* places a notable emphasis on interior space, not just in its use of mainly interior, domestic scenes, but in a preoccupation with household permeability, and with the question of how much exclusionary control it is proper to exercise over one's household.

Jonson's characteristic concern with doors and their significances becomes something like an obsession in *Epicoene*, which uses the word *door* nineteen times, more than any of his previous plays.[19] From its very outset, as Roger Holdsworth notes, the play exhibits a "preoccupation with doors as boundaries of one's private territory, dividing the world without from the world within."[20] Immediately the play opens, we encounter the emphasis on doors and exclusion, and the play's first act is a sustained discussion of various characters' behavior with regard to their own and others' private spaces. In the opening lines, the gallant Clerimont, employing his dramatically hermaphroditic boy servant as a go-between to Lady Haughty, is dismayed at the boy's ability, and his own failure, to penetrate her house (with an obvious sexual quibble): "No marvel if the door be shut against your master, when the entrance is so easy to you" (1.1.18–19). When Clerimont's friend Truewit arrives, the discussion of Haughty turns to a debate about the aesthetic and moral propriety of female cosmetic artifice, but their discussion is still focused through the lens of spatial control. Clerimont's complaint is not that Haughty uses cosmetics, but that her use of them prevents male access to her house: "There's no man can be admitted till she be ready nowadays, till she has painted and perfumed and washed and scoured, but the boy here" (81–84). Truewit's (possibly ironic) defense of feminine "painting" also focuses on women's control of their own private space: "nor when the doors are shut should men be inquiring," he says; "all is sacred within, then" (111–12). Truewit pushes his endorsement of the secret workings of female artifice to absurd levels, even insisting that

> a wise lady will keep a guard always upon the place, that she may do things securely. I once followed a rude fellow into a chamber, where the poor madam, for haste, and troubled, snatched at her peruke to cover her baldness and put it on the wrong way. (123–27)

This debate about female cosmetic artifice may seem curious, even superfluous to the play, especially to audience members unfamiliar with the surprise in store for them, the hasty snatching off of Epicoene's own peruke to reveal a boy actor. But given the importance of artificial, performed femininity to the play's resolution, the gallants' debate, with its equation of performative art with a secret inner chamber, a type of tiring house, is crucial to Jonson's insertion of himself and his own control of private space into the drama.

Following upon this opening discussion of doors and exclusivity, *Epicoene* quickly establishes a spectrum of household permeability among its characters, with a range of attitudes toward private, domestic space, the extremes of which represent differently monstrous and improper practices. On one end of this spectrum is Morose, to whom we are introduced by

report, by Truewit and Clerimont, in the first scene. His signature affliction, of course, is that "he can endure no noise" (142), but the gallants' discussion of Morose quickly shifts from the acoustical aspect of his humor
to the spatial aspect that accompanies it. Morose's abhorrence of noise has
determined, among other things, his dwelling place in the town: "he hath
chosen a street to lie in so narrow at both ends that it will receive no coaches
nor carts nor any of these common noises" (1.1.161–63). He has also come
to enact a darkly parodic version of the city's plague-time quarantine proce-
dure, in effect shutting up his own home like a grotesquely exaggerated sick-
house, not because of the plague itself, but because of the incessantly ringing
funeral bells whose noise is more threatening to him than the infection:

> now, by reason of the sickness, the perpetuity of ringing has made him
> devise a room with double walls and treble ceilings, the windows close
> shut and caulked, and there he lives by candlelight. (176–80)

His humor produces in Morose an obsession with the fortification and
defense of his door, the one weak spot in his domestic defenses. "Bar my
doors" is his frequent cry (2.2.144, 3.5.31), and we hear that when Clerimont's boy, as a practical joke, "practiced on him one night like the bell-
man," he provoked him to actual armed defense, "brought him down to the
door with a long sword, and there left him flourishing in the air" (1.1.157–
60). When we finally meet Morose in the second act, this obsession is one
of the most striking aspects of his instructions to his mute servant, whom he
has not only ordered to remove the doorbell (2.1.8) and to oil the lock and
hinges (25) but to fasten "a thick quilt or flock-bed on the outside of the
door, that if they knock with their daggers or with brickbats, they can make
no noise" (10–12). For Morose, noise threatens not only his own well being,
but the very integrity of his physical house: after driving Daw, La Foole, and
the Collegiate Ladies "out of [his] doors" with his trusty longsword, he complains that "[t]hey have rent my roof, walls, and all my windows asunder,
with their brazen throats" (2.5.110, 116–17).

Morose's insistence on complete exclusion, on complete domestic
prophylaxis, makes the normal commercial functions of the city outside
his walls into another sort of plague for Morose. He has "been upon divers
treaties" with the noisier mercantile professions—fishwives, orange-women,
chimney-sweepers—contracting them not to approach (1.1.144–46), and
as for smiths and other "hammermen," "A brazier is not suffered to dwell
in the parish, nor an armourer" (150–52). Morose usurps the place-making
functions of civic governmental power, becoming, in Gail Kern Paster's

apt phrase, a "city planner in reverse."[21] If, for Jonson, humor is often seen as a diseased practice of urban space, Morose's humor is a sort of cancer afflicting his whole neighborhood and threatening the spatial practice of the city itself.

If Morose's transgression is a domestic space that attempts to be impossibly impermeable, the Collegiate Ladies, also introduced by report in the first scene, inhabit the other end of the spectrum. A "foundation" or "order" of ladies "here in the town," they have, according to Truewit, an indistinct social place which also carries with it a topographical indeterminacy: they lie somewhere "between courtiers and country madams" (1.1.70–73). They manage to commit two damning (for Jonson) transgressions at the same time, against gender norms and against sound aesthetic judgment, "cry[ing] down or up what they like or dislike in a brain or a fashion with most masculine or rather hermaphroditical authority" (75–77), but more to the point, they inhabit private spaces that are all too permeable. The Collegiates "live from their husbands and give entertainment to all the Wits and Braveries o' the time" (73–74). That is, the fashionable gallants—like Truewit and Clerimont, presumably, or Dauphine, who declares himself in love with all the Collegiates at once (4.1.129)—have, Clerimont's temporary inability to enter Lady Haughty's house notwithstanding, an access to these ladies that heeds neither household boundaries nor prohibitions against adultery.

Like the Collegiates, the two knights, Sir John Daw and Sir Amorous La Foole, stand in direct opposition to Morose in their grotesque openness. Daw—perhaps we are to hear a pun on "door" in his name?—is anathema to Morose's humor, "the only talking sir i' th' town" (1.2.65), and his counterpart La Foole is the epitome of monstrous domestic openness, as transgressive at his extreme as Morose is in his obsessive acoustic prophylaxis. Adam Zucker aptly notes that "[i]f Morose is too isolated from the city in which he lives, La Foole, even within the confines of his own home, is too much in it."[22] As much as Morose's narrow street is a reflection of his humor, the location of La Foole's house in the Strand and his behavior therein is a reflection of his, as Clerimont describes:

> He does give plays and suppers, and invites his guests to 'em aloud out of his window as they ride by in coaches. He has a lodging in the Strand for the purpose, or to watch when ladies are gone to the china-houses or the Exchange, that he may meet 'em by chance and give 'em presents. . . . He is never without a spare banquet or sweetmeats in his chamber, for their women to alight at and come up to, for a bait. (32–40)

Where Morose eschews guests, La Foole entraps them with food as bait; where Morose blocks coaches from his street and insulates his windows, La Foole shouts at their passengers from his open windows; and where Morose can think of no greater punishment than to "sit out a play" (4.4.16–17), La Foole turns his own home into a playhouse. As a fan and amateur impresario, though not a creator, of drama, and a giver of plays with no discretion as to his audiences, La Foole is as calculatedly opposed to the ideals of Jonson the dramatist as Daw, who fancies himself a poet and critic—despite his confusion of the titles of books in his library with their authors—is opposed to the ideals of Jonson the poet. As we will see, although they are mainly confined to the subplot, these two knights and their ultimate defeat by means of dramatic art are as central to Jonson's argument as the discomfiture of Morose.

The first two acts introduce us to these two opposed, "humorous" households—Morose's obsessive and ineffectually controlled exclusion and La Foole's ludicrous and uncontrolled openness—in order to stage their collision in the third act by means of the invasion of Morose's house by the wedding feast that Dauphine tricks La Foole into managing. From that collision, eventually, emerges something like a Jonsonian ideal, but not before a thorough immersion in a chaos of uncontrolled individual practices of urban and domestic space.

After gleefully observing another humorously mismanaged household, that of Morose's neighbors the Otters, Dauphine and his companions engineer a "comedy of affliction" (2.6.35–36) whereby the troubling openness of La Foole's household will be transferred to Morose's. La Foole and his rival Daw are each made to think the other has snubbed him (or "given [him] the dor" [3.3.26], in another loaded pun) by insisting on hosting a wedding feast for Morose and Epicoene, and their hosting competition allows Morose's nightmare guests—the endlessly and loudly nagging Mistress Otter, her husband and his boisterous drinking game with the novelty cups, La Foole, Daw, and all the Collegiates—to penetrate Morose's tenuously maintained fortress of silence. La Foole literally usurps Morose's place in two senses, taking over both his house and his duty as host: the foolish knight is to behave like a "knight-sewer" (3.7.17–18), serving the meat and inviting the guests to enjoy themselves. This penetration, the gallants imagine, will cause a sort of chain reaction, with the newly open house permitting a sensory leakage and intermingling, both olfactory and acoustic, between private and public: once La Foole has pierced Morose's defenses with guests and meat, Clerimont reasons, "[t]he smell of the venison going through the street will invite one noise of fiddlers or other" (3.3.79–80).

The marriage begins a series of takeovers of Morose's house by various characters. Immediately upon marrying Morose, of course, Epicoene reveals that the silence that recommended her to her new husband has been an act. Perhaps as dismayingly to Morose, however, she also immediately usurps the house whose space Morose has so painstakingly tried to control: "I'll have none of this coacted, unnatural dumbness in my house," she declares (3.4.48–49). When Morose moves to defend his privacy from the invasion of the wedding feast, which he fears—and Truewit teasingly implies—will consist of "the whole town" (3.5.22), his new wife asserts her control over Morose's most fetishized locus, his doors:

MOROSE

. . . Bar up my doors, you varlets!

EPICOENE

He is a varlet that stirs to such an office. Let 'em stand open. I would see him that dares move his eyes toward it. Shall I have a barricado made against my friends . . . ? (33–36)

This question is entirely rational, as Truewit points out: "she speaks but reason, and methinks she is more continent than you" (40–41). The wordplay in Truewit's jest speaks to the central irony of Morose's spatial humor. No one is more obsessive about containment than Morose, but in opening the doors to friendship and the propriety of nuptial festivity, his new wife is paradoxically more "continent."

The stakes in the series of spatial usurpations are raised further by the entrance of the Collegiates. Lady Haughty, disappointed with the paucity of the marriage entertainments, demands, among other things, a masque (3.6.83), threatening to transform Morose's silent house into a stage for the sort of theatrical entertainments that he abhors, and Morose's sarcastic response to Haughty is not only a jibe at her sexual looseness, but also an indication of what he has lost, his control over private place. "Will it please your ladyship command a chamber and be private with your friend?" he asks, driven to surrender: "You shall have your choice of rooms to retire to after; my whole house is yours" (88–90). His defeat is driven home by his ceding the right to conduct in his guests—the control of his doors—to Epicoene (3.7.22–23), and when Mistress Otter, upon entering, declares "'Tis my place" (3.7.30), we may hear not only her jockeying for precedence with the other Collegiate Ladies, but the final collapse of Morose's spatial control.

Morose is literally driven from the stage by the revelers and their noise at the end of act three, and from that point he is effectively removed from the action of the play. We learn from Dauphine in the next scene that he has escaped to "a cross-beam o' the roof, like him o' the saddler's horse in Fleet Street, upright" (4.1.20–23). The metaphor is telling; not only has he been driven out of his private space, he has become like a shop sign, fixed by others as a marker of public commercial space, and without his own agency either to determine or to practice place.

Morose's flight to the rafters also surrenders his house to the invaders, an empty space to be played with and upon. In act four, the gallants transform the house into a theater of sorts, and it is this transformation that allows Jonson to posit dramatic authorship as the ideal relationship to domestic space, a medium between the monstrous extremes represented by Morose and La Foole, both of whom receive their punishment by means of theatrical art.[23] Truewit, who wrongly believes that he is a conspirator with Dauphine in the plot to disinherit Morose, is responsible for turning the gallants' discourse to the metatheatrical. "The ladies have laughed at thee most comically since thou went'st," he tells Dauphine (4.5.5–6), establishing the Collegiates in their function as onstage audience for Truewit's drama, and he "plots" revenge on Daw and La Foole, who have provoked this audience's "comic" laughter, thus entering a wit battle to win the Collegiates' favor for Dauphine.

This battle, and the gallants' victory, are achieved explicitly through the playwright's manipulation of space, making extempore use of Morose's house in a metatheatrical *mise en abîme*:

> Do you observe this gallery, or rather lobby, indeed? Here are a couple
> of studies, at each end one: here will I act such a tragicomedy between
> the Guelphs and the Ghibellines, Daw and La Foole. Which of 'em
> comes out first will I seize on. You two shall be the chorus behind the
> arras, and whip out between the acts and speak. (4.5.25–31)

With the same sort of knowing double reversal that Shakespeare employs in his rude mechanicals ("This green plot shall be our stage" [*A Midsummer Night's Dream* 3.1.3–4]), Jonson foregrounds the playwright's ability to transform playhouse space: Truewit's dialogue, in the usual way of theater, makes the Whitefriars into a room in Morose's house, a "gallery, or rather lobby," but then Truewit, stepping into Jonson's role as the author of dramatic place, transforms it back into a stage. The "studies," or side doors of the Whitefriars stage, become the side doors of Truewit's stage, and the central curtained stage space becomes a central curtained stage space, while the fictional representation of Morose's house flickers in and out of significance.[24] The concern with doors in the discourse of the play and their use as a recurring symbol becomes the practical, theatrical concern with entrances, and as Truewit manages the stage space and the doors that open onto it, he exerts a playwright's control over the exits and entrances of his actors, Daw and La Foole, achieving the spatial control that has eluded the play's humors characters.

Truewit's playlet collapses the larger play's spectrum of improperly controlled private space. In the mock duel that he directs between the two cowardly knights, La Foole's first impulse is to flee, but the doors of Morose's house prove to be a barrier to escape as well as to entry, as Truewit implies: "How will you get out o' the house, sir? He knows you are in the house" (175–76), and so La Foole turns to the Morosean extreme, planning to lock himself in the study for a week, with his back against the door, and laying up victuals and a chamber pot to withstand Daw's imagined siege (180–92). In La Foole's reduction to an even more absurd version of Morose's humor, Truewit's practical joke demonstrates the equivalence between La Foole's imperfect management of household permeability and Morose's.

As Truewit's jesting revelation of the two knight's natures reminds us of the gallants' exposure of the fools in *Every Man in His Humor*, it could be argued that his jest is merely of a piece with the exposure scenes in that earlier play, that his labeling the jest a "tragicomedy" does not in itself make the jest a play. With more theatrical terminology, however, Clerimont soon pushes the metatheatrical moment beyond metaphor. "Shall I make a motion?" he asks (213)—and his clever pun on the sense of *motion* as puppet show reminds us that a "motion" is just what the gallants are making, with La Foole and Daw as their puppets—"Shall I go fetch the ladies to the catastrophe?" (215). The Collegiate Ladies enter into the "gallery" (above), and become the audience that the "play" had been missing, the necessary condition for drama to occur.

This performance, the staging of this "motion," makes the gallants, in their audience's eyes, "wits," "braveries," and "very perfect gentlem[e]n" (4.6.12). The logic of the Collegiates is not meant to reflect Jonson's own, presumably, but the play and its audience's response does suggest the role of space in the gallants' easy victory. As Zucker puts it, the "quasi-theatrical scenario nicely articulates the basic social logic of the play: the three gallants move smoothly through their urban world, ordering their environment and the people in it."[25] Furthermore, this empowered practice of space that Zucker identifies with social success in the play is crucially aligned with the practices of dramatic authorship.

What emerges in *Epicoene*, in fact, is a competition between the privileged uses of space associated with successful dramatic art, and unsuccessful attempts to employ that privilege by others. For despite Morose's antipathy to plays, the powers over space and place that he usurps or imagines for himself are akin to the spatial practices of dramatic authorship, the power a playwright has over setting, stage space, and the practices of his characters: he claims the ability both to determine *lieu* and to exert control over the *espace* of others. Morose not only seeks to control fishwives and smiths through a strategic shaping of place; he also seeks to direct the space, in de Certeau's sense, of those few with whom he is intimately connected. When his plans to ensure Dauphine's disinheritance by marrying the "silent woman" are apparently assured and he is at his most triumphant, his fantasy of control over space is at its most fulsome. He is the master not only of his own private, household space, but that of his tenant, the barber Cutbeard, whom Morose gives "the lease of thy house free" (2.5.86) in exchange for providing him, as he thinks, with a silent wife. But in his soliloquy of revenge over Dauphine, he also imagines himself as a master of public space at not only the local, but even the international level:

> Oh my felicity! How I shall be revenged on mine insolent kinsman and his plots to fright me from marrying! This night I will get an heir and thrust him out of my blood like a stranger. He would be knighted, forsooth, and thought by that means to reign over me, his title must do it: no, kinsman. . . . Your knighthood itself shall come on its knees, and it shall be rejected . . . or it knighthood shall do worse, take sanctuary in Coleharbour, and fast. It shall fright all it friends with borrowing letters, and when one of the fourscore hath brought it knighthood ten shillings, it knighthood shall go to the Cranes or the Bear at the Bridge-foot and be drunk in fear . . . It shall not have hope to repair itself by Constantinople, Ireland, or Virginia. (96–125)

This is a fantasy of enforced exile for his nephew, in which Dauphine is driven further and further from the fashionable "town" in which he now jets it, to the city proper—the seedy Upper Thames street, with its maze of tenements called Coleharbour, a refuge from creditors, and its Three Cranes tavern—from thence over the river to the Bear tavern in Southwark, and ultimately from London, from England, and even from Christendom, to the very ends of the earth. The Dauphine of Morose's fantasy is controlled by the power (economic and cultural) of these marginalized places, as opposed to having the spatial mastery of the privileged locus that, as Zucker argues, is the primary means by which individual power is demonstrated in *Epicoene*.

Morose's attempts to exert authority are doomed, of course, by his humor. Morose maintains the kind of tight control over space that drama requires, but since his antipathy to noise admits no social discourse of any kind, he excludes all potential audiences, rendering him unable to attain the kind of "perfection" that this play espouses. Conversely, La Foole, with his indiscriminate giving of plays, dwells in a kind of bastardized playhouse, with performances for any and all comers and no thought of discernment or control. From the moment his enthusiasm is channeled into dramaturgy in act four, though, Truewit emerges as a playwright figure, and his and his cohort's dramatic practice of space comes to eclipse the chaos of dramatically-inflected, but unsuccessful practices of the other characters.

Indeed, Truewit's dramatic enthusiasm appears to take over the action of the play. He engineers the divorce—as he believes—as another theatrical trick, employing Cutbeard and Otter as amateur players, in the roles of lawyer and parson (4.7.39–46). The victory that his dramaturgical prowess seems certain to assure him, however, is denied Truewit at the play's resolution, as he is "lurched . . . of the better half of the garland" by Dauphine's revelation of Epicoene's true gender (5.4.208–9). That is to say, the gallants' successful employment of dramatic authority in their playlet for the Collegiates is not the final move of Jonson's argument. Truewit's plot is trumped by a better one, and his function as a potential author figure is usurped.

It is not Dauphine, however, who emerges as the final champion in the spatially focused competition for authority in the play, but Jonson himself. Dauphine's plot, after all, is Jonson's in the end, and the playhouse audience, no less than Truewit, is surprised by the removal of Epicoene's peruke. Moreover, despite the fact that they seem to be the only successful employers of the dramatist's authorial space, Jonson takes some pains to distance us from the gallants, and not simply by means of the alienating coldness with which Dauphine dismisses his defeated uncle to his grave. Many critics have identified the curious doubleness in Jonson's attitude to the gallants that keeps them from being pure author figures or exponents of a Jonsonian ideal.[26] They may be very perfect gentlemen in the Collegiates' terms, but the Collegiates are hardly an ideal Jonsonian audience. The gallants' moral authority as comic playwrights is questionable, as well, since Dauphine's attitude toward his audience is pointedly counter to Jonson's Sidneyan view of comedy as a means of moral reformation.[27] "Let them continue in the state of ignorance, and err still," says Dauphine of their Collegiate audience, "'Twere sin to reform 'em" (4.5.219). Jonson also, apparently, subtly compromises the gallants' spatial authority; Dauphine, though his victory would seem to be the final triumph of theatrical art, seems to have a tendency toward his uncle's humor. Dauphine is accustomed, Truewit complains in advising him in matters of love, to "live i' [his] chamber . . . a month together" (4.1.51–52). Dauphine's friends, however, have no consistent solution to this problem; while Truewit suggests he "come abroad where the matter is frequent" (53–54), Dauphine's unwise enthusiasm for the Collegiate Ladies, a few lines later, provokes Clerimont to the opposite extreme: "Out upon thee! We'll keep you at home, believe it, i' the stable, and you be such a stallion" (130–31).[28] The gallants' prowess in controlling space is enough for Jonson to assert the privileged status of the dramatic author, but it does not, apparently, exempt them from the imperfect practice of urban and domestic space that characterizes the play as a whole. In the play's final theatrical act, implicitly asserting Jonson's dramaturgical virtuosity through Dauphine's, we see where the play's chaotic competition of spatial relationships has led us all along: the only spatial practice that lives up to the Jonsonian ideal is Jonson's own, and we are the only audience that has a chance of discerning it.

"A HOUSE TO PRACTISE IN": *THE ALCHEMIST*

If, in *Epicoene*, Jonson implies a competition between his staging of private urban space and the practice, by the play's characters, of something very like dramatic authorship, in *The Alchemist* he makes this competition as explicit as possible. As has frequently been noted, the setting of the play in Lovewit's "house in town" with its "master quit, for fear" of the plague (Argument 1–2) coincides, with great precision, with the conditions of the play's original staging at the Blackfriars playhouse in late 1610 after the plague had lifted to the degree that the Kings' Men could return from provincial tours to their permanent London venues. The playhouse in the 'Friars is to be imagined as both representative of and equivalent to the house in which the cohort of rogues have set up, and the "absolute topicality and simultaneity" achieved by this equivalence—and by the fact that, as R. L. Smallwood notes, the play's action takes exactly as long as its performance would—draws an explicit parallel between the theatrics of Subtle, Face, and Dol on the one hand and Jonson's drama on the other:

> An audience in a theatre in the autumn of 1610 pays money to pass what the Prologue promises will be two hours (and an interval), to watch three masters of pretense, in the autumn of 1610, take two hours (and an interval) to deprive a number of representative gulls of their money.[29]

We will return to the significance of the dual nature of the house in this play, and to the significance of Jonson's contests for control of their space, but I introduce the equivalence here as a way into a larger discussion of what Smallwood calls the "constant theatrical self-awareness" of the play.[30] The double meaning of the house in the 'Friars is only one element in making *The Alchemist* Jonson's most systematicically and explicitly metatheatrical comedy.

The language of the play's argument hints that the "venture tripartite" (1.1.135) between Subtle, Face, and Dol is to be seen in terms not only dramatic, but in direct parallel to the business venture undertaken by professional London companies like the King's Men. Subtle and Dol, we learn, wanting nothing but "some / House to set up" have determined to "contract" with Face, "Each for a share, and all begin to act" (Argument 6–7). The rogues, that is, have become player-sharers, forming an economic arrangement like that of the Lord Chamberlain's, later the King's Men, in which principal actors were also part owners.[31]

We are to imagine the rogues not just as con men, but as players, and this is how they see themselves and present themselves to each other. Not only are they players in the sense that all characters are who don disguises or profit from seeming to be other than they are, but they repeatedly use the language of playing to describe themselves and their actions. In the opening argument between Subtle and Face that threatens to destroy the rogues' venture, for example, Dol insists to Subtle that all three are playing equally hard: "Do we not / Sustain our parts?" (1.1.144–45). And when the many costume changes start become too much for Face, he wishes he could shift clothes as easily as theatrical devices shift scenes: "O, for a suit, / To fall now, like a curtain: flap" (4.2.6–7). And the resolution of the play's plot involves the explicit acquisition of playhouse property, as Face employs Drugger and his "credit with the players" to borrow the costume of the imaginary Spanish Don that becomes the tool to win Dame Pliant's hand (4.7.68–71).

In addition to the material resources of playing, Subtle and Face borrow their primary roles, the Doctor and the Captain, from the tradition of professional theater, specifically the *commedia dell'arte* tradition with which Jonson demonstrated his familiarity throughout his career. Subtle's *Dottore* is a stock character of *commedia*, the same role that Volpone inhabits as Scoto of Mantua, and the "suburb-Captain" into which Jeremy the butler is "translated" (1.1.19) is a version of the swaggering braggart soldier, the *miles gloriosus* of New Comedy and *commedia's Capitano*.

The play constructs, then, as Mathew Martin puts it, "a small theatrical world . . . the dangerous double of the Globe and the Blackfriars,"[32] but giving the three rogues the perspective and the vocabulary of a playing company is only part of this construction. In the rogues' theater of *The Alchemist*, the audience is also invited to see potential versions of themselves. The miniature plays enacted in Lovewit's house depend on their audience's imagination as a motivating force, the fantasies of Dapper, Drugger, *et al* being a cynically satirical version of the "imaginary forces" the Chorus of Shakespeare's *Henry V* demands us to contribute to that play (Prologue 18). These fantasy dramas require the gull-audience's judgment to be cooperative (or faulty) enough to succeed. Moreover, as Robert Watson points out, the plots that the gulls' fantasies demand of the rogues in Lovewit's house are precisely those that

> packed Elizabethan theatres and bookstalls: not only coney-catching stories, but also versions of Marlowe's dramas of extravagant riches and supernatural pleasures, Sidney's and Middleton's stories of dynastic marriage, Shakespeare's and Spenser's adult fairy tales, even Deloney's chronicles of triumphant middle-class commercial diligence.[33]

To a certain extent, although he is disappointed in his quest for the philosopher's stone, Sir Epicure Mammon gets what he pays for: the performance of what even Surly acknowledges is "brave language . . . next to canting" (2.3.42). He is paying, in short, to "Believ't," the imperative with which Face bursts onto the stage in the play's opening line, and the imperative without which King's Men and confidence men alike cannot proceed.

The audience of *The Alchemist* may be disconcerted to discover that they are watching versions of themselves: eager fantasists being taken in—through a combination of their own imaginary forces and the virtuosity of others' performance—by theatrically adept rogues in a playhouse in the Blackfriars in 1610. This disturbing equivalence is nowhere more explicit than in the play's epilogue-like final speeches. First Lovewit and then Face are given lines in which the voice of the character seems to bleed into that of the player, and whose addressees are ambiguously defined as both the onstage spectators of the play's action—the fictional inhabitants of the Blackfriars—and the current visitors to the King's Men's house in the 'Friars. Lovewit's address to the "gentlemen, / And kind spectators" accomplishes a traditional role of epilogues, to apologize for any perceived lack of decorum in the action:

> If I have outstripped
> An old man's gravity, or strict canon, think
> What a young wife, and a good brain may do:
> Stretch age's truth sometimes, and crack it, too. (5.5.152–56)

It is Face, however, who gets the final word of the play, after Lovewit apparently cedes the right to the epilogue to him with "Speak for thyself, knave" (157). At first it seems that Face's epilogue will also be a traditional defense of the play's composition; he acknowledges, "Gentlemen, / My part fell a little in this last scene, / Yet 'twas *decorum*" (157–59). The final turn of the speech, however, reminds Jonson's audience that they are disturbingly related to, even complicit in, the process of theatrical gulling that they have just witnessed. Although Face—or more properly, the player of Face—is "clean / Got off" from both his fellow confidence men and their victims, "all / With whom [he] traded,"

> Yet I put myself
> On you, that are my country: and this pelf,
> Which I have got, if you do quit me, rests
> To feast you often, and invite new guests. (159–65)

The only remaining quasi-contractual agreement at the end of the play is that between the player and the audience of Londoners whom he considers "my country." The pelf that Face (or more properly now, "Face") has got is not Lovewit's winnings in the play's fiction, but the price of admission to the playhouse. One can easily imagine the player jangling the evening's receipts as he delivers these final lines, lines that serve as a reminder of our open invitation to return, gulls that we are, to pay to believe the theatrical lies on offer at the house in the 'Friars.

That house, whether it signifies more prominently Jonson's theater or Face's at any given time during our experience of the play, is necessarily entangled with the broader spatial practices of London. The play's argument presents us with a paradox of sorts. Subtle and Dol, the "cheater and his punk," when they are brought low, make the move from placeless, mobile inhabitants of London to place-dependent tricksters of a very particular sort. They move, that is, from an unbounded spatial practice in the suburban liberties to a place within the walls both of the city and of a specific house. The argument describes this move in terms that may seem backward: they "leav[e] their narrow practice" and "become / Cozeners at large" (5–6). This seeming paradox reflects a dynamic of the larger play, however, for if the plot of *The Alchemist*—with its uniquely strict adherence to the unities of place, time, and action, its setting in a single house, and its dependence on the absolute control of entrances and exits—seems to employ an obsessively narrow spatial focus, it is nevertheless dependent on the permeability of the household walls and on the interaction between private and public.

As Jonathan Haynes points out, this is only a surface level paradox. In *The Alchemist*, Jonson is still invested in demonstrating the social volatility of the theatrical and "fashionable demi-monde" of places like Paul's Walk, brothels, and ordinaries; the house itself having become a convenient microcosm of the public space of London.[34] There is a sense, moreover, in which the spatial practices of the apparent confinement of Lovewit's house are indeed more "at large" than the "narrow practice" of Subtle and Dol before they strike their deal with Face. Theatrical spaces like the Blackfriars playhouse, and like Lovewit's house in the hands of the rogues, have a broader spatial potential than actual, already-defined urban place. Jonson uses this paradox throughout *The Alchemist* to foreground the privileged nature of dramatic space and the consequently privileged position of those who can turn that dramatic space to their purposes. This play refrains almost entirely from the sort of ostentatious display of the transformative power of stage space that Jonson and his collaborators displayed in *Eastward Ho*. Indeed, *The Alchemist* goes to the opposite dramaturgical extreme; its only settings are the room just inside Lovewit's front door and the street just in front of that door. Rather than merely demonstrating that transformative power, as *Eastward Ho* did, *The Alchemist* takes a step back and stages it. Through its sparseness of setting, the play manages an extended examination of the power of dramatic space over the urban spaces and places that surround it.

This power is not confined to the interior of Lovewit's house. Mammon's fantasy of crossing to the Indies when he steps into the house seems familiar enough to a theatrical audience accustomed to a stage's significance being determined by the spatial practice of playwrights and players. That the house should also, from the perspective of outsiders, have transformative power over London place, is a bolder statement, but when Lovewit returns to his house, he finds that the activities within the house have made their neighborhood "Another Pimlico!" (5.1.6), a "second Hogsden" (5.2.19), making, that is, the Blackfriars into a place of suburban riot and holidaymaking, or turning the world into the madhouse of Bedlam or St. Katherine's (5.3.54–55). The house in the 'Friars allows Jonson to make the claim that the dramatic spatial practices of the theater can affect not only the potential worlds inside the playhouse, but also the urban world outside it.

The house—playhouse or alchemist's laboratory—is a special case, occupying the threshold between these two worlds, and capable of transforming either. In this way it is like Jonson's neighborhood itself. The Blackfriars, even after its very recent transfer into the city's jurisdiction, maintained its symbolically liminal associations. This is a point elided by Cheryl Lynn Ross's influential 1988 treatment of the play. Her essay, equating Subtle with the "sickness hot" and demonstrating similarities between his punishment and London's quarantine practices, correctly recognizes the play's emphasis on the interior and exterior, claiming that Subtle, as "the social equivalent of putrefaction and plague," invades the city walls and Lovewit's home.[35] Ross's conclusion, in the sort of Foucauldian gesture that characterized much of the new historicism, is that the institutionally authoritative internal, represented by Lovewit, contains, colonizes, and appropriates the subversive practices of the external, that London uses Subtle's dangerous marginality to define itself as civilized.[36] This binary of subversion and containment, however, necessarily ignores the liminal associations that the liberty of the Blackfriars retained, the ambiguity of being both inside and outside the city. Anthony Ouellette's argument, that *The Alchemist*, the first play performed by the King's Men at the Blackfriars, constitutes the declaration of the company's superiority as the first professional troupe allowed to play within London, nevertheless foregrounds the fact that the transitionally liminal nature of the Blackfriars district at the time of *The Alchemist*, two years after the change in jurisdiction, was still a prominent context in the minds of the King's Men and their new neighbors.[37]

Jonson explicitly foregrounds this ambiguous question of the Blackfriars's liberty status, the blurry boundaries of the play's spaces and the attendant contestation of authority over them, in Subtle's panicked accusation of Face when they hear of Lovewit's return:

> SUBTLE   You said he would not come,
>   While there died one a week, within the liberties.
> FACE
>   No: 'twas within the walls.
> SUBTLE   Was't so? Cry you mercy:
>   I thought the liberties. (4.7.115–18)

Lovewit will only return when the plague has ended in the city proper, though Subtle is not unreasonable in assuming that he would take the more cautious course of waiting until it had disappeared from the outlying liberties. Lovewit's conditions for returning, moreover, as absurdly restrictive as they may be—bills of weekly plague deaths rarely reached zero, even in periods between major visitations—are also the conditions for the return of playing companies to houses of their own that closed, as they had in most of 1610, by reason of the sickness. This short argument between the rogues is resolved quickly enough, but it serves as a reminder both of the dual nature of the Blackfriars, the liberty within the walls, and its significance as a place and space of theater.

I would contend that *The Alchemist's* spatial focus on walls, doors, and boundaries is less an echo of city-wide plague-time prophylaxis, as Ross would have it, than it is another Jonsonian demonstration of the space of the author. Subtle's powers are imagined by Abel Drugger, the "young beginner . . . building / Of a new shop" (1.3.7–8), to include a sort of magical *feng shui*:

> I would know, by art, sir, of your worship,
> Which way I should make my door, by necromancy.
> And, where my shelves. And, which should be for boxes.
> And, which for pots. (10–14)

Drugger is, of course, more right than he knows; Subtle's art not only includes, but consists almost entirely of the kind of authorial spatial manipulation that makes up so much of Jonson's own dramatic art. More even than *Epicoene*, *The Alchemist* is the sort of farce that depends on the playwright and the characters alike exerting a tight control over *lieu*, the place where the gulling takes place, and over *espace*, the ways in which other characters practice, inhabit, and imagine the place.

To an even greater extent than in *Epicoene*, a main focus of *The Alchemist* is on doors; the play's action depends on the working, material doors on the stage, but a door is also the central icon of the play's setting. "On Jonson's comic stage," as Christensen points out, "the door is less a passageway to someplace than it is a vital locus in its own right,"[38] and it is nowhere more apparent than in this play. If, as has often been noted, *The Alchemist* adheres more tightly to the unity of place than any other Jonsonian comedy, the central locus that underpins this unity is not so much a room as a door, Lovewit's front door, on both sides of which—inside the house and outside in the street—action occurs. The onstage door (the central door or "discovery space"?) serves as a fulcrum for the only scene changes in the play. In the remarkable shift from the first, exterior scene of act three to the second, interior scene, it actually changes significance, during Subtle's welcoming dialogue, from a door in to the house to a door out to the street, as Ananias and Tribulation somehow manage to enter and exit simultaneously while staying onstage. Lovewit's front door emblematizes the main tool of the rogues' (and Jonson's) virtuosity at controlling private space.

Doors and their control are crucial to the plot, for keeping the elements separate, keeping the gulls away from each other, timing their entrances and exits to the exact moment. The rogues' actions consists of such expedients as peeking through windows (2.4.20); speaking through keyholes or speaking tubes, as Dol does to the "bawd of Lambeth . . . in a voice . . . like one of your familiars" (1.4.3–5); leading Dapper out "by the back way" (1.2.163) and later stashing him blindfolded in the privy (3.5.78); keeping Ananias and Tribulation waiting at the door, thus satirically deflating their sense of martyrdom over the "rebukes" that "we of the Separation must bear" (3.1.2); and manipulating Dol's—at first apparently accidental—entrance to lure Mammon into further lust-induced gullery (2.3.210). The rogues constantly play, as does all good theater, on the promise of what can be imagined just offstage, addressing non-existent suitors just beyond the doors for Drugger's benefit (1.3.1–2) and maintaining the imaginative focus of all the gulls on Subtle's non-existent laboratory.

The Blackfriars' stage serves, in its representation of the main room in Lovewit's house, as the rogues' stage, but that main stage serves as their tiring house at the same time, since we see them preparing, getting into costume, consciously changing their vocal patterns, making noises "off" and speeches that, from the perspective of their onstage audiences, come from "within." The struggle for control of the entrances and doors is exerted from both sides of those doors, and it threatens to collapse the distinction between onstage and offstage space. We, the audience, alternate between a privileged backstage view of the rogues' theater, and the perspective of the gulls themselves, and this alternation serves both as a reminder of our own theatrical situation—almost a Brechtian alienation effect—and as an emphatic assertion of the mutable, transformative power of theatrical space.

The gulls, of course, are unaware of the theatrical nature of the house's magic. As Martin points out, the gulls are analogous to a bad playhouse audience, as unaware of the conventions of theatrical illusion as the Citizen and his wife in *The Knight of the Burning Pestle*, only more dangerously so: "[t]he rogues' customers frequent the house in the Blackfriars precisely because they do not think its magic to be illusion."[39] Like George the Grocer's, though, their incorrect responses remind us of our own awareness of theatrical illusion, even as we succumb to its power.

When Sir Epicure Mammon arrives at Lovewit's house, he expounds upon the magic to be produced and procured therein specifically in terms of this transformative space. He imagines the house—which promises to provide him that very day with the Philosopher's Stone—as the Americas, in a speech in which we may hear, along with satire on Mammon's greed, an acknowledgment of the spatial practices of theater:

> Come on, sir. Now, you set your foot on shore
> In *novo orbe*; here's the rich Peru:

And there within, sir, are the golden mines,
Great Solomon's Ophir! He was sailing to't,
Three years, but we have reached it in ten months. (2.1.1–5)

This sort of utterance reminds us of the conventional place-making function of characters' speeches on the non-representational Jacobean stage. Mammon's "here's the rich Peru" seems an echo of Rosalind's "this is the Forest of Arden" (*As You Like It* 2.4.15). For Mammon, of course, it is only metaphor; he knows, after all, that he is in a London house and not in America, but his speech reminds us of the power of this space's illusions. The fact that this house is not the rich Peru merely highlights the fact that theatrical space does usually work in this way, and although Mammon is the butt of ridicule, his enthusiastic response to the alchemist's playhouse foregrounds this transformative aspect of theatrical space.

What this magic house promises Mammon is the ability to extend this transformative quality into the real world via the Philosopher's Stone. His is a fantasy of transforming not just himself and his station, but the places and spatial practices of the world around him. He will "purchase Devonshire and Cornwall," he imagines, and "make them perfect Indies" (2.1.35–36). His fantasy of medicinal philanthropy, as described by Subtle, has him bravely pacing the streets in time of plague, throwing open doors, and healing not so much sick people as places with the associations of disease: "Methinks, I see him, entering ordinaries, / Dispensing for the pox; and plaguey-houses, / Reaching his dose; walking Moorfields for lepers" (1.4.18–20).[40] Mammon sees himself making London's plague-time quarantine practices obsolete—he will "fright the plague / Out o' the kingdom, in three months" (2.1.69–70)—and declares to Face that he will appropriate the traditional role of the civic government not just in dispensing medicine but in the kinds of philanthropy documented by the monuments to great men's charity in Stow's *Survey of London*, the kind of permanent imprint of virtue and fame onto the fabric of the city that *Eastward Ho*'s Touchstone imagines for his good apprentice Golding:

I shall employ it all, in pious uses,
Founding of colleges, and grammar schools,
Marrying young virgins, building hospitals,
And now, and then, a church. (2.3.49–52)

Mammon's dreams are an absurd parody of the ideal monumental construction of place celebrated by John Stow, as Surly's joke about a conduit running medicine attests (2.1.76), and his pretense of high-mindedness, a front for his more epicurean motives, is quickly abandoned. The fact, however, that his purchase of the alchemist's magic is imagined in terms of acquiring the power to define the spaces and places of the city puts him in a competition with Jonson's own assertion of theatrical power over place. That this competition is particular and personal is indicated by another of Surly's jokes. If Mammon can end the plague for good, Surly says, "the players shall sing your praises, then, / Without their poets" (2.1.71–72). Mammon, that is, will not merely replace the city fathers and their control over the places and practices of London; he will also replace the Ben Jonsons of the world in their capacity for supplying matter for the drama.

Mammon's imagined usurpation of the dramatic poet's job is only one of several contests of dramatic authority in *The Alchemist*. Like *Epicoene*, the play stages several competitions of theatrical prowess. Subtle and Face set up the day's action in the first scene with a gentleman's agreement to "prove, who shall shark best" (1.1.159), and in his abortive attempt to rescue Dame Pliant and expose the rogues, Surly enters the fray, playing the role of the Spanish Count and temporarily duping the dupers. As was the case with *Epicoene*, however, but if anything more explicitly here, the main theatrical competition in *The Alchemist* is between Jonson and his characters.

The most forceful recent articulation of this point comes from Mathew Martin, who argues that the larger opposition in the play is between types of theatrical practices, that Jonson performs an interrogation of theater through which he insists on "the distinction between the dangerous delusiveness of plague-time and plague-like theater and his own true, essential theater."[41] In the rogues' amalgam of "the dramatic styles and genres against which Jonson inveighs throughout the prefaces and dedications to his plays," the playwright creates a caricature to act as a foil to his own theatrical practices.[42] Martin's reading of Jonson is not anti-theatrical; he does not suggest an opposition between theater and "truth," only to more (Jonsonian) theater. For Martin, the upshot of this opposition is a kind of epistemological nihilism:

> Jonson offers no eternal, stable vantage point from which illusory existence might be distinguished from a higher reality, only equally illusory and groundless epistemologies competing in the theatrical marketplace. (407–8)

Instead of this groundlessness, I find in *The Alchemist*'s opposition of theatrical practices an assertion of authorial identity. What Jonson stages is not so much a morally determined competition between types of theater as it is a contest of dramatic virtuosity played out through the practices of theatrical space.

From the outset of the play this competition is clear. The explosive argument between Subtle and Face underscores the particular contributions of each to the "venture tripartite," and how necessary each is to the rogues' "republic" (1.1.110). When Face claims that "the place has made [Subtle] valiant," and Subtle responds that "No," his valor comes instead from Face's "clothes" (1.1.63), we see that Jonson has concisely divided the two aspects of the spatial practice of the dramatic author between the two: in de Certeau's terms, Face is associated with *lieu* and Subtle with *espace*. Before encountering Face, Subtle was placeless and unfixed, haunting the suburbs, dressed in rags and feeding only on the steam from cook's stalls in Smithfield's Pie-Corner (25–26). For all Subtle's knowledge of alchemy, astrology, and algebra, and for all his performative skills, he is powerless without Face's contribution, "A house to practise in" (47). Conversely, before taking Subtle in, Face was merely the caretaker of an abandoned building, his activities confined to "Sell[ing] dole-beer to aqua-vitae-men" and "convers[ing] with cobwebs" (53, 57). Subtle has given Face his role, alchemically "translated" him into a "suburb-Captain" (19), given him "[his] oaths, [his] quarreling dimensions . . . rules, to cheat at horse-race, cock-pit, cards, / Dice, or whatever gallant tincture else" (74–76). The author's spatial role in the rogues' theater, that is, is split. Face, providing the stage, defines place, and Subtle provides the script, the spatial practice.

This division of *lieu* and *espace* continues through the play, and ultimately proves fatal for the con artists' theater. Indeed, Jonson establishes this division in order to foreshadow his own final victory, and structures the play as a series of assertions of authority over the theatrical space and practices of Lovewit's house, each superceding the previous one. Subtle's strength is theatrical *espace*, the ability to create roles, not just for himself, but for his co-conspirators— Jeremy's translation from butler to Captain, Dol's Fairy Queen—and his gulls—Kastril's training as a roaring boy, Dapper's "hum" and "buz" (1.2.169–70). He even perceives himself as a shaper of others' practice of urban space: he promises to "hurry [Dame Pliant] through London, to th' Exchange, / Bedlam, the China-houses" (4.4.47–48), to teach her, that is, to make the city her stage and place of self-display, where "citizens [will] gape at her, and praise her tires" (49). For all Subtle's authoritative demeanor, however—the role of "Sovereign" of the rogues to Face's "General" (1.1.5)—he lives in fear of Face "overlook[ing him] like a tyrant" (4.3.19).

As it happens, Subtle's fear of Face is well founded. By the end of the play, with Lovewit's return, Face has proven himself to be a match for Subtle's manipulation of the characters' various spatial practices, able to give his widowed master Lovewit the costume and training required to win the prize of Dame Pliant's hand. Moreover, Face's control over the *place* of Lovewit's house trumps Subtle's authority. The role as housekeeper for which Subtle scorned Face at the beginning of the play eventually gives Face the power to heave Subtle and Dol unceremoniously over the back wall, taking away their "house to practise in" and ultimately expelling them from London entirely.

At the same moment that Face becomes a master of theatrical space and place, however, he has to submit himself to the reinscribed meaning of the place that has now become Lovewit's house again. In a line that anchors the play's resolution, Lovewit declares his legal and proprietorial claim to the place, banishing the rogues' theatrical control over the spaces of his house in almost ritualistic fashion: "The house is mine here, and the doors are open" (5.5.26). As Jonathan Haynes puts it, "as [Face] was to Subtle, Lovewit is to him: Lovewit's possession of the house is absolute, and allows him to subsume the wit which has provided such a handsome return on his investment."[43]

But is Lovewit's final triumph really as absolute as Haynes suggests? Considered carefully, his apparent ascendancy is somewhat troublesome. After all, his victory and his acquisition of Dame Pliant is absurdly sudden, and ensured by his willingness to don costumes (5.3.87), to play the roles of Spanish Count and roaring boy, to submit, in fact, to the theatrical control of his butler: "I will be ruled by thee in anything, Jeremy" (5.5.143). Critics have sometimes seen this submission as a reassertion of Face's power. Wayne Rebhorn, for example, argues that while Lovewit imagines himself to have outdone and replaced the rogues, he instead "has made himself into nothing less than Face's final dupe."[44] I believe, however, that we can look beyond the specific character of Face to a more general assertion of theatrical power, inverting the play's ostensible skepticism about theater—an inversion represented, perhaps, by the defeat of the arch-skeptic Surly—and celebrating what Martin calls the emergence of illusion as an "ineradicable constituent of reality."[45] Face, after all, has submitted as much as Lovewit has; the impromptu arrangement he strikes with Lovewit constitutes another theatrical "venture," with Lovewit this time controlling the place of the house and Face/Jeremy in charge of the theatrical spatial practices therein.

The Alchemist does not indiscriminately celebrate any and all theatrical illusion, however, but specifically Jonson and his authorial control. The dramaturgical virtuosity on display in the play demonstrates that unlike Face and Subtle, whose division of place and space between them leads to conflict and the destruction of their theatrical enterprise, Jonson can control both at once. Moreover, Jonson, more subtle than Subtle, inserts himself and his own poetic and dramatic prowess into the play. For example, when Mammon—who, we recall, was imagined to supplant dramatic poets, dreams of employing a poet himself, it is "[t]he same that writ so subtly of the fart" (2.2.63), a possible reference to Jonson's "On the Famous Voyage" (see chapter one). A more explicit instance of the playwright appearing in his own work is the crucial matter of the "Spanish suit," the costume that becomes itself a sort of sartorial Philosopher's Stone for winning its wearer a lucrative marriage to Dame Pliant. The first Spanish suit in the play is Surly's, which, Face implies, he acquired from one of London's many used clothing brokers (4.7.66), but the second is explicitly acquired from the theater: Face instructs Drugger to borrow, upon his "credit with the players" (68), "Hieronymo's old cloak, hat and ruff" (4.7.71). Face insists, that is, on the costume from Kyd's *Spanish Tragedy*, that most popular of Elizabethan plays, a costume owned by the same company that performed *The Alchemist* nearly twenty years later, and perhaps the very same costume worn by Ben Jonson in a role he is known to have taken himself.[46] The costume, therefore, becomes a metonym for Jonson himself, a reminder and a symbol of his own theatrical practices, and its continued presence on the stage enters him into the play's theatrical competition. As a material focus of the conflict between Subtle and Face over Dame Pliant, moreover, the costume stands for the destruction of the "venture tripartite." An onstage relic of Jonson's own theatrical experience and skill defeats the theatrical practices of his characters and ensures his own victory.

It is not, after all, Face who delivers that epilogue that highlights theater's power over its audiences and their spatial practices. It is the *player* of Face, whose part has fallen a little as the parts of epilogue speakers conventionally do. It is Jonson's authority, not Face's, that resonates in the play's final reminder that that playhouse has taken its audience's "pelf" and invites us gulls to come back any time.

Jonson's plague year plays represent a transition in the playwright's career with regard to the potential of dramatic space for his assertions of authority. Although Jonson's insertions of himself and the exercise of his own dramatic authority are subtle in these plays, the implicit competitions that he stages between himself and the would-be playwright figures in *Epicoene* and *The Alchemist* serve to hint at, if not directly to represent, the figure of the ideal dramatic author. As regards Jonson's illustration of the power of dramatic art and his championing of both that ideal author figure and its necessary corollary, the ideal audience, the plays of 1609–10 mark a crucial step towards Jonson's fullest achievement, which he would realize four years later. Despite its omission from Jonson's 1616 Folio, with its strategy of textual monumentalization, *Bartholomew Fair* (1614), the subject of the next chapter, constitutes Jonson's most vigorous demonstration of authorial space.

Chapter Five
"Practisers of their madnesse"
Bartholomew Fair and the Space of the Author

The authorial strategy I have been tracing through Jonson's career need not be seen as antithetical to the strategy of textual monumentalization that the 1616 Folio enacts. True, the Folio removes Jonson's plays from the immediacy of physical space, where audience censure and bad performance can damage them, into the space of the book. But if *Epicoene*, *The Alchemist*, and the revised *Every Man In* had positioned their author as a privileged interpreter of London space and theatricality as a potent shaper of the urban environment, this sense is not lost from the plays in their Folio publication. Rather, with the 1616 collection, Jonson could doubly assert his control by making his own poetic performance the plays' only expression.

One of Jonson's most vibrant and effective city comedies, *Bartholomew Fair* (1614), was not published in the Folio, however, and its omission is puzzling. As a play in which Jonson exerts supreme dramaturgical prowess, in which he inserts himself and his authorial practices more explicitly than in any previous play, *Bartholomew Fair* certainly seems as though it would fit Jonson's authorial project marvelously. The play was dedicated to King James himself and performed at court only a day after it opened at the Hope theater.[1] It would thus seem appropriate as the crowning achievement in Jonson's use of his drama to construct himself as a laureate, with the royal seal of approval serving as a climax to the crescendo of status of the other plays' Folio dedications to the universities, the Inns of Court, and aristocratic patrons. Why, then, is *Bartholomew Fair* missing from the Folio?

In answer to this question, most critics have cited the play's obvious differences in tone and technique from earlier Jonsonian comedy. It is seen as his last great play, but also as something of an experiment. K. Venkata Reddy cites these differences as the reasons for the play's deliberate omission, and is exemplary in her summation of them and in the implicit critical assumptions about Jonson's temperament:

> It is clear that Jonson, in the four years since *The Alchemist* (1610), had
> begun to move into a new comic world wherein he was prone to give
> more concession to popular taste than he did before. He creates in *Bar-*
> *tholomew Fair* a world into which he infuses more of sympathy, toler-
> ance and humanity than it is usually acknowledged he ever possessed.[2]

George Rowe follows Thomas Cartelli and Jonas Barish in pointing out
that *Bartholomew Fair* is essentially an attempt at Shakespearean romance
in theme and structure, despite the artful realism of its London setting, and
despite Jonson's explicit opposition of his play to Shakespeare's late offerings of "Tales, Tempests, and such like drolleries" (Induction 125).[3] Rowe
argues, however, that the play's apparently puzzling "affirmation of everything Jonson had spent much of his life opposing"—its romantic structure of
departure and return, its breakdown of social distinction and celebration of
communal folly—is actually an ironic and parodic *reductio ad absurdam* of
Shakespearean romance rather than the tribute that Cartelli sees. To Rowe
the play seems good humored and genial, but "its geniality is a function not
of acceptance but of disillusionment."[4] It seems to follow from Rowe's argument that *Bartholomew Fair*, "more the result of frustration over [Jonson's
failed tragedy] *Catiline* than a sign of a change in attitude," is too occasional
to fit into the Folio's project of career construction, a one-off parody whose
claim for Jonson's superiority and difference is too subtle, and ultimately
undermined by Jonson's parodic technique. The parody, Rowe suggests, is
in danger of lending authority to the target, of its audience missing the irony
and simply enjoying it as an example of the popular Shakespearean romance
it set out to debunk.[5]

I agree with Rowe that Jonson's strategy in *Bartholomew Fair* is at
odds with his strategy in the Folio, but the reasons for its omission from
Jonson's *Workes* are not as localized as Rowe's argument about Shakespearean parody would admit. I would contend that the play is not born simply
of the frustration of the post-*Catiline* moment. With *Bartholomew Fair*,
Jonson is no less concerned with the assertion of his authority as an author
than he is in the Folio project, but he is asserting it in a different arena,
with the parallel strategy that by 1616 he had come to recognize to be as
valid as, if not compatible with, the Folio's textual self-enshrinement. The
Folio performs a version of authority that seems to require Jonson to realize
his oft-cited wish to "leave the loathèd stage."[6] His book constructs Jonson
not primarily as a playwright, but as a *poet* attempting to control the meaning and the reception of the text on the page. Jonson's strategy of distancing himself from the stage, and the much discussed anti-theatrical pose it

requires, however, is paradoxically just that, a pose, one role of many that Jonson adopted. Jonson was a playwright and sometime actor, after all, and regardless of his critical stance toward the practices of his contemporary playmakers, the playhouse was Jonson's territory, and he was more than capable of using theater's own terms to assert his authority. Because the Folio was such a well-constructed and lasting cultural artifact, intended as a distillation of Jonson's poetic career, its distancing strategy is the most visible expression of Jonson's authority, but it was only one part of his authorial self-construction.

Bartholomew Fair allowed Jonson to articulate his ideal of authorship, and indeed of selfhood, not through the textualizing strategies of the Folio, but through an exploration of the authorial processes involved in producing theatrical space. Where the Folio textualizes and reifies Jonson's authority, *Bartholomew Fair* stages it. It depends, more than any other play in Jonson's canon, on the space of the playhouse, on the power of theater to control urban space, to establish Jonson as the privileged interpreter of London. In *Bartholomew Fair* he does not "leave the loathèd stage," but pursues with no little enthusiasm another strategy to control the meaning of his cultural product, a strategy that is bound up entirely in the space of the playhouse itself. In the play he exerts his authorial control over a general and varied *audience*, not just an exclusive readership, and the tactics that he employs in it involve and require his engagement with, and physical presence in, the space of the playhouse: stage, tiring house, and galleries alike.

Bartholomew Fair is the culmination and fullest expression of Jonson's career-long concern with space and place. Not only does it refer more frequently to specific locales than any other Jonsonian comedy—in the first act alone, before Jonson moves the action to Smithfield, he mentions particular local spots thirty times—but it also concerns itself with place as a concept, with recurrent quibbles on different meanings of the word: place as location, place as office, place as rank in social hierarchy. Indeed, the word *place* in all its forms and senses occurs forty-seven times in the play, more than any of the comedies in the Folio and more than twice as many as any Jonsonian play explicitly set in London.[7] Additionally, *Bartholomew Fair* pushes to its extreme city comedy's conceit of bringing London into the playhouse. For the majority of the play, Jonson's adherence to the unities of place and time, confining the action to one point in Smithfield on 24 August, St. Bartholomew's Day, establishes a one-to-one substitution of place for place. One spot of London, the Hope playhouse, is in effect donning the costume of another spot, a part of Smithfield adjacent to the market in the cloister of Christ Church. The play's Induction makes this bold substitution explicit, asking the audience to believe that the play *is* the Fair, and defending the play's slight strain on credulity by pointing out the olfactory verisimilitude of a bear-baiting arena playing the role of a horse market: "the place being as dirty as Smithfield, and stinking every whit" (Induction 151–54). In this most localized of comedies, where the playhouse becomes the world outside, Jonson breaks down the distinction between audience and actor, between the observation of the play and the inhabitation of the city, and he draws an analogy between the activities of the playhouse and the interpretation of the urban environment.

This is all the more important because for *Bartholomew Fair*, to an even greater degree than Jonson's other city comedies—even *Every Man in His Humor* where, as we have seen, the pseudo-psychology of humors is linked to spatial practice—place is intrinsic to identity and selfhood. The *dramatis personae* list pairs character to place of origin: Cokes is an "esquire of Harrow;" Knockem a "ranger o' Turnbull," i.e. a gamekeeper of Turnbull Street, notorious for prostitutes; Busy is a "Banbury man," synonymous with hypocritical Puritan. Other characters are linked to place by their speech; like Shakespeare's four captains in *Henry V*, Whit's Irish brogue, Puppy's West Country twang, and Northern's burr (like his name) mark them as representatives of their respective places. We hear of "the pretty wits of Paul's," the "cunning men of Cow-lane," and the "man of Moorfields," all of whose places serve as sufficient metonym for their function. Littlewit praises his wife's dress in terms that equate her body with specific places: he challenges all London's regions of fashionable consumption—Cheapside, Pimlico, Moorfields, the Exchange—to compete with her for appearance and habit (1.2.5–7), and her function in the play as object of desire and subject of capitalist "longing" makes his comparison apt.

The chief place that reflects its inhabitants' character is, of course, the Fair itself. When the characters of the play take on the roles of audience at the Fair, they illustrate the proper and improper responses of judgment available to the playhouse audience. Just as *Epicoene* and *The Alchemist* stage competitions between the playwright and his characters over interior theatrical spaces, *Bartholomew Fair* becomes an explicit contest of urban literacy, of how to read the city, and it is another contest that Jonson is guaranteed to win. The successful contestants are those characters in the play, and by the Induction's extension, the observers in the audience, who, like Jonson himself, have achieved the theatrical and authorial ability to reshape the urban environment to their own ends, to exceed the passivity of the ignorant spectator. The destined losers of the contest are all such ignorant spectators. Three characters in particular—Bartholomew Cokes, Zeal-of-the-land Busy, and Justice Adam Overdo, the descendants of Jonson's humors characters from Kitely to Morose—provide different versions of the faulty audience, and we are invited to judge them by their inability to judge the spectacles of the Fair correctly, by the degrees to which they are incapable of reading (and rewriting) the urban text.

This faulty audience judgment is perhaps best illustrated by Cokes, the foolish "esquire of Harrow," an obvious ass so little concerned with proper literacy that he only desires to look at his own marriage license to "see the length and breadth on't" (1.5.35). He is the very embodiment of a poorly judging audience, a passive sponge who thoughtlessly consumes and spits up everything he takes in. This spongelike nature is particularly dangerous when applied to his experience of the city. As his begrudging servant and self-appointed protector, the garrulous Wasp, complains,

> I dare not let him walk alone, for fear of learning of vile tunes, which he will sing at supper and in the sermon-times! If he meet but a carman i' the street, and I find him not talk to keep him off on him, he will whistle him and all his tunes over at night in his sleep! (1.4.73–78)

Cokes's illiteracy and his lack of judgment are strikingly represented by his inept mastery of London's places. He has, as Wasp disgustedly recounts, "walked London to shew the city to the gentlewoman he shall marry" (1.4.103–4), but his survey of London, unlike John Stow's, subjects the surveyor entirely to the mercy of place, so far as to rob him not only of any potential authorial agency, but of all intelligent discourse. "He would," Wasp continues,

> name you all the signs over, as he went, aloud; and where he spied a parrot or a monkey, there he was pitched with all the little long-coats about him, male and female. No getting him away! (108–12)

Cokes's incapacity to converse beyond reading street signs aloud is analogous to his incapacity to move physically beyond street novelties. Jonson presents his lack of judgment in terms of his spatial practice. Cokes's Christian name, Bartholomew, associates him with the eponymous Fair, and he proudly claims the Fair as his representative place, but his absolute subjection to the power of place ensures that the only aspects of the Fair he represents are its foolishness and excess.

The Puritan Zeal-of-the-Land Busy is the opposite extreme to Cokes, but he serves as another target of the same satire on bad audience judgment.

He admonishes his companions, with biblical echoes, to "walk on in the middle way, fore-right; turn neither to the right hand nor to the left. Let not your eyes be drawn aside with vanity, nor your ear with noises" (3.2.25–27). If Cokes is a willing and undiscerning sponge for the insipid novelty of every ballad, motion, and monkey, Busy is equally incapable of right judgment because of his refusal to interact with or even look at the Fair for fear of corruption. Nor can his refusal be attributed merely to principle. A consummate hypocrite, he is perfectly able, after a nominal resistance, to justify his eating Ursla's unclean pigs and becoming a beholder of Leatherhead's idolatrous puppet show. Busy's approach to the sights of the Fair is prophylactic pre-judgment, as Dame Purecraft approvingly notes: "so you hate 'em, as our brother Zeal does, you may look on 'em" (3.6.61–62).

As with Cokes, Jonson presents Busy's example of incorrect audience judgment in spatial terms. Busy's ludicrous Christian name, "Zeal-of-the-Land," explicitly ties his mental and spiritual limitations—his zealous humor—to place. "The Land" whose zeal he embodies is purposefully ambiguous, but whether it is meant to be Banbury, London, England, or some imagined Israel or New Jerusalem is irrelevant; he carries his zeal with him and uses it to color his interaction with every place he inhabits. This is illustrated in the argument with which he convinces himself that attendance at the Fair is morally permissible. Although at first he condemns the Fair in Old Testament terms as "no better than one of the high places" (1.6.51–52)—akin, that is, to the mountaintops where sinful Israelites practiced idolatrous worship—he concedes that the moral question is "[s]ubject to construction" (62) and ultimately resolves that "[t]he place is not much, not very much; we may be religious in the midst of the profane" (66–67). The logic is spurious, of course; Busy is hypocritically justifying his own desire to see the Fair on the grounds that his pregnant would-be daughter-in-law has a longing for pig. The passage, however, elucidates the issue at the heart of the play: the question of whether the will can have power over place. Busy falsely claims the ability to preserve the moral distance between himself and the Fair, and as a result he becomes its passive subject: the contradiction of his zealous condemnation of the place and his barely controlled desires lands him first in the stocks, and then, no less ridiculously, in the audience of Leatherhead's puppet show, as ignorant and spongelike an observer as Cokes.

The third character in the triad of faulty readers of the Fair is the Justice, Adam Overdo. He intends to spend the day under cover, disguised as the ranting lunatic "Mad Arthur of Bradley" and noting down the enormities of the Fair in his black book. Descending from the "high place" of his judicial office, he has apparently taken his cue from disguised dukes like Shakespeare's Vincentio and Marston's Altofront, or from the example of King James's attempted 1604 incognito visit to the Royal Exchange, to observe the iniquity of his underlings without the potentially corrupt mediation of an intelligencer.[8] This is his judicial and disciplinary ideal, to "see and not be seen" (2.1.45), a political twist on the play's central question of audience judgment, and to justify it Overdo claims the authority of history: "thus hath the wise magistrate done in all ages" (2.1.10). Overdo, however, is no wise magistrate; he falls short as a justice, and metatheatrically he fails both as audience and as player. The irony, of course, is that he *is* seen, both by the audience at the Hope—he is the play's only consistent soliloquizer— and by an onstage observer, as Quarlous eventually pierces his disguise. He utterly fails in his surveillance as well, first by mistaking the cutpurse Edgeworth as a virtuous youth in danger of being corrupted by the vice, not of larceny, but of the "terrible taint, poetry" (3.5.5), and then by accidentally abetting the picking of Cokes's pockets. He foolishly maintains his useless disguise through beatings and arrest, and fails to recognize his own wife's near conversion into a prostitute.

Overdo's failure as a detective, as a discoverer of enormities, is rendered more ironic by his repeated claims to associate enormity with place. The "black book" that he carries recalls the genre of rogue pamphlets that sought to catalogue rogues by the neighborhoods they inhabited, and the knowledge that he claims of London's bad neighborhoods echoes these pamphlets' moral warnings and their common slang names for disreputable areas: "Look into any angle o' the town—the Straits, or the Bermudas—where the quarreling lesson is read, and how do they entertain the time but with bottle ale and tobacco?" (2.4.70–72).[9] In practice, however, Overdo's pretended knowledge fails him. The Fair proves impenetrable to the magistrate's gaze, and the only thing he "discovers," in the end, is himself, removing his disguise in a fit of desperation to bring his tenuously held authority into the open. Far from being the unseen observer, the ideal disguised interpreter of the Fair's space that he intended, Overdo is reduced to impotence, an authority only in name, and in Quarlous's metaphor, not an interpreter of place, but a dumb, fixed marker of place: "Nay sir," Quarlous admonishes him, "stand not you fixed here, like a stake in Finsbury to be shot at, or the whipping post i' the Fair" (5.6.90–92). Anne Barton points out that by 1614, the disguised magistrate as an author figure and an agent of order was "a comic cliché." Barton suggests that Jonson "had for long avoided what he must have seen as an essentially romantic plot expedient," and uses Overdo to emphasize the play's lack of moral resolution.[10] I would go further, to suggest not only that Overdo fails as an author figure—a discoverer of enormities and restorer of order—but also that Jonson created him as a foil for his own presence in the play.

The presentation of the characters' lack of judgment in terms of spatial practice follows the particular logic of Jonsonian comedy, as we have seen from *Every Man In His Humor* onward. The analogy of the individual's mental capacity and his or her practice of space is nowhere made more explicit than in *Bartholomew Fair's* Induction, where it emerges that the one person in the play who truly has power over place is Jonson himself. If the play's characters are pitted against each other in an implicit contest of will over place, this contest has been foreshadowed in formal, indeed legal, terms by the Induction as a contest of wills between Jonson and his audience.

The Induction opens with a "Stage-keeper" begging the audience's patience for the delayed start of the play, but soon he advances his own traditional and lowbrow aesthetic agenda. Looking about furtively "lest the poet hear me . . . behind the arras" (7–8), the Stage-keeper confesses that the play is not so accurate to the festive experience of the real Bartholomew Fair, and complains that the bawdy, jig-making, and stage fighting that should be in such a play are missing in Jonson's: "But these master-poets, they will ha' their own absurd courses" (25–26).[11] The Stage-keeper is then interrupted and driven offstage by two surrogates for the author and representatives of textual authority: the Book-holder, responsible for ensuring the players' adherence to the script of the play Jonson wrote, and a Scrivener, who reads out a remarkable mock-legal contract, "drawn out in haste between our author and you" (58).

In these "Articles of Agreement" Jonson asserts his right to do more than rehearse traditional entertainments and bow to the whimsy of audience fashion; "no person here is to expect more than he knows" (110–11), the Scrivener reads, and though the Stage-keeper's wish for jugglers, apes, bawds, and sword-and-buckler men is disappointed, Jonson's contract promises entertainments as good. The Articles famously jibe at Shakespeare's contemporary output of "Tales, Tempests, and suchlike drolleries" (125), boasting that Jonson, unlike Shakespeare, is "loth to make Nature afraid in his plays" (124) merely to suit the preferences of the audience.

Further, the Articles constitute Jonson's dare to the audience to exercise the kind of correct judgment that the characters in the play fail at so woefully. The Scrivener insists upon individual exercise of wit, forbidding the audience to "censure by contagion, or upon trust, from another's voice or face that sits by him" (95–96). Jonson's articles also insist upon consistency of judgment, even ignorant judgment. Those who insist that such dated plays as *Titus Andronicus* and *The Spanish Tragedy* will never be surpassed are to be valued for the consistency of their opinion, if not their wisdom, for "[t]hough it be an ignorance, it is a virtuous and staid ignorance; and next to truth, a confirmed error does well. Such a one the author knows where to find him" (108).

One suspects that Jonson's equation of a staid though ignorant opinion with virtue is less than sincere, but this passage nevertheless reveals the ideal author-audience relationship that lies beneath the broad comedy of the Induction.[12] "Such a one the author knows where to find him": consistent ignorance makes an audience member as easy to control as one of Jonson's humors characters, precisely because it makes him locatable. The Articles of Agreement posit a hierarchy of wit and explicitly associate it with the audience's place in the playhouse. The Jonson figure imagined as hiding just behind the arras succeeds, where his Justice Overdo fails, at seeing but remaining unseen. For this author figure, knowing where to find each member of the audience, being able to place them according to the hierarchy of wit, is the ultimate expression of authority. The first of the Articles of Agreement binds the Hope audience to their physical places in the playhouse: the spectators, according to the contract, "do for themselves severally covenant and agree to remain in the places their money or their friends have put them in, with patience, for the space of two hours and a half, and somewhat more" (73–77).

Jonson thus reserves the right to mobility only for his play and its author. The remarkable scenic fluidity of *Bartholomew Fair*, with characters constantly moving in and out of the stage space, is to remain under the firm control of the author. While the characters in the fictional Fair have the choice to subject themselves to the power of the place or not, the audience is given no such opportunity. Jonson declares his control over the playhouse space and over the patrons' interpretive practice of it. Further, the equation of mental practices with spatial practices—so characteristic of Jonsonian comedy—is extended by the Induction's contract to the audience. Not only must they remain in their places in the playhouse, they are entitled to only so much censure of the play as their place—valued by the price of the seat—allows:

> It is further agreed that every person here have his or their free-will of censure, to like or dislike at their own charge; the author having now departed with his right, it shall be lawful for any man to judge his six penn'orth, his twelve penn'orth, so to his eighteen pence, two shillings, half a crown, to the value of his place—provided always his place get not above his wit. (82–88)

Jonson has "departed with his right" over the text; his play is out in the free market and open for censure, but with the Induction, he retains his right to control the audience. His Articles of Agreement express Jonson's ideal situation of control, not only over his own characters, but also over his audience and the playhouse they inhabit. By having the Stage-keeper establish that he, the master-poet, is just offstage behind an arras, keeping unseen surveillance over his audience and their judgments, Jonson retains the ultimate authority over his version of the Fair and its interpretation.

The play itself continues the Induction's association of judgment with fixity. As Richard Cave points out, the Fair draws a sharp distinction between static and fluid characters: the stall-keepers, who remain onstage for most of the central action, stand in contrast to the visitors, streaming in and out of the action as their desires, their senses, and the developing plot leads them. The "natives" of the Fair—the merchants, criers, pickpockets, bawds, and stall-keepers—are all portrayed as keen observers of humanity, where the objects of their observation (and the victims of their various scams and larcenies) are the visitors, whose fluidity and subjection to the (static and located) enticements of the Fair renders them incapable of judgment.[13] The ability to form correct judgments is therefore associated with *fixed* spectators, those who know their place, stay in it, and judge accordingly rather than being wrapped up in the action.

Jonson's association of stasis and detachment from the turbulent fluidity of life is not only his ideal for a theatrical audience; it is apparently a basis for virtue in all of life. In the *Discoveries*, he extends a common conceit of the *theatrum mundi*, the stage as a figure for human life, to a definition of human goodness in playhouse terms:

> *Good men* are the Stars, the Planets of the Ages wherein they live, and illustrate the times. . . . These ["good men," Abel, Enoch, Noah, and Abraham], sensuall men thought mad, because they would not be partakers, or practisers of their madnesse. But they, plac'd high on the top of all vertue, look'd downe on the Stage of the world, and contemned the Play of *Fortune*. For though the most be Players, some must be *Spectators*. (1100–1109)

Bartholomew Fair—both in the Induction and in the body of the play itself—makes this figure literally applicable to the audience at the Hope and the various spectators in the play by reversing the direction of the metaphor. If virtue in life is analogous to remaining a fixed spectator of the world among the stars and planets of the age, then remaining in place, as Jonson's

Induction enjoins, and staying detached from the madness of the Fair (or of *Bartholomew Fair*) would seem to be virtue.

Quarlous appears to be the character in the play who comes closest to inhabiting and interpreting the space of the Fair successfully; he "has the virtues," as Jonathan Haynes puts it, "that make one a master in this world."[14] Not taken in by the attractions of the place, he can establish enough distance from the object of his gaze not to be corrupted by it. His companion Winwife takes offense at being solicited by the Fair's merchants: "Do we look as if we would buy gingerbread? Or hobby-horses?" (2.5.12–13), but Quarlous counters that "our very being here makes us fit to be demanded, as well as others" (15–16). This is the magnanimity of a man who knows his role as the Fair's audience even as he recognizes the importance of maintaining a critical judgment. Quarlous, not Justice Overdo, is the character who correctly interprets and explains all the misunderstandings of the Fair, who discovers and resolves the confusions of the plot and brings the comedy to its conclusion.

Even though Quarlous comes out on top, however, his putative role as ideal critic and judge of the action would seem, in light of the *Discoveries*, to be compromised by his immediate immersion into the chaos of the Fair—donning a costume, speaking another man's lines, and placing his matrimonial fates into the arbitration of a madman's whim.[15] He certainly seems to bear no relation to Abel, Enoch, Noah, or Abraham, keeping aloof from his time like a distant planet; Quarlous does not scruple to become a "practiser of their madnesse." That phrase, indeed, could hardly be more apt, as Quarlous literally takes on the role, costume, and eccentricities of the madman Trouble-all.

The play, however, despite its insistence on its own audience keeping to their places, despite its apparent accordance with the *Discoveries'* ideal of detached spectatorship, does not judge Quarlous harshly for his involvement. Unlike the *Epicoene* gallants and the rogues of *The Alchemist*, Quarlous does not surrender his identity or compromise his virtue in exchange for the social potency that engagement in theatrical practices gains him. I would argue that this is because of his affinity to Jonson himself, and that Jonson exempts himself, as a superlative dramatic poet, a "laureate," from his own formulae of judgment and virtue. Quarlous is not only an ideal audience and critic; he is also apparently an ideal player and stage-manager, capable of using play, disguise, and theatricality to gain himself both a wife and an intellectual ascendancy over the rest of the characters. Quarlous is more suited than *Epicoene's* Truewit or *The Alchemist's* Subtle to stand for the creative aspect of theater and for the author himself.[16] He presents us

with a third way between the ostensible spectatorial ideal of good judgment—remaining detached and in *place*—and the failure of others like
Cokes, Busy, and Overdo to judge because their spatial practice is subjected
to and compromised by that of others.

From this third way, we can discern the expression of Jonson's ideal
of authorship, the mode of spatial practice that blends de Certeau's *lieu* and
espace. Quarlous, like Jonson, combines critic with playwright, writer with
reader, the production of space with the practical experience of it. He is not
only able to judge correctly as a spectator, but is able to reshape his world
by employing this dramatic, authorial mode of space. He retains his good
judgment even as he embroils himself in and takes control of the action. It
is a rare character in the Jonsonian canon who can perform this seemingly
contradictory feat, but it is Jonson's authorial ideal, the same balancing act
that he attempted to perform throughout his career.

Having given us a figure for himself in Quarlous, Jonson further
explores the dynamics of his own theater with a play-within-the-play and
a playmaker character to serve as another foil for the author. Littlewit is an
amateur dramatist as well as a proctor; he is the only main character who
must go to the Fair, having penned a puppet play to be performed there. We
are, of course, prepared by Littlewit's name to doubt any possible connec-
tions between him and Jonson, and the atrocious doggerel, vulgarity, and
barely contained chaos of the puppet play's performance hardly seem suited
to Jonson's poetic ideals. The puppet show, however, is not the unambiguous butt of satire that it might be; in many ways it is the climax of Jonson's
play, and its focus on the backstage proceedings of dramatic authorship and
the conditions of performance brings us back to the metatheatrical considerations of the Induction. "*A Puppet-play* must be shadow'd," wrote Jonson
in the *Discoveries*, "and seene in the dark: For draw the Curtaine, *Et sor-
det gesticulatio*" (240–41). Jonson, who remains imaginatively behind the
arras during the Induction to *Bartholomew Fair*, draws the curtain perhaps
unfairly on Littlewit's puppet play, but in revealing the *gesticulatio*, he more
clearly defines his own theater.

The puppet play is essentially an examination of Jacobean city comedy
within a Jacobean city comedy, and it explores in practice the Induction's
ideal, if ironized, relationship among dramatic poet, players, and audience.
The reduction of actors' bodies into "motions," or puppets, makes them a
burlesque. They live in baskets, and as Leatherhead bawdily implies, their
chief actor is little more than a glorified dildo: "he that acts young Leander
. . . is extremely beloved of the womenkind, they do so affect his action"
(5.3.77–78). The motions are, however, ostensibly easier for a playwright to

control than live actors. More, they are unassailable by puritan complaints against theatrical cross-dressing, as seen when the puppet Dionysius, in refutation of Busy's attack, "takes up his garment" to show that puppets "have neither male nor female amongst us" (5.6.93–94).

Littlewit's dramatization of Marlowe's *Hero and Leander* is, analogously to the puppet's burlesque of actors, a travesty of dramatic romance. Like Jonson in "On the Famous Voyage," but without the irony, Littlewit has transformed the London of the audience into a version of classical antiquity. The goal, however, is not a comedic heightening of the mundane for a perceptive and learned audience, but quite the opposite. Marlowe's poem, Leatherhead protests, "is too learned and poetical for our audience. What do they know what Hellespont is?" (5.3.97–98). Littlewit has taken "a little pains to reduce it to a more familiar strain for our people" (102–103), but he claims he means no insult to his audience by this reduction:

> I have only made it a little easy, and modern for the times, sir, that's all.
> As, for the Hellespont, I imagine our Thames here; and then Leander
> I make a dyer's son, about Puddle Wharf; and Hero a wench o' the
> Bankside, who going over one morning to Old Fish Street, Leander
> spies her land at Trig Stairs, and falls in love with her. (105–12)

Littlewit has in effect written a city comedy—all the tragedy of the original epyllion being purged by the puppet play's vulgarity, absurdity, and violence. The puppet play also seems distinctly Jonsonian, in that Littlewit has associated his characters with specific locales that help to define their natures.

Moreover, Littlewit himself echoes the situation that *Bartholomew Fair*'s Induction asks us to imagine. In attendance at his own play, he is concerned with how his wit will be received, and enacts a version of the hidden dramatist spying on his audience. The key distinction, however, is that Littlewit hides not behind a playhouse arras, but behind his anonymity. If Jonson "knows where to find" the ignorant censurers of *Bartholomew Fair*, at least his Articles of Agreement are even-handed; his audience also knows where to find him, and he remains confident in the quality of his art regardless of their opinions. Littlewit, on the other hand, "would not have any notice taken that I am the author, till we see how it passes" (5.3.21–22). Where Jonson draws up Articles fairly challenging his audience to censure him, Littlewit takes Leatherhead's advice not to "breed too great an expectation of it among your friends; that's the only hurter of these things" (5.4.10–12). Littlewit draws up no contract to keep his audience in their places according to their admission, and Jonson reminds us of his own contract by emphasizing the risk attendant on the puppet play's lack of one: told by the doorkeepers that it is "the best motion in the Fair," the ever-contrary Wasp snaps, "I believe you lie. If you do, I'll have my money again, and beat you" (70–71), audience behavior that Jonson's Induction contract forbids. Finally, the puppet play is, unlike *Bartholomew Fair*, too permeable to audience interaction, and to subversion by performers, even inanimate ones. Almost immediately, Leatherhead begins to joke extempore with the puppets, and as the audience becomes more and more intrusive and confrontational, he (and the puppets) abandon the *Hero and Leander* burlesque in favor of a comic public debate about theater, effectively removing and replacing Littlewit as author.[17]

Littlewit and his puppet play are thus an inverted and failed version of the authorial relationship to the playhouse and the audience that Jonson posits in *Bartholomew Fair*. The clumsy and perfunctory Londonization of *Hero and Leander* in the puppet play serves to highlight Jonson's own tightly structured and successfully mimetic representation of urban space in the playhouse. Littlewit's anxious concerns about reception emphasize by contrast Jonson's confidence in his own play and the implication that he holds the key to critical judgment. The puppet play proceeds through a series of interruptions by the audience bursting their bounds in order to confront the actors, the play, and theater itself, and ultimately it is not even allowed to finish, as Overdo interrupts it by revealing himself and accusing all and sundry of enormities. The puppet play's conclusion, however, is replaced by that of *Bartholomew Fair* itself, and it is Jonson, through his mouthpiece Quarlous—the playwright figure who wins the contest of dramatic spatial practice—who puts Overdo in his place and brings the proceedings to a somewhat happy close. Jonson's play is in the end controlled explicitly by the author's physical presence in the theater. In the climactic puppet play, Jonson deftly gives us a failed attempt at Jonsonian dramaturgy as laid out in the Induction, in order to showcase his success at bringing both London space and playhouse space under his control.

To our current picture of Jonson's career, to the critical model of Jonson's strategies of authorial definition, we must add the assertion of control over theatrical space that this chapter, and this book, have discussed. This inclusion does challenge received wisdom about Jonson's attitudes toward the theater, but such correctives have been long overdue. It is true that Jonson repeatedly complained about his necessary involvement with the stage, and critical tradition has taken these remarks, and the supposed anti-theatrical stance they imply, as a sign of divided selfhood, and of the impossibility of his authorial project. Richard Helgerson presents Jonson's career as a paradox precisely because successful theater simply does not allow for the constant presence of the author: "Like a ham actor, the author who refuses to disappear into the work distracts his audience from what should presumably be its object."[18] But need we make this presumption? Might not his refusal to disappear *be* the object of Jonson's drama? Jonson came to the theater first as an actor and he knew the theater business from the viewpoint of the stage as well as the study. If such an author exhibits anti-theatricality—when courting patronage, when attempting to reify his authority in an unchanging, exclusionary book, or when constructing his legacy as a poet in the classical tradition, rather than a jobbing playwright—surely it admits another interpretation than failure, political compromise, or neurosis.[19] It is as probably an example of playing a role as anything, an exercise in consciously theatrical masquerade. Despite his occasional anti-theatrical pose, theater gave Jonson a theoretical framework for authorship. He treated all writing like performance, and like a famous actor, maintained a balance between a perception of himself as an artist—present in the performance—and the authorial stance that the occasion demanded.

Authorship, for Jonson, consists not only in controlling textual meaning for a readership, but also, through the distinctly spatial poetics of theater, in shaping and directing the spatial practice of others, the individual character's or spectator's own experience of the environment. Although Jonson's ideal audience may be like the detached, superlunary "Good men" of the *Discoveries*, his ideal author (i.e. himself), like Quarlous, can acknowledge the virtue of detachment as a spectator and reader, but knows that to be able to guide readers and audiences to correct judgment, he must himself become a "practiser of their madnesse," actively working in the space of the stage, loathèd or not.

Epilogue

Beyond the 1616 Folio

> Die: seemes it not enough, thy Writing's date
> Is endlesse, but thine owne prolonged Fate
> Must equall it? For shame, engrosse not Age,
> But now, thy fifth Act's ended, leave the stage,
> And lett us clappe.
>
> Nicholas Oldisworth, "A letter to Ben. Johnson. 1629."[1]

In the decade after 1616, Jonson wrote no plays. His efforts to establish himself as a court poet had paid off, and in 1616 he received the title of poet
laureate, along with an accompanying pension. Along with his successful bid
for patronage from the Jacobean court and his work as the maker of masques
and royal entertainments from the beginning of James's reign, the success of
his Folio *Workes* played no small role in garnering him this honor. As Jennifer
Brady points out, however, the "very success of the Folio was double-edged,"
not because it failed to stand as a monument to his career, but because it suc-
ceeded.[2] The authorial strategy that has received most attention from Jonson's
critics, the textual monumentalization that the Folio enabled, had worked all
too well. Having become a "purely textual poet" had a cost; as Brady puts it,
the "[u]nprecedented closure of the kind Jonson engaged in by exploiting the
fixity of print had unforeseen consequences. To put it differently, tomes have
an uncanny way of mortifying their makers."[3] Shakespeare's posthumously-
published Folio of 1623 could stand as a combination of tombstone and
portrait, a replacement for his actual person. A reader who wished to know
Shakespeare could "looke / Not on his Picture, but his Booke," as Jonson's
own commendatory verse in the Shakespeare Folio admonished readers to
do. Jonson's book, on the other hand, erected a tombstone for a living poet;
he lived on for twenty-one more years, and as Nicholas Oldisworth, one of
Jonson's poetic "sons," suggests in his blunt poem, "Die Johnson," the longer
he lived, the greater a disjunction arose between the monument and the man.

If Jonson had exhausted his primary authorial strategy by 1616, however, he continued to experiment with the alternate strategy that has been the subject of this book. Neither the loss of his library to fire in 1623 nor the stroke he suffered in 1628 stopped him from using the dramatist's authority over space as an assertion of his poetic control. Thus, in *The Staple of News* (1626), Jonson gives us a satirical picture of a prototypical journalistic office, whose news-gathering employees reduce the city's meaningful spaces to "four cardinal quarters," corresponding to the points of the compass: "[t]he Court . . . Paul's, Exchange, and Westminster Hall" (1.2.58–60).[4] *The Staple of News* is thus the dramatic characters' attempt to control space through text, to make sense of the city by writing it, by managing the information associated with it. Characteristically, Jonson puts himself in competition with this attempt at spatial control, and when it becomes undisciplined, he exerts his authorial power over it; the fifth act sees the Staple destroyed by an earthquake *ex machina*. Despite its having an office and a patent, it turns out that news is just as windy and unreliable as the hearsay thrown about by the onstage audience of gossips that make up the play's interludes. As the Prologue for the Stage asserts, the only appropriate guides and navigators of the urban experience are true poets like Jonson himself, "those few can think, / Conceive, express, and steer the souls of men, / As with a rudder, round thus, with their pen" (22–24).

Even in *The New Inn*, written in 1629 after his stroke, Jonson maintains his interest in space, and the play, written for the King's Men to be played in "the old house," the Blackfriars (Prologue 2), returns to the concern with household space that marked his first play for that company in that playhouse.[5] Lord Frampul has abandoned his country house, the sort of ancestral pile celebrated by Jonson in "To Penshurst," in order to open the Inn of the Light Heart, a pseudo-domestic, commercial space too permeable as a house by virtue of its nature as an inn. In the course of the play's proceedings, dominated by theatrical games, a mock trial, and a doubly cross-dressed heroine, Jonson again exerts his authority over the theatrical space of the inn in order to ensure a return to proper domestic integrity, "with the characters converted from their wandering humours and ready to commit themselves to life together once more."[6]

Jonson's late plays, of course, are all too easily (and inaccurately) dismissed as "dotages," but if we return to the years of his vigor, the point about the continuation of his space-based authorial strategies will be more apparent. Long before the disillusionment of the Sons of Ben, before Oldisworth's complaint about his troubling longevity—in 1616 in fact, when his poetic achievements seemed most secure, Jonson wrote another play for the

King's Men, *The Devil is an Ass*. Like *Bartholomew Fair*, it does not appear
in the Folio, but it illustrates that Jonson's representational engagement with
the spaces of London was an authorial strategy as dominant in his mind as
his publication of the *Workes* earlier in the same year.

Like his earlier London comedies, *The Devil is an Ass* features ordinary
Londoners performing something very like theater; in fact, the play imagines the widespread eruption of theatrical practices beyond the walls of the
playhouse, and makes its characters' appropriation of those practices into an
object of satire. Moreover, the comedy, like its predecessors, derives much of
its point from its characters' inability to match Jonson himself in the theatrical manipulation of space.

The Devil is an Ass outdoes even *The Alchemist*'s metatheatrical experi-
mentation with exact correspondence between play and performance. The
joke, if anything, is more explicit in the later play: we learn that the chief
gull, Fitzdottrel, plans that day to make an appearance at the Blackfriars to
see a showing of a new play, called *The Devil is an Ass*. Fitzdottrel is a fool
precisely because he is more concerned with theater than with life. Plays
even contributes to his education: when Merecraft commends his knowledge
of history, Fitzdottrel confesses that "I ha't from the playbooks, / And think
they're more authentic" (2.4.13–14).[7] The action of the play is consistently
and explicitly theatrical, with false beards, female impersonation, and a final
coup de théâtre, Fitzdottrel's sham demonic possession, that makes use of the
special effects available to Jonson's stagecraft—squibs, soap, inflatable false
stomachs—while revealing their illusory mechanisms.

An entire subplot depends explicitly on Londoners attempting to
exploit the theater's potential for deception. When Merecraft, with an echo
of Dauphine's plot against Morose, needs a trained female impersonator to
play the "Spanish Lady" who will cozen Fitzdottrel out of his estate, he considers employing "one of the players" (2.8.60), in what becomes a keenly
metatheatrical running in-joke. When Merecraft learns that Dick Robin-
son—an actor once renowned for his female roles but now playing Wittipol
in *The Devil is an Ass*—is unavailable, he is forced to settle for Wittipol
to play the role of the Spanish Lady. Like *The Alchemist*, in which anyone,
apparently, can acquire Hieronimo's old cloak, *The Devil is an Ass* is set in
a London where the professional theater can supply plotters like Merecraft
with all the tools of its trade, including boy actors, for their theatrical activities in the city at large; it is also a London in which the citizens are more
than capable of doing the playing themselves.

In presenting such a version of London, and explicitly making it the
London in which his play is currently running, Jonson again puts those char-

acters who appropriate his theatrical practices symbolically into competition with his own theater. In *The Devil is an Ass*, however, these characters are not simply fictions; Fitzdottrel's implied attendance at his own play puts Jonson's theatricality in competition with the Blackfriars audience itself. And it should come as no surprise that the competition plays out in a spatial arena. Not coincidentally, this play about citizens appropriating theatricality for their own purposes begins with a prologue about gallants in the Blackfriars audience crowding into the stage space. In the prologue, an actor desires the "grandees" not to "grace / Our matter with allowing us no place. . . . Do not . . . force us act / In compass of a cheese-trencher. This tract / Will ne'er admit our vice, because of yours" (3–9). In *The Devil is an Ass*, Jonson's satirical version of the medieval morality play, where a devil comes to do mischief in London only to find that the city is more vicious even than hell, this play on "vice" in two senses—the stock device of the morality play, and the audience's habit of crowding the actors—serves to re-assert theatrical practices as the right of theater, in the face of the sort of audience appropriation of them that the ensuing play will illustrate. As becomes clear, Fitzdottrel is just the sort of "grandee" about which the prologue complains: he barters fifteen minutes of his wife's company for a new cloak, a "stage-garment" (1.6.186) or costume in which he can display himself onstage. Jonson, that is, places people like Fitzdottrel into competition with himself for the ability to control the meaning of playhouse space. In Jonson's hands, the stage can be anyplace in London or the netherworld, and indeed, as at 1.2.151–53 where Satan (in hell) gives Pug a vision of Fitzdottrel (in London), Jonson can make the infernal and the mundane occupy the same stage space at once. Fitzdottrel and his ilk in the audience, however, would hijack this potential and make the stage merely a showcase for their own frippery.

As much as the Londoners in the play attempt to appropriate the playwright's right to control theatrical space—both in the playhouse and in the streets of London—the play has no Wellbred, Truewit, or Quarlous to serve as a virtuoso producer of London space to rival Jonson himself. It is not the citizens whom *The Devil is an Ass* portrays as expert definers of London space, but the devils. Perhaps the most extensive survey of London in all of Jacobean drama takes place in the play's first act, set in hell, where the majority of the play's local references are concentrated. When Pug suggests that he should be allowed to go to London, Satan mockingly imagines an ineffectual tour of demonic mischief that amounts to a tour of the northern suburbs. Perhaps, Satan suggests, Pug has in mind "the crossing of a market-woman's mare / 'Twixt this and Tottenham?" (1.1.10–11). "This" is presumably hell, but comically imagined as a spot in Middlesex somewhat north of

Tottenham High Cross, a village six miles north of London. "Or some good ribibe [old woman]," Satan continues, "about Kentish Town, / Or Hoxton, you would hang now for a witch / Because she will not let you play round Robin?" (15–17). The sense—playing on Jonson's central joke that London is more evil than hell—is that Pug has no devilry good enough even for the suburbs, and would be more fit for the provincial backwaters of Lancashire or Northumberland (31–32).

This Satanic tour of the north suburbs is complemented by another, more complete, imagined practice of London's places a few lines later. Pug proposes that he will bring a Vice named Iniquity with him on his journey to London, and such a figure duly appears. This stock figure of medieval morality plays, with his jangling rhyme, is laughably out of place on the mature Jacobean stage, and his earnest devotion to the simple evils of a more innocent age is ill-suited to Jonson's (and Satan's) more complete knowledge of the fashions of evil in 1616. Iniquity's speech is notable, however, as a survey of London's places, a sort of Baedecker's guide to the city's vice, and it is worth quoting it at length. Iniquity offers to

> fetch thee a leap
> From the top of Paul's steeple to the Standard in Cheap:
> And lead thee a dance through the streets without fail,
> Like a needle of Spain, with a thread at my tail.
> We will survey the suburbs, and make forth our sallies
> Down Petticoat Lane, and up the Smock Alleys,
> To Shoreditch, Whitechapel, and so to Saint Katharine's,
> To drink with the Dutch there, and take forth their patterns.
> From thence we will put in at Custom House Quay there,
> And see how the factors and prentices play there
> False with their masters; and geld many a full pack,
> To spend it in pies at the Dagger and the Woolsack.
> . . . .
> Nay, boy, I will bring thee to the bawds and the roisters,
> At Billingsgate, feasting with claret wine, and oysters,
> From thence shoot the bridge, child, to the Cranes i' the Vintry,
> And see there the gimlets, how they make their entry!
> Or if thou hadst rather, to the Strand down to fall
> 'Gainst the lawyers come dabbled from Westminster Hall (55–73)

Satan condemns Iniquity's excesses as outdated dotages, but this survey of London is impressive in its scope, taking in both the center (the Standard in

Cheap) and the boundaries (Billingsgate, the bridge); both the official and exalted landmarks (Paul's and Westminster Hall) and the seediest neighborhoods (Smock Alley, Custom House Quay).

There is some irony in the fact that the most complete survey of the city and observation of place associations is put in the mouth of a Vice in hell, as there is irony in Satan acting as a direct mouthpiece for Jonson's satire. Satan is, however, in the position that Slitgut had occupied atop his pole in Cuckold's Haven, the position that Jonson claims for himself: that of a detached and privileged observer with an investment in celebrating the follies and evils of London. And Iniquity has the ability of a city comedy playwright to define the associations of London place from a broad, almost cartographic perspective. The devil in hell, in contrast to the characters in London, has no need for hypocrisy, and a broad enough view of the city to serve as the voice of satirical truth. Indeed, the devils are the closest things to author figures that *The Devil is an Ass* provides, and their appearance in the first scene is Jonson's answer to the rest of the characters' attempts to wrest the playwright's theatrical powers from him.

The 1616 Folio produced a reified, unchanging vision of Jonson the author, a textual monument to the ages. As I hope this book has shown, however, the narrative, or rather the synchronic and ahistorical portrait, provided by the Folio gives us an incomplete sense of Jonson and of his contribution to the development of early modern authorship. As importantly as his other authorial innovations, Jonson projected himself, the dramatic poet, as a privileged interpreter, and often as a maker, of the meanings of London's places, and his assertion of authorial agency in the medium of space, unlike his self-construction as a textual poet, was both flexible and versatile; he could and did continue to develop it, from the beginnings of his career, through and beyond the Folio, to the close, or shutting up of his circle.

Notes

NOTES TO THE INTRODUCTION

1. Martin Butler, "Jonson's London and its Theatres," in *The Cambridge Companion to Ben Jonson*, ed. Richard Harp and Stanley Stewart (Cambridge: Cambridge University Press, 2000), 15.
2. Steven Mullaney, *The Place of the Stage: License, Play, and Power in Renaissance England*. (Chicago: University of Chicago Press, 1988).
3. See, for example, Richard C. Newton, "Jonson and the (Re-)Invention of the Book," in *Classic and Cavalier: Essays on Jonson and the Sons of Ben*, ed. J. Summers and T. Pebworth (Pittsburgh: University of Pittsburgh Press, 1982), 31–55, and Alexandra Halasz, "Pamphlet Surplus: John Taylor and Subscription Publication," in *Print, Manuscript, & Performance* ed. Marotti and Bristol, 90–102.
4. Douglas A. Brooks, *From Playhouse to Printing House: Drama and Authorship in Early Modern England* (Cambridge: Cambridge University Press, 2000), 2. Douglas Bruster, similarly, argues that the modern author was created as a celebrity by the booming mass market for books. See "The Structural Transformation of Print in Late Elizabethan England," in *Print, Manuscript, & Performance: The Changing Relations of the Media in Early Modern England*, ed. Arthur F. Marotti and Michael D. Bristol (Columbus: Ohio State University Press, 2000), 49–89.
5. Loewenstein does issue a caveat against treating the early modern moment, and especially Ben Jonson's 1616 Folio *Workes* as a revolutionary, rather than a culminating, moment in the development of proprietary authorship, and his *Author's Due: Printing and the Prehistory of Copyright* (Chicago: University of Chicago Press, 2002) puts into a valuable diachronic context the work of his more focused study, *Ben Jonson and Possessive Authorship* (Cambridge: Cambridge University Press, 2002), but his major contribution to authorship studies is this focused analysis of the seventeenth century dramatic and book markets and the necessity for the individualized author that emerged from their competition over intellectual property.

6. Richard Helgerson, *Self-Crowned Laureates: Spenser, Jonson, Milton and the Literary System* (Berkeley: University of California Press, 1983). More recent work by Richard Dutton likewise locates the transitions in early modern dramatic authorship in the technological and accompanying social changes between manuscript and print. See Richard Dutton, "The Birth of the Author," in *Texts and Cultural Change in Early Modern England*, ed. Cedric C. Brown and Arthur F. Marotti (New York: St. Martin's Press, 1997), 153–78.

7. Not all histories of authorship focus on early seventeenth-century England, of course, but regardless of their divergence over the precise factors or the implications, one major strain of authorship studies among literary historians presupposes that Renaissance Europe more broadly was indeed the birthplace of modern authorship. Thus, for example, Michael D. Bristol and Arthur F. Marotti's collection of essays, *Print, Manuscript, & Performance: The Changing Relations of the Media in Early Modern England* (Columbus: Ohio State University Press, 2000), while impressive in its contributors' range of treatments, takes "the newly emerging practice of individualized authorship" in early seventeenth-century England as a given (8).

8. Raymond Williams, *Keywords* (Oxford: Oxford University Press, 1976), 47.

9. Jean Howard, *Theater of a City: The Places of London Comedy, 1598–1642* (Philadelphia: University of Pennsylvania Press, 2007), 5.

10. One of the best recent discussions of the direct relationship between the move from mobile to fixed playing spaces in London comes from Andrew Hiscock's *The Uses of this World: Thinking Space in Shakespeare, Marlowe, Cary and Jonson* (Cardiff: University of Wales Press, 2004), which argues from an impressive array of primary and archival evidence for theater's defining, almost didactic cultural function: "[t]he theatre in London played a significant part in [the] revision of the capital's spatial practice." After the first purpose-built playing place in 1575–76, "the theatre begins to occupy defined spaces in the urban environment and it continued to have an interest through performance in how society chooses to organize its living spaces" (11). Douglas Bruster links urbanization and theater in a similar vein, in *Drama and the Market in the Age of Shakespeare* (Cambridge: Cambridge University Press, 1992), arguing that the institutionalization of theater, and the structural fixity of the playhouses built in Elizabethan and Jacobean London, were responses to the overwhelming pressures of social change (1). And Jean Howard's recent monograph, *Theater of a City*, explores the ways in which the theater business helped establish the meanings of London locales and make them knowable to the city's inhabitants. See also Henry S. Turner's *The English Renaissance Stage: Geometry, Poetics, and the Practical Spatial Arts 1580–1630* (Oxford: Oxford University Press, 2006), which argues that all "urbanization is empirically invisible or inaccessible *except* through formal abstractions

that are of an iconic nature," and that theater, intimately involved with the practical, mechanical spatial arts that underlay both the historical processes and the representational epistemology of that urbanization, was therefore "one of the most important modes of iconic representation during the period" (148).

11. Bruster argues that the "placelessness of the Renaissance platform stage worked to exoticise and commodify space" (*Drama and the Market*, 8). My related point is that this foregrounding of space as produced allowed for a contemporary authorial consciousness drawn from the playwrights' status as purveyors of this abstract commodity.

12. David Riggs, *Ben Jonson: A Life* (Cambridge: Harvard University Press, 1989), 352.

13. Roland Barthes, "The Death of the Author," in *Authorship: From Plato to Postmodernism: A Reader*, ed. Seán Burke (Edinburgh: Edinburgh University Press), 125–30. W. K. Wimsatt and Monroe C. Beardsley, "The Intentional Fallacy," in *The Verbal Icon: Studies in the Meaning of Poetry*, edited by W. K. Wimsatt (Lexington: University of Kentucky Press, 1954), 3–18. Michel Foucault, "What Is an Author?" *The Foucault Reader*, ed. Paul Rabinow (New York: Pantheon Books, 1984), 101–20.

14. Barthes, "Death of the Author," 126.

15. Foucault, "What Is an Author?" 119.

NOTES TO CHAPTER ONE

1. Citations from Shakespeare are taken from *The Riverside Shakespeare*, ed. G. Blakemore Evans and J. J. M. Tobin, 2nd ed (Boston: Houghton Mifflin, 1997).

2. For a useful summary of these traditional unfavorable critical comparisons and their underlying assumptions, see Jonas Barish's introduction to *Ben Jonson: A Collection of Critical Essays*, ed. Barish (Englewood Cliffs: Prentice Hall, 1963), 1–13.

3. *Ben Jonson*, ed. C. H. Herford and Percy Simpson, 11 vols. (Oxford: Clarendon Press, 1925–52), 1:119. Unless otherwise stated, citations of Jonson's non-dramatic writings are taken from this edition.

4. Helgerson, in the third chapter of his *Self-Crowned Laureates*, discusses Jonson's career as one of self-deception and internal conflict whereby his very insistence on transcendence prevented transcendence, and calls his work as "an agon, an unresolved struggle of the self against the very conditions of its expression" (184).

5. This is a point emphasized by Sara van den Berg's biographical sketch, "True Relation: The Life and Career of Ben Jonson," in *The Cambridge Companion to Ben Jonson*, edited by Richard Harp and Stanley Stewart (Cambridge: Cambridge University Press, 2000), 1–14.

6. Douglas A. Brooks, in *From Playhouse to Printing House*, 104–39, traces the critical calcification of the notion that the 1616 Folio represents a watershed event in the development of authorship, but he also demonstrates that the idealization of Jonson's involvement in the printing process—largely exaggerated, or even "fashioned for him by his Oxford editors" (109)—can be dangerously reductive. Brooks seeks to reposition Jonson and his book as transitional, rather than "the embodiment of the modern notion of the author" (107), and while his project, unlike my own, focuses on the historical contexts of printed drama, and the effect of critical reception of Shakespeare on our idea of Jonsonian authorship, I hope to complement his goals by further broadening our sense of Jonson's authorial innovations to include physical, as well as textual space.

7. Foucault, "What Is an Author?" 111.

8. The exception is *Sejanus*, a collaboration in its original version, which was revised in print to exclude the product of the second pen. In the Folio, Jonson omits a note to the reader that had explained this revision in the quarto text, thus effectively removing any trace of collaboration. See Timothy Murray, "Ben Jonson's Folio as Textual Performance," in *Proceedings of the Xth Congress of the International Comparative Literature Association*, ed. Anna Balakian (New York: Garland, 1982), 329. Jonson's impulse to downplay or erase evidence of collaboration has traditionally been seen as another proto-modern aspect of his authorial attitude, anticipating Romantic idealizations of lone, inspired authorship. His expressions of antipathy toward collaboration did not, of course, keep him from collaborating as much as his contemporaries, and perhaps the importance of such antipathy to an authorial strategy is itself anachronistic: the word "collaborator" in its strictly literary sense did not come into use in English until 1802 (*OED* 1; see also Andrew Bennet, *The Author* [London: Routledge, 2005], 94). Stephen Dobranski, in his discussion of Miltonian authorship, usefully reminds us that we must be aware of the collaborative processes through which, paradoxically, seventeenth-century authors constructed themselves as a solitary individuals (*Milton, Authorship, and the Book Trade* [Cambridge: Cambridge University Press, 1999], 9, 133).

9. Jerome McGann, "The Monks and the Giants: Textual and Bibliographical Studies and the Interpretation of Literary Works," *Textual Criticism and Literary Interpretation*, ed. Jerome McGann (Chicago: University of Chicago Press, 1985), 192–94.

10. Joseph Loewenstein puts this claim into the larger context of an early modern competition between theater professionals and stationers: "at the end of the century . . . the press and the stage discover each other as competitors" (*Possessive Authorship*, 23). Loewenstein's focus, however, is on the influence of censorship and market forces in producing and encouraging this competition; as I will argue below, Jonson positions himself within this

competition as capable of exerting his authorial control over the spatial practices of both the press and the stage.

11. Gerald E. Bentley, *The Profession of Dramatist in Shakespeare's Time, 1590–1642* (Princeton: Princeton University Press, 1971), 261.

12. See James K. Bracken, "Books from William Stansby's Printing House, and Jonson's Folio of 1616," *The Library* 10 (1988): 25–26.

13. Bracken, "Stansby's Printing House," 21–22.

14. The issue of the relationship between publication and "class" in the early modern period is complicated and a discussion of all its implications is beyond the scope of the current project, but it has been discussed comprehensively by Richard Helgerson in *Self-crowned Laureates*, and more recently by Wendy Wall, whose nuanced critique of the intersection of culture, technology and gender in the development of early modern authorship is premised in part on assumptions about the class implications of the coexisting and competing modes of manuscript and print literature in the Renaissance. See Wall, *The Imprint of Gender* (Ithaca: Cornell University Press, 1993), 11–17.

15. Sara van den Berg, "Ben Jonson and the Ideology of Authorship," in *Ben Jonson's 1616 Folio*, edited by J. Brady and W. H. Herendeen (Newark: University of Delaware Press, 1991), 116–17.

16. Newton, "(Re-)Invention," 44.

17. Newton, "(Re-)Invention," 44.

18. See James A. Riddell, "Ben Jonson's Folio of 1616," in *The Cambridge Companion to Ben Jonson*, ed. Harp and Stewart, 154. Some recent criticism, however, has downplayed Jonson's status as an innovator in this regard. Joseph Loewenstein, for example, notes that Thomas Coryat, Samuel Daniel, and George Wither all anticipated Jonson in appropriating some of the stationer's traditional functions (*Possessive Authorship*, 7), although Loewenstein's qualifications also strengthen the sense of Jonsonian innovation by relocating Jonson's Folio in the context of an entire career of "author-centered publishing" (*Author's Due*, 87). David Scott Kastan, in *Shakespeare and the Book* (Cambridge: Cambridge University Press, 2001), 17–20, shows that even other playwrights—Webster, Barnes, Heywood, and Brome—asserted proprietary rights over their works in the same way that Jonson did, and that his "desire for a printed text that will preserve the intended form" is not unique. Both Richard Dutton ("Birth of the Author") and, more extensively, Lukas Erne (*Shakespeare as Literary Dramatist* [Cambridge: Cambridge University Press, 2003]) add Shakespeare to this list of playwrights, arguing that he meticulously prepared manuscript versions of his plays for circulation. From a different angle, Douglas Brooks has shown that our sense of Jonson as anomalously obsessive about his printed text has been exaggerated (*From Playhouse to Printing House*, 107). My point about Jonson's importance in the development of

the authorial control of texts, however, holds true whether we consider his editorial practices an innovation or the culmination of a trend.

19. Murray, "Textual Performance," 327.

20. W. H. Herendeen, "A New Way to Pay Old Debts: Pretexts to the 1616 Folio," in *Ben Jonson's 1616 Folio*, ed. Brady and Herendeen, (Newark: University of Delaware Press, 1991), 53.

21. Critics have begun to challenge the assumption of Jonson's sincere, unambiguous anti-theatricality that Jonas Barish did much to solidify with *The Antitheatrical Prejudice* (Berkeley: University of California Press, 1981). See, for example, Sean McEvoy's effective counterargument in "Hieronimo's Old Cloak: Theatricality and Representation in Ben Jonson's Middle Comedies," *Ben Jonson Journal* 11 (2004): 67–88. Barish's portrait of the dualism in Jonson's career as a purportedly stage-hating playwright dies hard, however. Even Anne Barton (*Ben Jonson, Dramatist* [Cambridge: Cambridge University Press, 1984]) and Peter Womack (*Ben Jonson* [Oxford: Blackwell, 1986]), who both attempt to position Jonson primarily as a dramatist and focus on his plays as "scripts for the theatre" endorse the idea of a dualistic quality in Jonson's personality. Joseph Loewenstein, while he adheres to the narrative of Jonson's "growing allegiance to the page" in opposition to the stage (*Possessive Authorship*, 180), contends that the playwright's ideal of the book as a *melior theatrum* is not necessarily adversarial or antitheatrical (144) and complicates Jonson's stance toward the theater as containing "some grudging appreciation of the players" and their craft (146n). I would go further, to suggest that the apparent antitheatricality on Jonson's part is merely a role played by a consummate theater man, useful for particular rhetorical stances at points in his career, but belied by the robust celebration of his characters' proteanism.

22. Edward S. Casey, "How to Get from Space to Place in a Fairly Short Stretch of Time: Phenomenological Prolegomena," in *Senses of Place*, edited by Steven Feld and Keith H. Basso (Santa Fe: School of American Research Press, 1996), 19. See also Casey, *The Fate of Place: A Philosophical History* (Berkeley: University of California Press, 1997).

23. Bernhard Klein, *Maps and the Writing of Space in Early Modern England and Ireland* (Houndmills: Palgrave, 2001), 5. On the rise of cartographic consciousness in early modern Europe, see also the work of cartographic historians J. B. Harley and David Woodward, eds., *Cartography in Prehistoric, Ancient, and Medieval Europe and the Mediterranean*, vol. 1, *The History of Cartography* (Chicago: University of Chicago Press, 1987), 7–12, and P. D. A. Harvey's discussion of the "cartographic revolution" in early modern England: "Far more than a revolution in the ways maps were made it was a revolution in the ways of thought of those who used them" (P. D. A. Harvey, *Maps in Tudor England* [Chicago: University of Chicago Press, 1993], 15). Perhaps no one has more forcefully demonstrated English

theater's debt to these early modern innovations in geometry, cartography, and other practical spatial arts than Henry S. Turner (*The English Renaissance Stage*, especially chapters 2 and 6).

24. For detailed discussions on the importance of the chorographic tradition to the emergence of English nationalism and the production of spatial awareness in England, see, respectively, Richard Helgerson, *Forms of Nationhood: The Elizabethan Writing of England* (Chicago: University of Chicago Press, 1992), 105–47, and Klein, *Maps and the Writing of Space*, 137–48.

25. Douglas Bruster, *Drama and the Market*, 22.

26. John Twyning, *London Dispossessed: Literature and Social Space in the Early Modern City* (New York: St. Martin's, 1998), 3.

27. Howard, *Theater of a City*, 5. Henry Turner, similarly, argues that the development of the "city" play in the period is a response to the "material changes associated with London's urbanization produc[ing] new conceptions of the city as a representational space" and, further, that social tensions were self-consciously translated into and realized as dramatic form (*The English Renaissance Stage*, 38). For a more general discussion of the theater's role in helping to articulate the early modern conceptions of space, see Russell West's excellent *Spatial Representations and the Jacobean Stage: From Shakespeare to Webster* (New York: Palgrave, 2002), which demonstrates how theater, "an ostentatiously spatial art form, interacts with the context of early modern society" (3). West argues that theater offered its practitioners nothing less than a new kind of selfhood, "a tangible, performed theory of the new subjective moment lived by the audience well before any comparable social analysis was available," and explained for them "the bewildering phenomena of experienced space in an age in the throes of turbulent processes of transformation" (241).

28. Yi-Fu Tuan, *Space and Place: The Perspective of Experience* (Minneapolis: University of Minnesota Press, 1977).

29. See especially Alan Dessen, *Elizabethan Stage Conventions and Modern Interpreters* (Cambridge: Cambridge University Press, 1984), 84–104.

30. Dessen, *Stage Conventions*, 95.

31. Hiscock makes a similar warning against the all-too-easy association of Tuan's definition of space with the spatial practices we usually assign to early modern theater, arguing that even playhouse space is not an inert container but something continually produced by the ideological, economic, cultural, and historical baggage that it carries with it (*Uses of this World* 3–4).

32. For the sake of clarity, I use de Certeau's French terms throughout the book when referring to his rather specific definitions of place and space. My metaphor of the spatial palimpsest is drawn from Henri Lefebvre, for whom space is not a "blank page," but a "rough draft, jumbled and self-contradictory. Rather than signs, what one encounters here are direc-

tions—multifarious and overlapping instructions" (*The Production of Space*, trans. Donald Nicholson-Smith [Oxford: Blackwell, 1991], 142).

33. Michel de Certeau, *The Practice of Everyday Life*, trans. Steven Rendall (Berkeley: University of California Press, 1984), 117.

34. De Certeau, *Practice*, 117.

35. De Certeau, *Practice*, 117 (de Certeau's italics). This aphorism may have been less surprising to Jonson's ear than it is to our own. Among the senses of the verb *practise/practice* listed in the *Oxford English Dictionary* is a sense available to Jonson, though now obsolete: "To frequent or habitually visit (a place)" (*OED* 4b).

36. De Certeau, *Practice*, xviii-xix.

37. De Certeau, *Practice*, 36 (de Certeau's italics).

38. De Certeau, *Practice*, 38.

39. Importantly for my purposes, Harvey emphasizes the fluidity and constant constructedness of place—of *lieu* in the terms I am using—that the illusion or goal of permanence implicit in projects of place (de Certeau's "strategies") is never complete, and that what exists instead is a series of, or a competition between, "permanences." (*Justice, Nature, and the Geography of Difference* [Oxford: Blackwell, 1996], 261). Doreen Massey goes a step further, arguing that intersecting expressions of space (in de Certeau's definition), interactions of individual and social processes, are the building blocks in the ongoing process of place-production. For Massey, places are not simply "areas with boundaries around," but "articulated moments in networks of social relations and understandings" ("Power-Geometry and a Progressive Sense of Place," in *Mapping the Futures: Local Cultures, Global Change*, ed. Jon Bird et al. [London: Routledge, 1993], 66).

40. The authorial production of space that I am ascribing to Jonson here can be seen to correspond to what the geographer Edward W. Soja has called "thirdspace," a term that grew out of his rethinking of dialectics of space in *Postmodern Geographies* (London: Verso, 1989). In that book, as well as in *Thirdspace* (Oxford: Blackwell, 1996), which extends the theoretical potential of spatial "trialectics" to feminism, postcolonialism, and historicism, Soja builds primarily on the work of Henri Lefebvre. Also impatient with the limitations of binaries, Lefebvre had made a similar move in 1974 with *The Production of Space* (first translated into English in 1991), positing a trinary of terms to describe conceived, perceived, and lived space. Two of his terms are roughly analogous to de Certeau's: "Representations of Space" (conceived space) represents the order imposed by institutions of political and economic power, and corresponds in some ways to de Certeau's *lieu*. "Spatial Practice" (perceived space) is analogous to *espace*, in that it is the province of the individual and his or her reaction to this imposed order. The relationship between these is also much like de Certeau's model: "Every space is already in place before the appearance in it

of actors . . . this pre-existence of space conditions the subject's presence, action and discourse, his competence and performance" (57). Lefebvre's third term, however, while it is also akin to de Certeau's *espace*, brings with it the possibility of describing the position filled by Jonson's spatial strategy of authorship: "Representational Space" (lived space) is linked in his model to the clandestine, underground side of social life, and also, importantly, to art. Emerging from Lefebvre's triad, and essential for my purposes of determining the relation of dramatic authorship to the production of London space, is the question of "what intervenes, what occupies the interstices between representations of space and representational spaces." Lefebvre temptingly suggests that the answer might be "culture," "imagination," or "artistic creation . . . but that leaves unanswered the queries 'By whom?' and 'How?'" (43). I hope to answer these questions by situating Jonson's dramatic authorship in the interstices that Lefebvre's model identifies. For Jonson, the playwright participates in shaping the conceived, perceived, and lived space of London both for himself and his audiences.

41. For an extensive discussion of the early modern conceptual relationship between the artisanal and the aesthetic, focused on the confluence of Renaissance theories of surveying, poetics, and the overdetermination of the word *plot*, see Henry S. Turner, "Plotting Early Modernity," in *The Culture of Capital*, ed. Turner (London: Routledge, 2002), 85–127. Turner furthers this discussion, focusing on Jonson's artisanal metaphors and their derivation from his reading of Vitruvius, in *The English Renaissance Stage*, 246–61 .

42. Martial's epigram (12.94), with the possible exception of line 10 ("hinc etiam petitur iam mea palma tibi"), is entirely without spatial metaphors. The translation of D. R. Shackleton Bailey reads as follows (Martial, *Epigrams*, Loeb Classical Library [Cambridge: Harvard University Press, 1993], 3:166–67):

    I was writing an epic; you started to write one: I gave up, so that my poetry should not stand in competition with yours. My Thalia transferred herself to tragic buskins; you too fitted the long train on yourself. I stirred the lyre strings, as practiced by Calabrian Muses; eager to show off, you snatch my new quill away from me. I try my hand at satire; you labor to be Lucillus. I play with light elegy; you play with it too. What can be humbler? I start shaping epigrams; here too you are already after my trophy. Choose what you don't want (modesty forbids us to want everything), and if there's anything you don't want, Tucca, leave it for me.

43. On Jonson's frequent valorization of stasis and dwelling, see Thomas Greene, "Ben Jonson and the Centered Self," *Studies in English Literature* 10 (1970): 325–48, and Ian Donaldson, *Jonson's Magic Houses* (Oxford: Oxford University Press, 1997), 42.

44. Herford and Simpson, *Ben Jonson*, 6:511.

45. "Centre and circle become symbols, not only of harmony and completeness but of stability, repose, fixation, duration, and the uncompleted circle comes to symbolize a flux or a mobility, grotesquely or dazzlingly fluid" (Greene, "Centered Self," 326).

46. *Conversations with Drummond*, 578–79 (Herford and Simpson, *Ben Jonson* 1:148). See also the epilogue of L. A. Beaurline, *Jonson and Elizabethan Comedy: Essays in Dramatic Rhetoric* (San Marino: Huntington Library, 1978).

47. Heyden has been identified as Sir Christopher Heyden, and Shelton as the Sir Ralph Shelton commemorated by Epigram 119, although since Jonson says of both men "I cannot call 'hem knights" (22), these identifications may be questionable.

48. Bruce Boehrer discusses this poem, and Jonson's uses of digestive and excremental imagery more generally, in *The Fury of Men's Gullets: Ben Jonson and the Digestive Canal* (Philadelphia: University of Pennsylvania Press, 1997). See also Leah Marcus, "Of Mire and Authorship," in *The Theatrical City*, ed. David L. Smith, Richard Strier and David Bevington (Cambridge: Cambridge University Press, 1995), 170–82.

49. The actor Will Kemp's *Nine Daies Wonder* (London, 1600) documents his morris-dancing voyage from London to Norwich during Lent of 1600. It also records Kemp's meeting with a man named Foskew (Fortescue) who walked to Berwick and may be the adventurer mentioned here, although Kemp makes no note of his having undertaken to walk the journey backward. Other putting out voyages made by water include Richard Ferris's journey from London to Bristol in a wherry in 1590, and an unidentified rower's journey to Antwerp (both mentioned in "On the Famous Voyage," 39–40). The waterman-poet John Taylor made wherry voyages to York in 1622 and Salisbury in 1623, but his most famous and outlandish putting out voyage was a journey down the Thames to Quinborough in 1619 in a boat made of brown paper. For a further argument on the satirical scope Jonson found in the representation of such "adventures," both in "On the Famous Voyage" and in *Eastward Ho*, see Anne-Julia Zwierlein, "Shipwrecks in the City: Commercial Risk as Romance in Early Modern City Comedy," in *Plotting Early Modern London: New Essays on City Comedy*, ed. Mehl, Stock, and Zwierlein (Aldershot: Ashgate, 2004), 75–94.

50. The processes of commodification may be at work in cartography and chorography as well, of course. The distinction I draw is between chorography's marketing of *place* and the attendant ideological construction of nationhood or provincial/civic consciousness, and the marketing of *space*, that may partake in, but is not centered around, this construction. On the putting out voyage's function of marketing celebrity, see Max Thomas,

"*Kemps Nine Daies Wonder*: Dancing Carnival into Market," *PMLA* 107 (1992), 511–32.

NOTES TO CHAPTER TWO

1. See David Bergeron, *English Civic Pageantry 1558–1642* (London: Edward Arnold, 1971), 104.
2. For another extensive, but differently inflected, treatment of the implications of the conflicts and competitions—both political and poetic—surrounding the 1604 royal entry, see Sara van den Berg, "The Passing of the Elizabethan Court," *Ben Jonson Journal* 1 (1994), 31–62. Van den Berg traces a change in the way Londoners represented their interests over the course of the three main events that marked 1603–4: Queen Elizabeth's funeral, the plague epidemic, and James's royal entry. She suggests that these changes mark nothing less than "a change in the creation of meaning" in early modern London (32). The communal, impersonal rhetoric used to describe the funeral gives way to a picture of London as a collection of suffering Londoners during the plague, a picture that challenges courtly, civic, ecclesiastical, and judicial models of authority, and allows for the emergence of individual subjectivity. Finally, she argues, the inherently competitive nature of the royal entry provides a picture of the renewal of the city's communal life, but "its meaningful events are now acknowledged as the creation, even the contestation, of individual citizens—the urban authors and their architect" (32–33). My argument here complements van den Berg's by tracing the mechanisms of spatial practice through which the authors articulate their competition, and reading it not only in terms of the subversion of institutional authority, but as a claim for authorial agency.
3. Mimi Yiu, building on Eve Sedgwick's formulation of homosocial desire, coins the term "homospatial" to describe a "regime in Western philosophy . . . in which space acquires value precisely because it permits endless exchange between men" ("Sounding the Space Between Men: Choric and Choral Cities in Ben Jonson's *Epicoene; or, The Silent Woman*," *PMLA* 122 [2007], 76). I would suggest that the competition between Dekker and Jonson over the interpretive control of London's spaces prefigures and informs such homospatial dynamics of exchange, not only in *Epicoene*, but recurrently in Jonson's London comedies.
4. Indeed, Manley observes, "[t]he history of London street pageantry is practically identical with the history of collaboration between the twin jurisdictions of the Crown and the City" (*Literature and Culture in Early Modern London* [Cambridge: Cambridge University Press, 1995], 216).
5. This tradition, indeed, continued with real political significance—especially in periods of baronial struggle—even after William the Conqueror's

attempts to establish the crown's sovereignty over London. See Francis Sheppard, *London: A History* (Oxford: Oxford University Press, 1998), 90–91.

6. The recorder, as this implies, was an important civic office, and his speech was the most obvious outlet through which the city could participate in a political discourse with the new king. On 25 May 1603, when the city's plans for his royal entry were underway, King James heightened political tensions by writing to the Lord Mayor and aldermen asking them to appoint a royal favorite, Sir Henry Montague, to the position of recorder. The aldermen quickly complied, but this was not usual practice—a similar request from Elizabeth in 1594 had occasioned complaints from the city officials over royal incursion into their prerogatives—and the incident represents a bold attempt by James to prevent any potentially oppositional political rhetoric at the most ritually charged spot in the progress. See John Nichols, ed., *The Progresses, Processions, and Magnificent Festivities of King James the First*, 4 vols. (London: J.B. Nichols, 1828), 1:333 and note.

7. Manley, *Literature and Culture*, 223–24. For a discussion of the early modern civic tradition of "keeping Gyants" as a representation of the collective identity of a city, see Michael D. Bristol, "Theater and Popular Culture," in *A New History of Early English Drama*, ed. John D. Cox and David Scott Kastan (New York: Columbia University Press, 1997), 238–39.

8. *Repertory of the Court of Aldermen* 26, pt. 1, fol. 120^v. In February 1604 James was still writing to the city government to postpone repayment (*Calendar of State Papers Domestic*, 6:50), and the inherited debt was not entirely repaid until 1608, by which time James had received two more loans from the Corporation of London. For details, see Robert Ashton, *The Crown and the Money Market 1603–1640* (Oxford: Clarendon Press, 1960) 114–18.

9. The leisurely pace of James's progress was viewed with some concern in the south. Pains had been taken for the ordering of the queen's funeral, but until the arrival of her successor she could not be buried and continued to lie in state at Whitehall for more than a month. A letter from John Chamberlain on 12 April attests that "We have no certaintie where the King is" (John Chamberlain, *Letters*, ed. Norman McClure, 2 vols. [Philadelphia: American Philosophical Society, 1939], 1:192), and an anonymous balladeer captures popular sentiment, pleading "O noble King to England haste . . . For nothing now breedes our despight / but that we want our Prince his sight." For the balladeer, "though her Corpse be wrapped in Lead"—and indeed the queen lay in state so long that her body burst its cerements and began to offend despite these wrappings (see G. B. Harrison, *A Jacobean Journal* [London: Routledge, 1941], 5)—"King James

is hee by whose sweete breath / wee still possesse Queene Elizabeth" (*An excellent new Ballad shewing the Petigree of our Royall King IAMES* [London, 1603]). The only trouble was the lack of the king's physical presence to replace the queen's, and to compound the anxiety, the slowly-traveling king sent letters to his new privy council ordering them to bury his predecessor without him.

10. See F. P. Wilson, *The Plague in Shakespeare's London* (Oxford: Oxford University Press, 1927), 87–88.

11. *Stuart Royal Proclamations: Royal Proclamations of King James I 1603–1625*, ed. James Larkin and Paul Hughes (Oxford: Clarendon Press, 1973), 38.

12. The court had been emptied of suitors on 1 August and began a progress of necessity that only served to carry the plague to the estates that it visited, as a letter from the courtier Sir Thomas Edwards attests: "The Court hath ben so contynuallie haunted wth the sicknes, by reason of the disorderlie companie that doe followe us, as we are forced to remove from place to place, and doe infect all places where we come" (Nichols, *Progresses of James*, 1:258).

13. Indeed, given the practical interdependence between city and crown in James's English reign, little open political conflict between the two institutions could exist. As Curtis Perry points out, whatever "oppositional potential" the literature of London had concerning the Stuart court served only to renegotiate the city's relationship to royalty, laying the groundwork for political conflict that would become overt in the 1630s, but remained nascent in Jacobean England. Perry does, however, trace a shift from London's "habitual royalism" under Elizabeth to a rivalry of ostentatious magnificence between civic elites and an increasingly withdrawn King James. See Curtis Perry, *The Making of Jacobean Culture* (Cambridge: Cambridge University Press, 1997), 184.

14. Graham Parry, *The Golden Age Restor'd: The Culture of the Stuart Court, 1603–42* (Manchester: Manchester University Press, 1981), 1.

15. See Manley, *Literature and Culture*, 237–41.

16. This iconic moment was documented by Richard Mulcaster in *The queens maiesties passage through the citie of London to Westminster the daye before her coronacion* (London, 1559). See also Manley, *Literature and Culture*, 248–51.

17. Such an alignment is understandable, if reductive. It seems logical enough to characterize Dekker—who went on to write several civic pageants, who chronicled of the vibrancy of London life in his prose, and whose *Shoemakers' Holiday* celebrates the values of London's mercantile class—as a city poet. Conversely, Jonson's career as a masque writer and poet of the Stuart court would seem to place him on the side of the crown. Lawrence Manley draws just this distinction between a pro-city Dekker and a pro-crown Jonson, seeing Dekker's text as a celebration of the economic, material power

of urban labor (*Literature and Culture*, 252–53), and Jonson "subject[ing] the city to the monarch's own messianic agency" (254). The question of the two playwrights' ideological alignment could not but be complicated, however, considering the varied audiences both had to please. Jonson does seem, especially with the benefit of hindsight, to be making an ultimately successful play for court patronage with his pageants, but his contributions to the royal entry are not without their notes of praise for civic virtues, and like Dekker he walked a fine line between praising either the city or the king to the detriment of the other.

18. Jonson's text was entered in the Stationers' Register to Edward Blount on 19 March, and Dekker's to Thomas Mann Jr. on 2 April. Although Jonson included only his contributions to the day's events, Mann complained that Blount's sale of Jonson's text was an infringement of his right to publish the official account of the royal entry, and on 14 May the company of stationers fined Blount and ordered him to hand over his copies of Jonson's pamphlet to Mann, who duly printed a corrected quarto of Dekker's account under the emphatic title *The Whole Magnificent Entertainment*. Joseph Loewenstein sees in this controversy an intense and explicit competition between stationers over the proprietary rights to the pageant that parallels the one I am tracing between the poets (*Possessive Authorship*, 170–72). See also Richard Dutton, ed., *Jacobean Civic Pageants* (Keele University Press, 1995), 20; Herford and Simpson, *Ben Jonson* 7:67, 77–9; Thomas Dekker, *The Dramatic Works*, ed. Fredson Bowers (Cambridge: Cambridge University Press, 1953–61), 2:231.

19. Clifford Geertz, *Local Knowledge* (New York: Basic Books, 1983), 125.

20. James's lack of participation during the royal entry has been frequently exaggerated into a general portrait of dour aloofness and compared unfavorably to the popular image of his predecessor. Seventeenth-century historian Arthur Wilson's *Life and Reign of King James the First* (London, 1653) depicts a king who values privacy above public display and only grudgingly participates in the requisite shows of royal pomp, who "naturally did not love to be looked on . . . the accesses of the people made him so impatient, that he often dispersed them with *frowns*, that we may not say with *curses*" (12–13). This image of James I has become almost canonical, especially among literary historians, but it should be treated with suspicion. Although Wilson's view may have some basis given the king's behavior later in his reign, we must remember that Wilson—just eight years old at James's accession in 1603—was hardly a reliable eyewitness, and that his history's anti-Stuart bias was conditioned by his having lived through the civil war. The most valuable corrective to the biases of the traditional English historiography of James is Jenny Wormald's "James VI and I: Two Kings or One?" *History* 68 (1983): 187–209, which traces the negative English views of James to the conflict between English expectations,

conditioned by Elizabeth's ruling style, and the very different style of rule James brought with him from Scotland.

21. Turner (*The English Renaissance Stage*, 133–52), in a similar argument to the one I make below, compares the playwrights' different representational techniques in the pageant, presenting Jonson's as emblematic and textual and Dekker's as quantitative and practical, the latter being (as Turner shows throughout his study) more unapologetically indebted to the "practical spatial arts"—cartography, architecture, geometry, etc.—than was Jonson.

22. Ben Jonson, *Part of King James his Royall and Magnificent Entertainement* (London, 1604), C1; all subsequent signature references to Jonson's text in this chapter will be parenthetical.

23. Harrison was the architect and joiner who carried out the erection of the triumphal arches, and his folio *The Arch's of Trivmph* (London, 1604) gives a brief description of the day's events as well as seven elaborate engravings of his work by William Kip.

24. The allegorical conceit—"that those cloudes were gathered vpon the face of the Citty, through their long want of his most wished sight: but now, as at the rising of the Sunne, all mistes were dispersed and fled"—may take its cue from the rhetoric of T. M. (Thomas Millington?) the year before in *The True Narration of the Entertainment of his Royall Maiestie* when describing the king's approach to Berwick after a ceremonial ordnance discharge: "as all darknesse flies before the face of the Sunne, so did these clouds of smoake and gun-powder vanish at his gracious approach" (C1ᵛ).

25. For the identity of the players we are indebted to Dekker, *The Magnificent Entertainment* (London, 1604), C1.

26. Dekker, *The Magnificent Entertainment*, C1.

27. Jonson's sidenote explains that "these" are the silent daughters of Genius (B3ᵛ).

28. The act of translating the temple also has the added bonus of rendering the ominous Ides of March harmless, by claiming the date as a feast day for James and his wife: "And may these *Ides* as fortunate appeare / To thee, as they to *Caesar* fatall were" (D2ᵛ).

29. Parry, *Golden Age Restor'd*, 6, 18.

30. Parry, *Golden Age Restor'd*, 8.

31. Joseph Loewenstein (*Possessive Authorship*, 168) makes a similar point about Jonson's use of printed glosses in the masque:

    Jonson does all he can to produce a printed text that will function as a kind of pre-requisite supplement, the necessary adjunct to an ostensibly self-sufficient performance, one which will make up the gaps in the masquers' (again, ostensibly) total understanding. . . . In essence, Jonson uses print to complete the event.

32. All subsequent signature references to Dekker's *The Magnificent Entertainment* will be parenthetical.

33. Compare Jonson's "Court- Towne- and Countrey-Reader" (B2ᵛ).
34. This 1604 title page marks the first recorded occurrence of Jonson's name with the distinctive spelling—dropping the "h"—by which he was afterwards known. David Riggs makes much of this intentional change in spelling, arguing that it implies his uniqueness among the many Johnsons in Jacobean London, autonomy from familial attachments, and a new authorial identity suited to his new role as Jacobean court poet (Riggs, *Ben Jonson*, 114). See also Richard Dutton, *Jacobean Civic Pageants*, 23.
35. Parry, *Golden Age Restor'd*, 3. Reading and walking are of course arguably distinct in important ways; reading is guided, as we see particularly in this Jonsonian text, in ways that walking usually is not. De Certeau, however, compares the reader's practice of page place with the walker's practice of urban space (see *Practice*, xxi), and in any case the royal entry, a highly controlled and plotted walk through the city, gives Jonson an opportunity to explore a specialized act of walking that is closer to reading than urban walking generally is.
36. Dekker also wrote (and preserved in his text) what was to have been the first device of the pageant, a pseudo-martial meeting on horseback between Saints George and Andrew, the two patrons of James's kingdoms, whose amicable union would be achieved by the approach of the king. Intended to be performed outside Bishopsgate, this device was preempted by Jonson's Fenchurch Street arch, but elements of it may have been recycled. The Chester pamphleteer Gilbert Dugdale preserved an eyewitness account (*The Time Triumphant*, [London, 1604]), in which it seems that the Bishopsgate pageant, or at least its characters and costumes, were used in some truncated form in 1604 before the procession encountered the Fenchurch arch: "There also Saint George, and Saint Andrew, in compleat Armour, met in one combate & fought for the victorie" (Dugdale, B2ᵛ). It is difficult to determine how much, if any, of Dekker's script was used, and it is just as hard to imagine this saintly joust not conflicting with the silent decorum of Jonson's device.

     One would expect Dekker's intended device outside the city to be especially fitting in March 1604 to welcome the now twice-crowned king into London. In the event, however, the king and his train began their progress from the Tower, inside the city, with Dekker's device put aside, and the reasons for this change are open to speculation. Since the Bishopsgate pageant focused on the unification of England and Scotland the previous spring, perhaps the novelty of the unification had worn off in the interim. More importantly, I would argue, the change in the route, bringing the first pageant within the city walls, was part of a concerted effort by the city government to structure the procession so as to emphasize London's ritual importance. James's coronation had gone on in July 1603 without the traditional pomp, and the new occasion for the royal entry, the opening of parliament, had little or nothing to do with London. There was no traditional symbolic role for the city in such an occasion, and the royal entry thus seemed to have been transformed from a ritual of mutual affirmation for city and crown into one whose only significance was royal display. In restructuring the event with James starting in the Tower, however, the royal entry could be made to *look* like a coronation. London would host the king, lead him through its streets, and include all the ritual-laden elements—the reciprocal acknowledgement of authority—that had been missing from the coronation the previous summer.

37. Although Peace presides over the transformation of London into garden, Dekker, mindful that the civic elites are also part of his audience, is careful not to efface the glories specific to the city: despite all the pastoral trappings of a *locus amoenus*, two central figures of the Garden of Plenty are the commercial and un-pastoral personifications of Silver and Gold, forming a somewhat incongruous core of mercantile truth amidst the allegorical transformation.

38. This is an example of what Paula Johnson, in "Jacobean Ephemera and the Immortal Word," *Renaissance Drama* 8 (1977), calls Dekker's "rhetoric of presence," a strategy of foregrounding the immediacy and ephemerality of the event that Johnson contrasts with Jonson's efforts to produce an entirely textual, ahistorical, and permanent version of the pageant. But inasmuch as Dekker "returns us in memory to the lost moment, transforms history into present story," his chattier, more readerly approach, Johnson argues, is not "any less serious an attempt to conquer time than is Jonson's universalizing" (156).

NOTES TO CHAPTER THREE

1. The first fifteen years of James's reign saw a boom in the genre unprecedented in the history of European drama. As Jonathan Haynes points out in *The Social Relations of Jonson's Theater (Cambridge: Cambridge University Press, 1992)*, the "hunger for contemporary realism and novelty on the Elizabethan stage" was "radically and spectacularly new" and the contemporary London setting, almost unheard of in 1598, became standard in less than a decade (7). As a category, "city comedy" is still difficult to designate precisely, but most critical debates, following the lead of Brian Gibbons's first systematic treatment of the genre, *Jacobean City Comedy* (Cambridge: Harvard University Press, 1968) center on class conflict as the genre's primary concern. For example, Alexander Leggatt's study, *Citizen Comedy in the Age of Shakespeare* (Toronto: University of Toronto Press, 1973), as its title suggests, focuses more on the portraits of merchant citizens—both as heroes and villains—than on city comedy's critique of London society, but his two main categories rely on class antagonisms. Susan Wells discusses

the genre as a means of defining the mercantile class, a response to the disjunction between traditional, communal ideals of the city and the burgeoning commercial realities of Jacobean London ("Jacobean City Comedy and the Ideology of the City, *ELH* 48 [1981]: 37–38). Lawrence Venuti's nuanced Marxist critique ("Transformations of City Comedy: A Symptomatic Reading," *Assays* 3 [1985]: 99–134), does not ascribe a consistent class-based ideology to the genre, arguing that it reflects the contradictions and discontinuities in emergent Jacobean capitalism. Similarly, Andrew Gurr has recently argued that city comedy as a genre is too large a category to be understood in simple polarities, and has reminded us that "the 'city' was never an organism, a coherent single-minded entity" with easily traceable attitudes and allegiances ("'Within the compass of the city walls': Allegiances in Plays for and About the City," in *Plotting Early Modern London*, ed. Mehl, Stock, and Zwierlein [Aldershot: Ashgate, 2004], 116). Both Venuti and Gurr do acknowledge that individual plays take stands and do focused ideological work, championing the values of one class or another, if in complex and sometimes contradictory ways, but they are right to say that class ideology is inadequate to characterize the genre. I agree with Theodore Leinwand that "the playwrights do not unthinkingly champion one status group over another" (*The City Staged* [Madison: University of Wisconsin Press, 1986], 7), and I would argue that the best examples of the genre, particularly Jonson's, tend to be less about celebrating the victory of one class than about the victory of theater as a set of practices and theatricality as a set of values, an ideological claim, to be sure, but based on the dramatist's profession rather than social hierarchy and economic relations.

2. Wells, "Ideology," 42–45.

3. Theodore Leinwand, "London Triumphing: The Jacobean Lord Mayor's Show." *CLIO* 11 (1982): 137.

4. Jonson always had an ambivalent attitude toward the sort of flattery of London's ruling citizen class that this kind of bourgeois drama, like the Lord Mayor's Shows, required. Although in 1628, in poor financial circumstances, he accepted an annual pension of one hundred nobles from the city government to replace Thomas Middleton in the post of city chronologer, a job that required him to "collect and set down all the memorable acts of this City," he seems to have neglected the post. The pension was withheld three years later "vntill he shall have presented . . . some fruits of his labours" (Herford and Simpson, *Ben Jonson*, 1:240–41). In late 1604 Jonson was employed, as many of his fellow playwrights would be in the ensuing years, to write a Lord Mayor's Show, for the newly elected haberdasher Sir Thomas Low. Unlike most such pageants, however, no script for his one and only Lord Mayor's Show survives. Jonson was consciously wooing the patronage of the new king's court at that time, demonstrably more interested in employment creating courtly entertainments than civic

ones, and he either neglected to have a printed record of the show produced or sought to suppress it.

5. Joseph Loewenstein places this 1599 Order into the context of a late Elizabethan "see-saw" effect; the escalation in the output of satirical *books* that prompted the 1599 ban (and the attendant boom in satirical *plays*) was itself a response to the earlier suppression of theatrical satire (*Possessive Authorship*, 23).

6. Indeed, as Theodore Leinwand points out, "it is possible, though not probable, that Jonson moved his gulls from Florence to London at about the same time he was working on *Eastward Ho*" (*City Staged*, 115).

7. The controversy over the date of revision of the F version of *Every Man in His Humor* has still not been settled, with any year from 1601 to 1616 a possibility, but the better evidence points to a later revision date, probably beginning around 1612 (Herford and Simpson's estimation), and possibly continuing as late as the publication process. For an excellent summary of the arguments see Robert S. Miola's introduction to his 2000 edition of the play (The Revels Plays [Manchester: Manchester University Press], 1–3).

8. J. W. Lever, introduction to Ben Jonson, *Every Man in His Humour: A Parallel-Text Edition of the 1601 Quarto and the 1616 Folio*, ed. J. W. Lever (London: Edward Arnold, 1971). All citations of the play will be taken from this edition.

9. Richard Dutton, *Ben Jonson: To the First Folio* (Cambridge: Cambridge University Press, 1983), 28.

10. See Stow, *A Survey of London: Reprinted from the Text of 1603*, ed. C. L. Kingsford, 2 vols. (Oxford: Clarendon Press, 1908), 2:54; and Lever, introduction to *Every Man in His Humour*, 25n.

11. Stow, *Survey*, 2:128–29.

12. See, for example, Barton, *Dramatist*, 46.

13. Dutton, *Ben Jonson*, 28.

14. G. B. Jackson, introduction to *Every Man in His Humor* (New Haven: Yale University Press, 1969), 1, 22.

15. See, for example, Jackson, introduction to *Every Man in His Humor*, 25, and Dutton, *Ben Jonson*, 37.

16. Ben Jonson, *Every Man Out of His Humour*, ed. Helen Ostovich, The Revels Plays (Manchester: Manchester University Press, 2001).

17. Jonson portrays an elaborately choreographed version of the sort of microcosmic adventuring that took place in Paul's in *Every Man Out*, act three. Epigram 88, "On English Movnsievr," in which he compares a pretentious, Frenchified gallant to a mannequin paraded around the middle aisle as advertisement, further suggests Jonson's contempt for "Paul's men" and their turning: the "English Monsieur" "needs must proue / The new *french*-taylors motion, monthly made, / Daily to turne in Pavls, and helpe the trade" (14–16).

18. Dutton, *Ben Jonson*, 32.
19. Impossible, that is, unless we associate it with the neighborhoods of the Whitefriars or the Blackfriars, both having the status of liberties, outside the civic government's jurisdiction since they were seized by Henry VIII from the monastic orders that gave them their names, and both the sites of playhouses. For more on the potent dual nature of the liberty of the Black-friars, see Chapter Four, below.
20. See Lever, introduction to *Every Man in His Humour*, 141n.
21. Anne Barton points out that this awareness of the exhibitory function of theater was a part of the play from its beginnings, that "the principal activity of the comedy [is] the exhibition of fools," and further, that Jonson made this more emphatic in the Folio version by excising Old Kno'well's 2.2 soliloquy in praise of reason, precisely because "Looked at rationally, there is indeed something both aimless and morally doubtful about the time and energy expended by Prospero, Lorenzo Junior—and, by extension, the dramatist himself—in arranging a display of other people's harmless eccentricities" (*Dramatist*, 53).
22. Dutton, *Ben Jonson*, 32.
23. The term refers to the easily purchased knighthoods that James was widely criticized for granting. The crown was quite sensitive to such criticism, and satirical comments on the practice in *Eastward Ho* were the cause of the playwrights' temporary imprisonment.
24. The acceptance of the play's "neat moral paradigm" (Jackson I. Cope, "*Volpone* and the Authorship of *Eastward Hoe*," *Modern Language Notes* 72 [1957]: 256), and the insistence that it unironically champions the bourgeois values of thrift and duty, have persisted from the eighteenth century onward, a critical tradition that R. W. Van Fossen traces in the introduction to his Revels Plays edition (Manchester: Manchester University Press, 1979), 21–23. Reactions to the play's perceived didactic morality have ranged from Anthony Trollope's complaints about its tedium (1825, cited by Van Fossen, 22) to T. M. Parrott's influential interpretation in 1914, where he approvingly contrasts it with the amorality of Middleton and Dekker: "instead of the laxness and confusion of morals which we have noted in *Westward Ho*, we have here a sharp differentiation between vice and virtue—the latter, to be sure, presented in a somewhat bourgeois form—an open conflict, and the final triumph of the good" (*The Plays and Poems of George Chapman*, ed. Parrott [London: Routledge, 1910–14], 2:840).
25. C. G. Petter, ed., *Eastward Ho!*, The New Mermaids (London: A & C Black, 1973), xii.
26. Citations are taken from Chapman, Jonson, and Marston, *Eastward Ho*, ed. R.W. Van Fossen, The Revels Plays (Manchester: Manchester University Press, 1979).

27. Leinwand, *The City Staged*, 64.
28. Louis B. Wright, *Middle-Class Culture in Elizabethan England* (Chapel Hill: University of North Carolina Press, 1935), 631.
29. Una Ellis-Fermor, *The Jacobean Drama: An Interpretation* (London: Methuen, 1936), 136; H. W. Wells, *Elizabethan and Jacobean Playwrights* (New York: Columbia University Press, 1939), 208–209; M. C. Bradbrook, *The Growth and Structure of Elizabethan Comedy* (Cambridge: Cambridge University Press, 1955), 128; Marchette Chute, *Ben Jonson of Westminster* (New York: Dutton, 1953), 150; Jill Phillips Ingram, "Economies of Obligation in *Eastward Ho*," *Ben Jonson Journal* 11 (2004): 22–23.
30. See *Conversations*, 274–75 (Herford and Simpson, *Ben Jonson*, 1:140).
31. Petter, introduction to *Eastward Ho!*, xxvii.
32. Leinwand, *The City Staged*, 115.
33. Ralph Alan Cohen, "The Function of Setting in *Eastward Ho*," *Renaissance Papers* (1973): 83, 88.
34. Cohen, "Function of Setting," 91.
35. Cohen, "Function of Setting," 95–96. Turner argues that the play's "cyclical spatial and moral trajectory" are a virtue of the framework of the prodigal play, which in turn may have been an expedient of collaboration, "the simplest way to provide a minimum of structure so that the business of writing individual scenes and lines could be parceled out" (*The English Renaissance Stage*, 211).
36. Both Petter (introduction to *Eastward Ho!*, xiii-xxi), after evaluating earlier arguments about division of authorship, and more extensively D. J. Lake in "*Eastward Ho*: Linguistic evidence for Authorship," *Notes and Queries* 226 (1981): 158–66, break down the allocation of scenes with Marston responsible for act one, Chapman for acts two and three, all three contributing to 4.1, and Jonson writing 4.2–5.5. See also R. W. Van Fossen's Appendix 3 (*Eastward Ho*, 226).
37. Turner, *The English Renaissance Stage*, 212–13.
38. As Helen Ostovich has observed, Golding only flourishes as an admirable character when he "bursts into imaginative flower," becomes "exuberantly theatrical . . . abandons his puritan philosophy of hard work and restraint, and leaps into enthusiastic pretence" (introduction to *Eastward Ho!*, Royal Shakespeare Company Edition [London: Nick Hern Books, 2002], xiii). Moreover, as Jill Phillips Ingram argues, Golding's theatrical metamorphosis in *Eastward Ho*'s concluding "burlesque of tidy morality-play reconciliations" ("Economies of Obligation," 22) seems consciously modeled on the prodigals' enactment of festive misrule (35–36).
39. Howard, *Theater of a City*, 102.
40. Gibbons, *City Comedy*, 11.
41. Leggatt, *Citizen Comedy*, 52.

42. Angela Stock expands this view of *Eastward Ho*'s spatial inversion of civic ceremony. She argues that the prodigals' washing-up spots are systematically chosen as "satirically inverted equivalents" to the sacred spaces of city pageants: Baynard's Castle, St. Paul's, Cheapside and the Guildhall. Angela Stock, "'Something done in honour of the city': Ritual, Theatre, and Satire in Jacobean Civic Pageantry," in *Plotting Early Modern London*, ed. Mehl, Stock, and Zwierlein (Aldershot: Ashgate, 2004), 140.
43. Van Fossen, introduction to *Eastward Ho*, 36.
44. Leggatt, *Citizen Comedy*, 53.

NOTES TO CHAPTER FOUR

1. Dutton, *Ben Jonson*, 102. See also Dutton's introduction to the Revels Plays edition of *Epicene* (Manchester: Manchester University Press, 2003), 12.
2. These Chapel Children were not those who had played in a private space in the Blackfriars district in the 1570s, but a new boys company established in 1600 by Henry Evans. Evans had leased from William Burbage the Blackfriars playhouse, which had stood empty since 1596, when the residents of the Blackfriars district petitioned the privy council to prevent professional theater there. See E. K. Chambers, *The Elizabethan Stage*, 4:319–20. The turn-of-the-century boys' company still, however professional their practices, maintained the cachet of being nominally a part of the royal household; see Riggs, *Ben Jonson*, 68.
3. For an excellent history of the playing spaces in the Blackfriars district, see Reaveley Gair, "Takeover at the Blackfriars: Queen's Revels to King's Men," in *The Elizabethan Theatre X*, ed. C. E. McGee (Port Credit, ON: P. D. Meany, 1988), 37–54. See also Rosalind Miles, *Ben Jonson: His Life and Work* (London: Routledge & Kegan Paul, 1986), 127, 130.
4. Jonson signed his prefatory epistle in the 1607 quarto of *Volpone* "From my house in the Black-friars."
5. Anthony Ouellette, in "*The Alchemist* and the Emerging Adult Private Playhouse," *Studies in English Literature* 45, 2 (Spring 2005): 375–99, makes much of this potential unease, and sees in *The Alchemist* a comment on the King's Men's tension with their new neighbors and on their ascendancy over their rival playing companies, still restricted to the suburban liberties.
6. Ann C. Christensen, "'The doors are made against you': Domestic Thresholds in Ben Jonson's Plays." *Journal of the Rocky Mountain Medieval and Renaissance Association* 18 (1997): 176.
7. Civic arguments for closing the theaters could partake of both types of argument, as illustrated by the neat catch-22 in the Corporation of London's 1584 answer to the Queen's Men's petition to the Privy Council: "To play in plagetime is to encreasce the plage by infection: to play out of plagetime

is to draw the plage by offendinges of God vpon occasion of such playes" (Chambers, 4:301). See also F. P. Wilson, 51–55.

8. See Wilson, *Plague*, 55–71.

9. Wilson, *Plague*, 118. See also Patrick Phillips, "'You Need Not Fear the House': The Absence of Plague in *The Alchemist*," *Ben Jonson Journal* 13 (2006): 45–46.

10. Citations of *The Alchemist* are taken from Elizabeth Cook's New Mermaids edition (London: A & C Black, 1991).

11. Dutton, *Epicene*, 6, 92. See also Gair, "Takeover," 47–48.

12. On the dimensions and layout of the Whitefriars playhouse, about which very little is known, see Jean MacIntyre, "Production Resources at the Whitefriars Playhouse, 1609–1612," *Early Modern Literary Studies* 2.3 (1996) 2.1–35, #3, http://purl.oclc.org/emls/02-3/maciwhit.html; on the influence of this space on *Epicoene*, see Dutton, *Epicene*, 52–53.

13. The 1616 Folio claims that the first performance was in 1609, but since the company had not been granted its patent until 4 January 1610, it is likely that the 1609 date reflects old style reckoning, with the new year starting on 25 March.

14. Donaldson, *Magic Houses*, 66–88, 71.

15. Citations from *Epicoene* are taken from R. V. Holdsworth's New Mermaids edition (New York: W. W. Norton, 1979).

16. John Dryden, "Examen of *The Silent Woman* (1667–1668)," in *Critical Essays on Ben Jonson*, ed. Robert N. Watson (New York: G.K. Hall, 1997), 110; Edmund Wilson, "Morose Ben Jonson," in *Ben Jonson: A Collection of Critical Essays*, ed. Jonas Barish, (Englewood Cliffs, NJ: Prentice-Hall, 1963), 60–74.

17. For excellent arguments on the significance of the play's representation of this newly fashionable inter-urban area, see Janette Dillon, *Theatre, Court, and City 1595–1610: Drama and Social Space in London* (Cambridge: Cambridge University Press, 2000), 124–36; Howard, 21–22, 162–208; P. K. Ayers, "'Dreams of the City': The Urban and the Urbane in Jonson's *Epicoene*," *Philological Quarterly* 66 (1987): 73–86, especially 74; Emrys Jones, "The First West End Comedy," *Proceedings of the British Academy* 68 (1982): 215–58.

18. Adam Zucker, "The Social Logic of Ben Jonson's *Epicoene*." *Renaissance Drama* 33 (2004): 46, 48. This idea, that the play demonstrates urban cultural competency via its characters' production of space, also forms the basis of Mimi Yiu's argument. Yiu's concern, like mine, is primarily with domestic space, though she sees the play as more explicitly didactic: "Jonson's *Epicoene* presents a scene to teach viewers how to design their own homes, how to structure social and spatial relations in the uncertain landscape of Jacobean London" (Yiu, "Sounding the Space," 79).

19. Tellingly, of the eight plays published in the 1616 Folio, only the other plague year play, *The Alchemist*, contains more occurrences of the word,

with twenty-nine, and only *Every Man in His Humor,* with eleven occurrences, comes close.

20. Holdsworth, introduction to *Epicoene,* xxxvii.
21. Gail Kern Paster, *The Idea of the City in the Age of Shakespeare* (Athens: University of Georgia Press, 1985), 162.
22. Zucker, "Social Logic," 50.
23. Among the recent critics who have insisted upon the identity of Morose's house with the space of the stage is Mimi Yiu, who argues that the equivalence, and the barrage of noise that explodes within both houses, serves both to equate the audience with Morose and to distance us from the antitheatrical attitudes that he espouses (Yiu, "Sounding the Space," 74, 79).
24. For an excellent discussion of the physical nature of the "studies" on the Whitefriars stage, see MacIntyre, "Production Resources," #15–17.
25. Zucker, "Social Logic," 54.
26. Ayers, for example, argues that *Epicoene* offers in the gallants "only doubtful models of emulation" ("Dreams," 84), and that they are "inevitably compromised by their position in the world about them" (78). Richard Dutton, despite his lengthy argument for the identification of the gallants with Jonson's friends, including John Donne, acknowledges the inescapable ambiguity of Jonson's attitude toward the characters (*Epicene,* 59).
27. In the epistle to the quarto text of *Volpone,* for example, Jonson famously argues that it is "the office of a *comic-Poet* to imitate justice, and instruct to life, as well as purity of language, or stir up gentle affections" (Epistle 119–21, in *Volpone,* ed. Philip Brockbank, The New Mermaids [London: Ernest Benn, 1968]).
28. The gallants' (and the play's) ambivalence toward the moral question of Dauphine's and Morose's habit of obsessive withdrawal from public might be illuminated by Patricia Fumerton's description of the "aesthetics of detachment" among the aristocracy of Jacobean England (in *Cultural Aesthetics* [Chicago: University of Chicago Press, 1991], 111–68). Tracing the gradual subdivision of great houses' eating spaces and their tendency toward withdrawing further and further from public—culminating in James's fully detached banqueting house at Whitehall, the performance site of Jonson's court masques, Fumerton argues for a new subjectivity defined by withdrawal: "the aristocratic self in James's era absented itself" (112). She finds in Jonson something like the ambivalence toward withdrawal to private space that I read in *Epicoene,* showing that Jonson's masques, which tended to support the aesthetic of detachment, are undercut by the Jacobean masquing tradition in which, at a masque's end, walls are torn down and sets are cannibalized by audience and masquers alike, in a fashion analogous to the invasion of Morose's house by the wedding party.
29. R. L. Smallwood, "'Here, in the Friars': Immediacy and Theatricality in *The Alchemist," Review of English Studies* 32 (1980): 147.

30. Smallwood, "'Here, in the Friars,'" 152.
31. See Riggs, *Ben Jonson*, 171.
32. Mathew Martin, "Play and Plague in Ben Jonson's *The Alchemist*," *English Studies in Canada* 26 (2000): 394. The idea that the play equates alchemy with dramatic art and that the activities in Lovewit's house are a version of Jonson's own comedy is a critical commonplace, though the uses to which Jonson puts this equation are up for debate. See, for example, C. G. Thayer's claim that Lovewit is a model of an ignorant Jonsonian audience (*Ben Jonson: Studies in the Plays* [Norman: University of Oklahoma Press, 1963], 88), Robert W. Witt's treatment of *The Alchemist* as a series of "plays within" (*Mirror within a Mirror: Ben Jonson and the Play Within* [Salzburg: Institut für English Sprache und Literatur, 1975], 66–72, 108–9), and Peter Womack's discussion of Lovewit's house as a "disgraceful and cynical" image of Jonson's theater (*Ben Jonson*, 118).
33. Robert N. Watson, *Ben Jonson's Parodic Strategy: Literary Imperialism in the Comedies* (Cambridge: Harvard University Press, 1987), 114.
34. Jonathan Haynes, "Representing the Underworld: *The Alchemist*," *Studies in Philology* 86 (1989): 36–37.
35. Cheryl Lynn Ross, "The Plague of *The Alchemist*," *Renaissance Quarterly* 41 (1988): 443.
36. Ross, "Plague," 444. More recently, Andrew Hiscock (*Uses of this World*, 171–97) makes a similar argument, that the play offers an "encounter with a fantasied Other, which penetrates the familiar landscape of plague-ridden Blackfriars," but for Hiscock, who owes more, perhaps, to British cultural materialism than to American new historicism, the upshot of this "penetration" is the emergence of new individual and communal subjectivity, not (as for Ross) on the reinforcement of power: the encounter with the Other "leads to a radical interrogation of the identities on offer in this dramatic world," and the play ultimately "reflects upon how changing economic and demographic relationships . . . caused communities to reinvent themselves in order to insure their cultural survival" (*Uses of this World*, 16).
37. See Ouellette, "Emerging Adult Playhouse," 381.
38. Christensen, "Domestic Thresholds," 176.
39. Martin, "Play and Plague," 396.
40. For the argument that the spatial practices of theater itself served as the same kind of therapy against the plague as Mammon's imagined "labours," see Phillips, "Absence of Plague," 43–62.
41. Martin, "Play and Plague," 393.
42. Martin, "Play and Plague," 395.
43. Haynes, "Representing the Underworld," 40.
44. Wayne Rebhorn, "Jonson's 'Jovy Boy': Lovewit and the Dupes in *The Alchemist*," *Journal of English and Germanic Philology* 79 (1980): 356. In general, critical discussion of the resolution of *The Alchemist* has fallen into two

camps, those who see Lovewit as the final victor, and those, like Rebhorn, who see his victory compromised by his dependence upon Face. In the former camp, with Haynes, are Cheryl Lynn Ross, Francis Mares in the introduction to his 1967 Revels Plays edition of the play (xliii), and Alan C. Dessen, "*The Alchemist*: Jonson's 'Estates' Play," *Renaissance Drama* 7 (1964): 48–50). Robert Smallwood, conversely, argues unequivocally that Jonson resolves the play in Face's favor ("'Here, in the Friars,'" 152), and more recently Ouellette ("Emerging Adult Playhouse") has expanded this argument with the view that Face represents the King's Men in a subtextual assertion of the company's ascendancy in their new playhouse.

45. Martin, "Play and Plague," 393.
46. See Miles, *Life and Work*, 27–28; Riggs, *Ben Jonson*, 20.

NOTES TO CHAPTER FIVE

1. The play's Induction (65–66) gives the date of the first performance as 31 October 1614; the Chamber Accounts and Revels Accounts list the court performance as 1 November 1614. See Chambers, *Elizabethan Stage*, 4:183. All citations of *Bartholomew Fair* are taken from Ben Jonson, *Bartholmew Fair [sic]*, ed. G. R. Hibbard, The New Mermaids (New York: W. W. Norton, 1977).
2. Venkata Reddy, *Ben Jonson: His Dramatic Art* (New Delhi: Prestige Books, 1994), 198.
3. See Jonas Barish, *Ben Jonson and the Language of Prose Comedy* (Cambridge: Harvard University Press, 1960), 236, and Thomas Cartelli, "*Bartholomew Fair* as Urban Arcadia," *Renaissance Drama* 14 (1983): 172.
4. George E. Rowe, *Distinguishing Jonson: Imitation, Rivalry, and the Direction of a Dramatic Career* (Lincoln: University of Nebraska Press, 1988), 157.
5. Rowe, *Distinguishing Jonson*, 158.
6. "Ode to Himself," Herford and Simpson, *Ben Jonson*, 6:492.
7. Of Jonson's plays, only two come close to this frequency, with *Sejanus* having forty-seven occurrences and *Cynthia's Revels* forty-four, though in these plays the sense is usually place as office. My survey is by no means comprehensive, but Jonson does seem to have used the word considerably more frequently than his contemporary playwrights. For example, it occurs in *A Chaste Maid in Cheapside*, arguably Middleton's most localized London play, only nine times.
8. For James's attempt to visit the Exchange with Queen Anne in early March of 1604 "for their recreation, and thinkeing to passe vnknowne" we are indebted again to Gilbert Dugdale (*Time Triumphant*, B1ᵛ). According to Marchette Chute, there was an even more immediate and comically relevant precedent for Overdo's activities:

> ... in this same year of 1614 the new mayor of London sent a proud
> report to the government in which he announced that he had not
> only ferreted out many brothels through his spy service but "had
> gone himself disguised to divers of them," thus striking a note of
> unconscious humor that the most satirical playwright could hardly
> have bettered. (*Jonson of Westminster*, 215–16)

Presumably this "new mayor" is the Draper Sir Thomas Hayes, elected just
three weeks before *Bartholomew Fair*'s first performance.

9. Peter Lake puts *Bartholomew Fair* into the much wider context of pamphlet literature, both moralizing and sensationalist, arguing that the play
   enters into, even as it parodies, the discourse of Puritan moral reform.
   See Peter Lake and Michael Questier, *The Antichrist's Lewd Hat: Protestants, Papists and Players in Post-Reformation England* (New Haven:
   Yale University Press, 2002), especially chapter 11. For examples of
   rogue pamphlets, see Arthur Kinney's anthology, *Rogues, Vagabonds, and
   Sturdy Beggars* (Amherst: University of Massachusetts Press, 1990). For
   an extended comparison of the genre's depiction of the London underworld to that provided by city comedy, and a discussion of the early modern revolution in thinking about crime, see Haynes, "Representing the
   Underworld."

10. Barton, *Dramatist*, 204.

11. As Tiffany Stern demonstrates in "Behind the Arras: The Prompter's Place
    in the Shakespearean Theatre," *Theatre Notebook* 55, (2001): 110–18,
    the conceit of the playwright lurking backstage was something of a com-
    monplace at opening performances of new plays (see also Tiffany Stern,
    "'A Small-Beer Health to His Second Day': Playwrights, Prologues, and
    First Performances in the Early Modern Theater," *Studies in Philology* 101
    [2004]: 172–98). In most cases, however, the conceit carries a joke about
    the poet's anxiety about the play's reception; the Induction to *Bartholomew
    Fair* is notable for its construction of a confident, even aggressive author,
    using the conceit to urge the dramatist's disciplinary authority over the
    space of the playhouse and its inhabitants.

12. I am inclined to read this passage, and the Induction more generally, as
    more ironically satirical toward the audience than do Herford and Simp-
    son and critics such as Alexander Leggatt, who argues that "Jonson's stance
    in *Bartholomew Fair* is generally conciliatory" and that the Induction's
    "tone is light, the audience is more teased than bullied, and Jonson shows
    himself prepared to be accommodating" (*Ben Jonson: His Vision and His
    Art* [London: Methuen, 1981], 208, 207).

13. Richard Allen Cave, *Ben Jonson* (New York: St. Martin's, 1990), 114.

14. Jonathan Haynes, *Social Relations*, 129.

15. One strain of *Bartholomew Fair* criticism has seen Quarlous, because of
    his plotting, as only a dubiously effective author figure or example of

good judgment. Alexander Leggatt sees the character as illustrative of the universally debasing nature of the Fair (*Ben Jonson*, 66–72), and Richard Cave (*Ben Jonson*, 118) says that the play requires us to doubt his motives and the degree to which he is changed for the better by the Fair.

16. Peter Lake makes this association between Quarlous and Jonson as well, but in terms of antipuritanism, not practice of space: "Like Quarlous, the play and perhaps Jonson himself seem, if not happiest, then at least morally at ease, excoriating puritans" (*Antichrist's Lewd Hat*, 599).

17. Herford and Simpson (*Ben Jonson*, 1:146–48) argue that Leatherhead is a satirical portrait of Inigo Jones, Jonson's longtime collaborator on royal court masques, with whom he frequently had quarrels of authorship and authority; if so, his easy usurpation of Littlewit's authority reinforces the latter's role as a foil for Jonson and a failed version of Jonsonian authorship. For a discussion of the Jonson-Jones quarrel, and an opposing view on Leatherhead's representation of Inigo Jones, see D. J. Gordon, "Poet and Architect: The Intellectual Setting of the Quarrel between Ben Jonson and Inigo Jones," in *The Renaissance Imagination*, ed. Stephen Orgel (Berkeley: University of California Press), 77–101.

18. Helgerson, *Self-Crowned Laureates*, 156.

19. Turner's *The English Renaissance Stage* pursues a different, if analogous explanation for apparent contradictions in Jonson's attitude toward poetics and form on the one hand, and his stagecraft on the other: he consistently favored a classicizing, rhetorical, emblematic, and polemic attitude toward the composition of drama, masque and pageant, most notable in his quarrels and collaborations with Inigo Jones in court masques. Jonson's attempt to distance himself from the spatial, mechanical arts upon which the evolution of early modern drama depended, however, was compromised by "the fact that he continued to occupy the position both of 'practitioner' and 'critic' simultaneously and uneasily throughout his career" (245–46). As should be clear by now, I believe that Turner is right to see spatial practices of theater as the central focus of Jonson's ambivalence to theater, though, as I have argued, *Bartholomew Fair* offered Jonson an opportunity to balance these two roles.

NOTES TO THE EPILOGUE

1. Herford and Simpson, *Ben Jonson*, 11:397.
2. Jennifer Brady, "'Noe Fault, but Life': Jonson's Folio as Monument and Barrier," in *Ben Jonson's 1616 Folio*, ed. Brady and Herendeen, 195.
3. Brady, "Monument and Barrier," 194–95.
4. Ben Jonson, *The Staple of News*, ed. Anthony Parr, The Revels Plays (Manchester: Manchester University Press, 1988).

5. Ben Jonson, *The New Inn*, ed. Michael Hattaway, The Revels Plays (Manchester: Manchester University Press, 1984).

6. Hattaway, introduction to *The New Inn*, 5.

7. Ben Jonson, *The Devil is an Ass*, ed. Peter Happé, The Revels Plays (Manchester: Manchester University Press, 1996).

Bibliography

An excellent new Ballad shewing the Petigree of our Royall King IAMES. London, 1603.

Arber, Edward, ed. *Transcript of the Registers of the Company of Stationers of London: 1554–1640 A.D.* 5 vols. London, 1876.

Ashton, Robert. *The Crown and the Money Market 1603–1640.* Oxford: Oxford University Press, 1960.

Ayers, P. K. "'Dreams of the City': The Urban and the Urbane in Jonson's *Epicoene.*" *Philological Quarterly* 66 (1987): 73–86.

Barish, Jonas. *The Antitheatrical Prejudice.* Berkeley: University of California Press, 1981.

———, ed. *Ben Jonson: A Collection of Critical Essays.* Englewood Cliffs: Prentice Hall, 1963.

———. *Ben Jonson and the Language of Prose Comedy.* Cambridge: Harvard University Press, 1960.

Barthes, Roland. "The Death of the Author." In *Authorship: From Plato to Postmodernism: A Reader,* edited by Seán Burke, 125–30. Edinburgh: Edinburgh University Press, 1995.

Barton, Anne. *Ben Jonson, Dramatist.* Cambridge: Cambridge University Press, 1984.

Beaurline, L. A. *Jonson and Elizabethan Comedy: Essays in Dramatic Rhetoric.* San Marino: Huntington Library, 1978.

Bennet, Andrew. *The Author.* London: Routledge, 2005.

Bentley, Gerald Eades. *The Profession of Dramatist in Shakespeare's Time, 1590–1642.* Princeton: Princeton University Press, 1971.

Bergeron, David M. *English Civic Pageantry 1558–1642.* London: Edward Arnold, 1971.

Boehrer, Bruce. *The Fury of Men's Gullets: Ben Jonson and the Digestive Canal.* Philadelphia: University of Pennsylvania Press, 1997.

Bracken, James K. "Books from William Stansby's Printing House, and Jonson's Folio of 1616." *The Library* 10 (1988): 18–29.

Bradbrook, M. C. *The Growth and Structure of Elizabethan Comedy.* 2nd ed. Cambridge: Cambridge University Press, 1973.

Brady, Jennifer. "'Noe Fault, but Life': Jonson's Folio as Monument and Barrier." In *Ben Jonson's 1616 Folio*, edited by Jennifer Brady and W. H. Herendeen, 192–216. Newark: University of Delaware Press, 1991.

Bristol, Michael D. "Theater and Popular Culture." In *A New History of Early English Drama*, edited by John D. Cox and David Scott Kastan, 231–48. New York: Columbia University Press, 1997.

Brooks, Douglas A. *From Playhouse to Printing House: Drama and Authorship in Early Modern England.* Cambridge: Cambridge University Press, 2000.

Bruster, Douglas. *Drama and the Market in the Age of Shakespeare.* Cambridge: Cambridge University Press, 1992.

———. "The Structural Transformation of Print in Late Elizabethan England." In *Print, Manuscript, & Performance: The Changing Relations of the Media in Early Modern England*, edited by Arthur F. Marotti and Michael D. Bristol, 49–89. Columbus: Ohio State University Press, 2000.

Butler, Martin. "Jonson's London and Its Theatres." In *The Cambridge Companion to Ben Jonson*, edited by Richard Harp and Stanley Stewart, 15–29. Cambridge: Cambridge University Press, 2000.

Calendar of State Papers, Domestic Series, of the Reigns of Edward VI, Mary, Elizabeth, and James I 1547–1625. Edited by Robert Lemon. 12 vols. Vol. 6. London: Her Majesty's Stationery Office, 1856.

Cartelli, Thomas. "*Bartholomew Fair* as Urban Arcadia: Jonson Responds to Shakespeare." *Renaissance Drama* 14 (1983): 151–72.

Casey, Edward S. *The Fate of Place: A Philosophical History.* Berkeley: University of California Press, 1997.

———. "How to Get from Space to Place in a Fairly Short Stretch of Time: Phenomenological Prolegomena." In *Senses of Place*, edited by Steven Feld and Keith H. Basso, 13–52. Santa Fe: School of American Research Press, 1996.

Cave, Richard Allen. *Ben Jonson.* New York: St. Martin's Press, 1991.

Chamberlain, John. *Letters.* Edited by Norman McClure. 2 vols. Philadelphia: American Philosophical Society, 1939.

Chambers, E.K. *The Elizabethan Stage.* 4 vols. Oxford: Clarendon Press, 1923.

Chapman, George. *The Plays and Poems of George Chapman.* Edited by Thomas Marc Parrott. 2 vols. London: Routledge, 1910–14.

Chapman, George, Ben Jonson, and John Marston. *Eastward Ho!* Edited by C. G. Petter, New Mermaids. London: A & C Black, 1973.

———. *Eastward Ho.* Edited by R. W. Van Fossen, The Revels Plays. Manchester: Manchester University Press, 1979.

Christensen, Ann C. "'The Doors Are Made against You': Domestic Thresholds in Ben Jonson's Plays." *Journal of the Rocky Mountain Medieval and Renaissance Association* 18 (1997): 153–78.

Chute, Marchette. *Ben Jonson of Westminster.* New York: Dutton, 1953.

Cohen, Ralph Alan. "The Function of Setting in *Eastward Ho.*" *Renaissance Papers* (1973): 83–96.

Cope, Jackson I. "*Volpone* and the Authorship of *Eastward Hoe.*" *Modern Language Notes* 72 (1957): 253–56.

de Certeau, Michel. *The Practice of Everyday Life.* Translated by Steven Rendall. Berkeley: University of California Press, 1984.

Dekker, Thomas. *The Dramatic Works.* Edited by Fredson Bowers. 4 vols. Cambridge: Cambridge University Press, 1953–61.

———. *The Magnificent Entertainment.* London, 1604.

Dessen, Alan C. "*The Alchemist*: Jonson's 'Estates' Play." *Renaissance Drama* 7 (1964): 35–54.

———. *Elizabethan Stage Conventions and Modern Interpreters.* Cambridge: Cambridge University Press, 1984.

Dillon, Janette. *Theatre, Court, and City 1595–1610: Drama and Social Space in London.* Cambridge: Cambridge University Press, 2000.

Dobranski, Stephen B. *Milton, Authorship, and the Book Trade.* Cambridge: Cambridge University Press, 1999.

Donaldson, Ian. *Jonson's Magic Houses: Essays in Interpretation.* Oxford: Oxford University Press, 1997.

Dryden, John. "Examen of the Silent Woman (1667–1668)." In *Critical Essays on Ben Jonson,* edited by Robert N. Watson, 108–11. New York: G. K. Hall, 1997.

Dugdale, Gilbert. *The Time Triumphant.* London, 1604.

Dutton, Richard. *Ben Jonson: To the First Folio.* Cambridge: Cambridge University Press, 1983.

———. "The Birth of the Author." In *Texts and Cultural Change in Early Modern England,* edited by Cedric C. Brown and Arthur F. Marotti, 153–78. New York: St. Martin's Press, 1997.

———, ed. *Jacobean Civic Pageants.* Stafford: Keele University Press, 1995.

Ellis-Fermor, Una Mary. *The Jacobean Drama: An Interpretation.* London: Methuen, 1936.

Erne, Lukas. *Shakespeare as Literary Dramatist.* Cambridge: Cambridge University Press, 2003.

Finlay, Roger. *Population and Metropolis: The Demography of London 1580–1650.* Cambridge: Cambridge University Press, 1981.

Foucault, Michel. "What Is an Author?" In *The Foucault Reader,* edited by Paul Rabinow, 101–20. New York: Pantheon Books, 1984.

Fumerton, Patricia. *Cultural Aesthetics: Renaissance Literature and the Practice of Social Ornament.* Chicago: University of Chicago Press, 1991.

Gair, Reaveley. "Takeover at Blackfriars: Queen's Revels to King's Men." In *The Elizabethan Theatre X: Papers Given at the Tenth International Conference on Elizabethan Theatre,* edited by C. E. McGee, 37–54. Port Credit, ON: P. D. Meaney, 1983.

Geertz, Clifford. *Local Knowledge: Further Essays in Interpretive Anthropology.* New York: Basic Books, 1983.

Gibbons, Brian. *Jacobean City Comedy: A Study of Satiric Plays by Jonson, Marston, and Middleton*. London: Rupert Hart-Davis, 1968.

Gordon, D. J. "Poet and Architect: The Intellectual Setting of the Quarrel between Ben Jonson and Inigo Jones." In *The Renaissance Imagination*, edited by Stephen Orgel, 77–101. Berkeley: University of California Press, 1975.

Greene, Thomas. "Jonson and the Centered Self." *Studies in English Literature* 10 (1970): 325–48.

Gurr, Andrew. "'Within the Compass of the City Walls': Allegiances in Plays for and About the City." In *Plotting Early Modern London: New Essays on Jacobean City Comedy*, edited by Dieter Mehl, Angela Stock and Anne-Julia Zwierlein, 109–22. Aldershot: Ashgate, 2004.

Halasz, Alexandra. "Pamphlet Surplus: John Taylor and Subscription Publication." In *Print, Manuscript, & Performance: The Changing Relations of the Media in Early Modern England*, edited by Arthur F. Marotti and Michael D. Bristol, 90–102. Columbus: Ohio State University Press, 2000.

Harrison, G. B. *A Jacobean Journal; Being a Record of Those Things Most Talked of During the Years 1603–1606*. London: Routledge and Kegan Paul, 1941.

Harrison, Stephen. *The Arch's of Trivmph*. London, 1604.

Harley, J. B., and David Woodward, eds. *Cartography in Prehistoric, Ancient, and Medieval Europe and the Mediterranean*. Vol. 1, *The History of Cartography*. Chicago: University of Chicago Press, 1987.

Harvey, David. *Justice, Nature and the Geography of Difference*. Oxford: Blackwell, 1996.

Harvey, P. D. A. *Maps in Tudor England*. Chicago: University of Chicago Press, 1993.

Haynes, Jonathan. "Representing the Underworld: *The Alchemist*." *Studies in Philology* 86 (1989): 18–41.

———. *The Social Relations of Jonson's Theater*. Cambridge: Cambridge University Press, 1992.

Helgerson, Richard. *Forms of Nationhood: The Elizabethan Writing of England*. Chicago: University of Chicago Press, 1992.

———. *Self-Crowned Laureates: Spenser, Jonson, Milton and the Literary System*. Berkeley: University of California Press, 1983.

Herendeen, W. H. "A New Way to Pay Old Debts: Pretexts to the 1616 Folio." In *Ben Jonson's 1616 Folio*, edited by Jennifer Brady and W. H. Herendeen, 38–63. Newark: University of Delaware Press, 1991.

Hiscock, Andrew. *The Uses of This World: Thinking Space in Shakespeare, Marlowe, Cary and Jonson*. Cardiff: University of Wales Press, 2004.

Howard, Jean E. *Theater of a City: The Places of London Comedy, 1598–1642*. Philadelphia: University of Pennsylvania Press, 2007.

Ingram, Jill Phillips. "Economies of Obligation in *Eastward Ho*." *Ben Jonson Journal* 11 (2004): 21–40.

Johnson, Paula. "Jacobean Ephemera and the Immortal Word." *Renaissance Drama* 8 (1977): 151–72.

Jones, Emrys. "The First West End Comedy." *Proceedings of the British Academy* 68 (1982): 215–58.

Jonson, Ben. *The Alchemist*. Edited by F. H. Mares, The Revels Plays. Manchester: Manchester University Press, 1988.

———. *The Alchemist*. Edited by Elizabeth Cook, New Mermaids. London: A & C Black, 1991.

———. *Bartholmew Fair*. Edited by G. R. Hibbard, New Mermaids. New York: W. W. Norton, 1977.

———. *Ben Jonson*. Edited by C. H. Herford and Percy Simpson. 11 vols. Oxford: Clarendon Press, 1925–52.

———. *The Devil Is an Ass*. Edited by Peter Happé, The Revels Plays. Manchester: Manchester University Press, 1994.

———. *Epicene*. Edited by Richard Dutton, The Revels Plays. Manchester: Manchester University Press, 2003.

———. *Epicoene, or, the Silent Woman*. Edited by Roger Victor Holdsworth, New Mermaids. New York: W. W. Norton, 1979.

———. *Every Man in His Humor*. Edited by Gabriele Bernhard Jackson, The Yale Ben Jonson. New Haven: Yale University Press, 1969.

———. *Every Man in His Humour: A Parallel-Text Edition of the 1601 Quarto and the 1616 Folio*. Edited by J. W. Lever. London: Edward Arnold, 1971.

———. *Every Man in His Humour*. Edited by Robert S. Miola, The Revels Plays. Manchester: Manchester University Press, 2000.

———. *Every Man Out of His Humour*. Edited by Helen Ostovich, The Revels Plays. Manchester: Manchester University Press, 2001.

———. *His Part of King James His Royall and Magnificent Entertainement*. London, 1604.

———. *The New Inn*. Edited by Michael Hattaway, The Revels Plays. Manchester: Manchester University Press, 1984.

———. *The Staple of News*. Edited by Anthony Parr, The Revels Plays. Manchester: Manchester University Press, 1988.

———. *Volpone*. Edited by Philip Brockbank, New Mermaids. London: A & C Black, 1968.

———. *Workes*. London, 1616.

The Journal of the Court of Common Council. London: Guildhall Library.

Kastan, David Scott. *Shakespeare and the Book*. Cambridge: Cambridge University Press, 2001.

Kemp, William, *Kemps Nine Daies Wonder*. London, 1600.

Kinney, Arthur F. *Rogues, Vagabonds, and Sturdy Beggars: A New Gallery of Tudor and Early Stuart Rogue Literature*. Amherst: University of Massachusetts Press, 1990.

Klein, Bernhard. *Maps and the Writing of Space in Early Modern England and Ireland*. Houndmills: Palgrave, 2001.

Lake, D. J. "*Eastward Ho*: Linguistic Evidence for Authorship." *Notes and Queries* 226 (1981): 158–66.

Lake, Peter, and Michael Questier. *The Antichrist's Lewd Hat: Protestants, Papists and Players in Post-Reformation England*. New Haven: Yale University Press, 2002.

Lefebvre, Henri. *The Production of Space*. Translated by Donald Nicholson-Smith. Oxford: Blackwell, 1991.

Leggatt, Alexander. *Ben Jonson: His Vision and His Art*. London: Methuen, 1981.

———. *Citizen Comedy in the Age of Shakespeare*. Toronto: University of Toronto Press, 1973.

Leinwand, Theodore. *The City Staged: Jacobean Comedy, 1603–1613*. Madison: University of Wisconsin Press, 1986.

———. "London Triumphing: The Jacobean Lord Mayor's Show." *CLIO* 11 (1982): 137–53.

Loewenstein, Joseph. *The Author's Due: Printing and the Prehistory of Copyright*. Chicago: University of Chicago Press, 2002.

———. *Ben Jonson and Possessive Authorship*. Cambridge: Cambridge University Press, 2002.

M., T. *The True Narration of the Entertainment of His Royall Maiestie*. London, 1603.

MacIntyre, Jean. "Production Resources at the Whitefriars Playhouse, 1609–1612." *Early Modern Literary Studies* 2.3 (1996): 2.1–35. <http://purl.oclc.org/emls/02-3/maciwhit.html>

Manley, Lawrence. *Literature and Culture in Early Modern London*. Cambridge: Cambridge University Press, 1995.

Marcus, Leah. "Of Mire and Authorship." In *The Theatrical City*, edited by David L. Smith, Richard Strier and David Bevington, 170–82. Cambridge: Cambridge University Press, 1995.

Marotti, Arthur F., and Michael D. Bristol, eds. *Print, Manuscript, & Performance: The Changing Relations of the Media in Early Modern England*. Columbus: Ohio State University Press, 2000.

Martial. *Epigrams*. Edited and translated by D. R. Shackleton Bailey. 3 vols. Cambridge: Harvard University Press, 1993.

Martin, Mathew. "Play and Plague in Ben Jonson's *The Alchemist*." *English Studies in Canada* 26 (2000): 393–408.

Massey, Doreen. "Power-Geometry and a Progressive Sense of Place." In *Mapping the Futures: Local Cultures, Global Change*, edited by Jon Bird, Barry Curtis, Tim Putnam, George Robertson and Lisa Tickner, 59–69. London: Routledge, 1993.

McEvoy, Sean. "Hieronimo's Old Cloak: Theatricality and Representation in Ben Jonson's Middle Comedies." *Ben Jonson Journal* 11 (2004): 67–88.

McGann, Jerome. "The Monks and the Giants: Textual and Bibliographical Studies and the Interpretation of Literary Works." In *Textual Criticism and Literary Interpretation*, edited by Jerome McGann, 180–99. Chicago: University of Chicago Press, 1985.

Miles, Rosalind. *Ben Jonson: His Life and Work*. London: Routledge & Kegan Paul, 1986.

Mulcaster, Richard. *The queens maiesties passage through the citie of London to westminster the daye before her coronacion*. London, 1559.

Mullaney, Steven. *The Place of the Stage: License, Play, and Power in Renaissance England*. Chicago: University of Chicago Press, 1988.

Murray, Timothy. "Ben Jonson's Folio as Textual Performance." In *Proceedings of the Xth Congress of the International Comparative Literature Association*, edited by Anna Balakian, 325–30. New York: Garland, 1982.

Newton, Richard C. "Jonson and the (Re-)Invention of the Book." In *Classic and Cavalier: Essays on Jonson and the Sons of Ben*, edited by J. Summers and T. Pebworth, 31–55. Pittsburgh: University of Pittsburgh Press, 1982.

Nichols, John, ed. *The Progresses, Processions, and Magnificent Festivities of King James the First*. 4 vols. London: J.B. Nichols, 1828.

Ouellette, Anthony J. "*The Alchemist* and the Emerging Adult Playhouse." *Studies in English Literature* 45 (2005): 375–99.

Parry, Graham. *The Golden Age Restor'd: The Culture of the Stuart Court, 1603–42*. New York: St. Martin's, 1981.

Paster, Gail Kern. *The Idea of the City in the Age of Shakespeare*. Athens: University of Georgia Press, 1985.

Perry, Curtis. *The Making of Jacobean Culture: James I and the Renegotiation of Elizabethan Literary Practice*. Cambridge: Cambridge University Press, 1997.

Phillips, Patrick. "'You Need Not Fear the House': The Absence of Plague in *The Alchemist*." *Ben Jonson Journal* 13 (2006): 43–62.

Rebhorn, Wayne. "Jonson's 'Jovy Boy': Lovewit and the Dupes in *The Alchemist*." *Journal of English and Germanic Philology* 79 (1980): 355–75.

Reddy, K. Venkata. *Ben Jonson: His Dramatic Art*. New Delhi: Prestige Books, 1994.

The Repertory of the Court of Aldermen. London: Guildhall Library.

Riddell, James A. "Ben Jonson's Folio of 1616." In *The Cambridge Companion to Ben Jonson*, edited by Richard Harp and Stanley Stewart, 152–62. Cambridge: Cambridge University Press, 2000.

Riggs, David. *Ben Jonson: A Life*. Cambridge: Harvard University Press, 1989.

Ross, Cheryl Lynn. "The Plague of *The Alchemist*." *Renaissance Quarterly* 41 (1988): 439–58.

Rowe, George E. *Distinguishing Jonson: Imitation, Rivalry, and the Direction of a Dramatic Career*. Lincoln: University of Nebraska Press, 1988.

Shakespeare, William. *The Riverside Shakespeare*. Edited by G. Blakemore Evans and J. J. M. Tobin. 2nd ed. Boston: Houghton Mifflin, 1997.

Sheppard, F. H. W. *London: A History*. Oxford: Oxford University Press, 1998.

Smallwood, Robert L. "'Here, in the Friars': Immediacy and Theatricality in *The Alchemist*." *Review of English Studies* 32 (1980): 142–60.

Soja, Edward W. *Postmodern Geographies: The Reassertion of Space in Critical Social Theory*. London: Verso, 1989.

———. *Thirdspace: Journeys to Los Angeles and Other Real-and-Imagined Places.* Oxford: Blackwell, 1996.

Stern, Tiffany. "Behind the Arras: The Prompter's Place in the Shakespearean Theatre." *Theatre Notebook* 55, no. 3 (2001): 110–18.

———. "'A Small-Beer Health to His Second Day': Playwrights, Prologues, and First Performances in the Early Modern Theater." *Studies in Philology* 101, no. 2 (2004): 172–98.

Stock, Angela. "'Something Done in Honour of the City': Ritual, Theatre, and Satire in Jacobean Civic Pageantry." In *Plotting Early Modern London: New Essays on Jacobean City Comedy*, edited by Dieter Mehl, Angela Stock and Anne-Julia Zwierlein, 125–44. Aldershot: Ashgate, 2004.

Stow, John. *A Survey of London: Reprinted from the Text of 1603.* Edited by C. L. Kingsford. 2 vols. Oxford: Clarendon Press, 1908.

Stuart Royal Proclamations: Royal Proclamations of King James I 1603–1625. Edited by James Larkin and Paul Hughes. Oxford: Clarendon Press, 1973.

Thayer, C. G. *Ben Jonson: Studies in the Plays.* Norman: Oklahoma University Press, 1963.

Thomas, Max W. "*Kemps Nine Daies Wonder*: Dancing Carnival into Market." *PMLA* 107 (1992): 511–32.

Tuan, Yi-fu. *Space and Place: The Perspective of Experience.* Minneapolis: University of Minnesota Press, 1977.

Turner, Henry S. *The English Renaissance Stage: Geometry, Poetics, and the Practical Spatial Arts 1580–1630.* Oxford: Oxford University Press, 2006.

———. "Plotting Early Modernity." In *The Culture of Capital: Property, Cities, and Knowledge in Early Modern England*, edited by Henry S. Turner, 85–127. London: Routledge, 2002.

Twyning, John. *London Dispossessed: Literature and Social Space in the Early Modern City.* New York: St. Martin's, 1998.

van den Berg, Sara. "Ben Jonson and the Ideology of Authorship." In *Ben Jonson's 1616 Folio*, edited by Jennifer Brady and W. H. Herendeen, 111–37. Newark: University of Delaware Press, 1991.

———. "The Passing of the Elizabethan Court." *Ben Jonson Journal* 1 (1994): 31–62.

———. "True Relation: The Life and Career of Ben Jonson." In *The Cambridge Companion to Ben Jonson*, edited by Richard Harp and Stanley Stewart, 1–14. Cambridge: Cambridge University Press, 2000.

Venuti, Lawrence. "Transformations of City Comedy: A Symptomatic Reading." *Assays* 3 (1985): 99–134.

Wall, Wendy. *The Imprint of Gender: Authorship and Publication in the English Renaissance.* Ithaca: Cornell University Press, 1993.

Watson, Robert N. *Ben Jonson's Parodic Strategy: Literary Imperialism in the Comedies.* Cambridge: Harvard University Press, 1987.

Wells, Henry Willis. *Elizabethan and Jacobean Playwrights.* New York: Columbia University Press, 1939.

Wells, Susan. "Jacobean City Comedy and the Ideology of the City." *ELH* 48, (1981): 37–60.

West, Russell. *Spatial Representations and the Jacobean Stage: From Shakespeare to Webster*. New York: Palgrave, 2002.

Williams, Raymond. *Keywords*. Oxford: Oxford University Press, 1976.

Wilson, Arthur. *The History of Great Britain, Being the Life and Reign of King James the First*. London, 1653.

Wilson, Edmund. "Morose Ben Jonson." In *Ben Jonson: A Collection of Critical Essays*, edited by Jonas Barish, 60–74. Englewood Cliffs, NJ: Prentice-Hall, 1963.

Wilson, F. P. *The Plague in Shakespeare's London*. Oxford: Oxford University Press, 1927.

Wimsatt, W. K., and Monroe C. Beardsley. "The Intentional Fallacy." In *The Verbal Icon: Studies in the Meaning of Poetry*, edited by W. K. Wimsatt, 3–18. Lexington: University of Kentucky Press, 1954.

Witt, Robert W. *Mirror within a Mirror: Ben Jonson and the Play Within*. Salzburg: Institut für English Sprache und Literatur, 1975.

Womack, Peter. *Ben Jonson*. Oxford: Blackwell, 1986.

Wormald, Jenny. "James VI and I: Two Kings or One?" *History* 68 (1983): 187–209.

Wright, Louis B. *Middle-Class Culture in Elizabethan England*, Huntington Library Publications. Chapel Hill: University of North Carolina Press, 1935.

Yiu, Mimi. "Sounding the Space between Men: Choric and Choral Cities in Ben Jonson's *Epicoene; or, the Silent Woman*." *PMLA* 122 (2007): 72–88.

Zucker, Adam. "The Social Logic of Ben Jonson's *Epicoene*." *Renaissance Drama* 33 (2004): 37–62.

Zwierlein, Anne-Julia. "Shipwrecks in the City: Commercial Risk as Romance in Early Modern City Comedy." In *Plotting Early Modern London: New Essays on City Comedy*, edited by Dieter Mehl, Angela Stock and Anne-Julia Zwierlein, 75–94. Aldershot: Ashgate, 2004.

Index

www.ingramcontent.com/pod-product-compliance
Ingram Content Group UK Ltd.
Pitfield, Milton Keynes, MK11 3LW, UK
UKHW020429010325
455677UK00029B/1076